Advisory Editor

Lawrence A. Cremin
Frederick A. P. Barnard Professor of Education
Teachers College, Columbia University

AMERICAN EDUCATION: *Its Men, Ideas, and Institutions*
presents selected works of thought and scholarship that have
long been out of print or otherwise unavailable. Inevitably, such
works will include particular ideas and doctrines that have been
outmoded or superseded by more recent research. Nevertheless,
all retain their place in the literature, having influenced educational thought and practice in their own time and having provided
the basis for subsequent scholarship.

AMERICAN EDUCATION

Its Men,

Ideas,

and

Institutions

The Century Studies in Education
W. L. UHL, Editor

EDUCATION
AND THE PHILOSOPHY
OF EXPERIMENTALISM

BY

JOHN L. CHILDS, Ph.D.

ARNO PRESS & THE NEW YORK TIMES
*New York * 1971*

Reprint Edition 1971 by Arno Press Inc.

Copyright © 1931 by John L. Childs
Reprinted by permission of Appleton-Century-Crofts

Reprinted from a copy in
  The Newark Public Library

American Education:
  Its Men, Ideas, and Institutions - Series II
ISBN for complete set: 0-405-03600-0
See last pages of this volume for titles

Manufactured in the United States of America

Library of Congress Cataloging in Publication Data

Childs, John Lawrence, 1889-
    Education and the philosophy of experimentalism.
    (The Century studies in education) (American
education: its men, ideas, and institutions.
Series II)
    Originally presented as the author's thesis,
Columbia, 1931.
    Includes bibliographical references.
    1. Pragmatism. 2. Education--Philosophy.
3. Experience. I. Title. II. Series.
III. Series: American education: its men, ideas,
and institutions. Series II.
LB875.C48 1971   370.1   76-165735
ISBN 0-405-03604-3

EDUCATION AND THE PHILOSOPHY
OF EXPERIMENTALISM

The Century Studies in Education
W. L. UHL, Editor

EDUCATION AND THE PHILOSOPHY OF EXPERIMENTALISM

BY

JOHN L. CHILDS, Ph.D.

Instructor in Philosophy of Education
Teachers College, Columbia University

WITH A FOREWORD BY

WILLIAM HEARD KILPATRICK

THE CENTURY CO.

NEW YORK   LONDON

PRINTED IN U. S. A.

To
G. F. C.

EDITOR'S INTRODUCTION

American institutions, industry, and science have evolved from a panorama of changing life. He who seeks finality, the absolutist, sees our nation quite askew—to him chaos here plays havoc with ideals, traditions, and standards of worthy living. He who lets come what will and seeks only for success, the instrumentalist, finds here an opportunity for exploitation, narrow individualism, and fame. He who ventures forth upon the course of life itself, the experimentalist, discovers here a sumptuous laboratory, ever challenging to his powers of clear vision and interpretation.

To the experimentalist Dr. Childs directs the first volume of The Century Studies in Education. His pages bear the distinctive imprint of American life and thought. He interprets both this life and this thought. He develops basic conceptions for the student and the educator who would equip themselves with instruments for further discovery and for the progressive reconstruction of American life.

WILLIS L. UHL.

PREFACE

Although Experimentalism is an indigenous American philosophy, it was in China that my attention first was called to it. During the World War, a brilliant group of young Chinese thinkers launched a movement which soon became nation-wide in its influence. This movement was called in Chinese the "Hsin Szu Ch'au" which literally translated means the "New Thought Tide." Because many of its features were similar to those of the earlier European awakening, it became popularly known in English as "The Chinese Renaissance."

While the sources of this intellectual and social movement were various, it is undoubtedly true that some of its most able leaders had been influenced profoundly by the ideas of John Dewey. These Chinese educators desired to reconstruct the ancient culture of their people. They found intellectual tools almost ideally suited to their purposes in Dewey's philosophy. Among these tools were his belief that philosophy should concern itself primarily with the present problems of men, his view of the instrumental character of thought, his demand that all traditions, beliefs, and institutions be tested continuously by their capacity to meet contemporary human needs, and his faith that the whole-hearted use of the experimental attitude and method could achieve results in the social field similar to those already secured in the field of the natural sciences.

At about the time of the close of the World War, Professor Dewey visited China. For two years through lectures, writing, and teaching he gave, in person, a powerful reinforcement to the work of the Chinese Renaissance leaders. Living as I was in Peking at that time, my first introduction to Experimentalism came as I watched it grapple with the complex and difficult problems of present-day China.

Later while on furlough I studied at both Teachers College and Union Theological Seminary. Under the stimulating leadership of Professors George A. Coe and Harrison S. Elliott the implications of this philosophy for religious life and thought became more apparent. During this same period, I studied in philosophy of education with Professor William H. Kilpatrick. From him I received suggestions for a new approach to education and to philosophy which after years of exploration seem constantly to grow in meaning and in significance.

In the preparation of the materials for this book I have also had the advantage of many valuable criticisms and suggestions from Professor Robert B. Raup, a colleague in the department of philosophy of education at Teachers College. I wish to acknowledge my deep obligation to all of the above-named individuals. This book owes its existence to their sympathetic encouragement.

Special thanks are due to the various authors whose writings are quoted so freely in these pages. The large number of direct quotations is explained by the fact that the nature of the study made it desirable to give both the ideas of the Experimentalists and those of their critics in their own words wherever possible. I also wish to acknowledge my indebtedness to the following publishing houses and periodicals for their generous permission to use selections from their publications: The University of Chicago Press, Clark University

Press, Columbia University Press, Harcourt, Brace and
Company, Harvard University Press, D. C. Heath and Company, Henry Holt and Company, *The Journal of Philosophy,*
Longmans, Green and Company, The Macmillan Company,
Minton, Balch and Company, *The Nation, The New Republic,* W. W. Norton and Company, University of North
Carolina Press, Open Court Publishing Company, Progressive Education Association, *The Saturday Review of Literature,* Charles Scribner's Sons, Frederick A. Stokes Company,
and The Viking Press.

J. L. C.

FOREWORD

This book of penetrating inquiry and constructive criticism comes opportunely. A shift of attitude in thought is now upon us. Wise advance depends on a deeper and closer scrutiny of our presuppositions. In education such a scrutiny is much overdue, the reaction appears already at hand. In but recent times the tide ran strong against the ultimate human element and factor in life. Things were indeed in the saddle, not merely in a rank industrial outlook but as well in science and explanation. Conscious action was brought under suspicion as merely subjective. The unavowed aim in education was in effect to abolish thinking, at least for the many; for if thinking were possible, the few could do it for the rest. Purposing became peculiarly suspect, "conditioning" must supplant it. A science born of physics and its conceptions claimed sufficiency for all needs. "Facts," if only objectively recorded and treated, would give adequate guidance. Tests and measures would give such facts, statistics would treat them. Philosophy was at last outmoded. Education would thus advance to effectual control.

But a reaction has set in. Ebb follows flow. Science is remaking itself, astonishingly so. The material thing is no longer the ultimate. An all-inclusive prior determinism does not hold. The old arrogance of physics is gone. Man is freed to take again his rightful place. Psychology moves to give up its atomistic trend. Education has learned that test and measure at most but furnish data which thought must interpret for use. Moreover,—as the leaders have always known, at least for themselves—statistics offers no substitute for thinking. These husks have now been tried and found wanting. On such fare life shrivels. More is needed. Constructive philosophy comes to its own. Education wakes.

And this is the timeliness of the book before us. As education feels new need to understand and build, the way forward proves hard. To go down deep enough and find therein new bearings on *what* and *how* and *why* is no easy task. A guide and interpreter helps. Here Dr. Childs serves. We have among us in this country the most significant living philosophy of education. In Peirce, James, and Dewey, a true school of indigenous thought is, to all appearances, in process of becoming. It is this developing outlook and method which Dr. Childs has chosen to discuss under the title of Experimentalism. And the name is fitting. Life is in fact lived experimentally. Always we face uncertainty in a world ever on the go. Our efforts to deal with such a world are but trials. In this world, ends as well as means must be held subject to review as events continually develop. If education is to go forward, no road more promising lies open than this experimental approach.

It is then this philosophy of experimentalism in relation to education that is here examined and discussed. The study is both critical and constructive. Critical, first of all, in that Dr. Childs is no mere disciple. Accepting as he does the main position of experimentalism, he none the less thinks his own thoughts fearlessly at whatever cost of difference. If, for example, some insiders have said that experimentalism is method only and has no metaphysic, then Dr. Childs is ready to hold the opposite—and convincingly so. Critical also is the study in opposition and attack. In active opposition, various positions are examined which this philosophy would correct: a denial of freedom in man responsibly to affect affairs, a denial of thinking in the rank and file of men, the tendency toward an atomistic psychology, a too narrow $S \rightarrow R$ bond theory, "conditioning" as the unit element in learning. In critical answer, an examination is also made of certain attacks upon the experimentalist position: that in it individual men are unduly loosed from social obligations, or contrariwise that experimentalism binds us to the industrial order as now it is, or that the position so commits itself to instrumentalism as to leave no essential place to life itself on its qualitative or esthetic side. All these points Dr. Childs discusses with a penetration and a balance which are disarming by their fairness. The position which experimentalism holds in these matters receives at his hands excellent definition.

But everywhere are criticism and discussion constructive in intent, as befits regard for education and belief in its processes. At each point Dr. Childs is concerned to find dependable ways of thinking on which life and education may go more fruitfully forward. Many who in our shifting times are groping for a surer outlook will find here help in their quest. Hard is that reader to please or instruct who from these honestly argued pages does not find himself upbuilt in fruitful outlook. In the portrayal here given life and education—two interacting aspects of one dynamic process—find a surer road toward better things.

WILLIAM H. KILPATRICK.

CONTENTS

CONTENTS   xix

EDUCATION AND THE PHILOSOPHY
OF EXPERIMENTALISM

EDUCATION AND THE
PHILOSOPHY OF EXPERIMENTALISM

CHAPTER I

AN INDIGENOUS AMERICAN PHILOSOPHY

"Whoever is interested in the future should especially study America. To my mind, the best work that has been done anywhere in philosophy and psychology during the present century has been done in America."

"Sophisticated America, wherever it has succeeded in shaking off slavery to Europe (which is too common among the sophisticated), has already developed a new outlook, mainly as a result of the work of James and Dewey."

Bertrand Russell.

It was probably inevitable that sooner or later the American people should produce an indigenous philosophy. The story of their national existence represents too profound a departure from the social experience of the Old World to be satisfactorily formulated through the exclusive use of the traditional European intellectual molds. It was also highly probable that when such an indigenous philosophy did arise, it would have something important to say about education. The experiment in social and political democracy to which the United States is committed is closely linked with the faith of the American people in education. As will be shown later, a philosophy with its roots in the vital activities of the youthful American life would come in time to develop its own distinctive traits. Among these it was almost sure to make central an interest in democracy, in education, and in their mutual inter-relations.

There is to-day rather general recognition, both here and in foreign countries, that such an indigenous American philosophy has emerged. While many have contributed to its development, there would be common agreement that the most fundamental and original contributions have come from the works of Charles Sanders Peirce, William James, and John Dewey. Important differences, to be sure, are to be found in the ideas of these three men. Such differences, however, are not of primary concern to this study, which is interested in the educational implications of their common philosophic positions. For our purposes we may consider all of these men as members of the same school of thought. In this we seem to have the approval of Dewey, who stands to-day as the most eminent leader in this new approach both to philosophy and to education. Building on the important work of Peirce and James in logic and psychology, Dewey has not only made fundamental contributions in both of these fields, but he has also used these fresh insights to elicit the deeper meanings imbedded in the raw, but vital, social experiences of the American people. Without Dewey, it is doubtful if the ideas of Peirce and James would have developed into an indigenous American philosophic movement. On the other hand, no one more than Dewey recognizes the important connections between his thought and that of Peirce and James.

This new movement in philosophy has encountered difficulty in finding a suitable name. Part of this difficulty may be due to the character of the philosophy itself. As a philosophy it is more of an attitude and a method—or a principle of orientation to experience—than it is a final system of philosophic doctrines. Moreover, its specific emphases have shifted from time to time, and unfortunately some of these partial emphases have been permitted to give a name to the whole movement.

The movement first appeared as "Pragmatism," and it is still almost exclusively known to the general public under that name. There are, however, serious objections to the use of this term. Most obvious is the popular belief that pragmatism sanctions anything immediately expedient in the sense that it "gets by." While this is absurd, there remains the more fundamental difficulty that pragmatism is often considered to be merely a method for testing the meaning of our ideas. As thus defined, the pragmatic method is only one element in the total position of this philosophy.

An English thinker, F. C. S. Schiller of Oxford, much attracted by some of the ideas of William James, has maintained consistently that this philosophy would be more fittingly described as "Humanism." It must be admitted that the broad social sympathies of the leaders of this movement do give a certain appropriateness to this name. On these shores, however, the term *humanism* has latterly been commandeered to give fighting leadership to such conflicting programs that it would only compound confusion to ask it do duty in this, still another, movement.

There was a period when attention was primarily given to matters of logic and more specifically to the instrumental character of ideas, in which Dewey's philosophy labored under the somewhat unhappy title of "Instrumentalism." Of late relatively less emphasis has been given to this aspect of his thought.

Recently there has been some tendency among the leaders of this movement to call it the philosophy of "Experimentalism." It appears that the temper and character of its radically experimental approach to both the world of nature and the world of man is more adequately suggested in this latter name than in any other yet proposed. It is partly because of this that the term *experimentalism* is used throughout this study.

Another reason for using *experimentalism* rather than other names more widely current lies in the fact that our interest in this book is primarily with the implications of this philosophy for education. Certainly in the field of education it is the experimental character and method of this philosophy which is of largest significance. In fact, it is its radically experimental way of construing life and knowledge which has led to its searching challenge to traditional school procedures. As naturally would be expected, it is also this and closely related phases of its educational program which are most under attack at the present time. Inasmuch as this study is chiefly concerned with an evaluation of this philosophy in the light of its educational proposals and consequences, it has seemed advisable to use the name which most sharply calls attention to the features here specifically under review. In the opinion of the writer, *experimentalism* is the term which best serves this purpose.

However, the question of the particular name to be used is not of fundamental importance. The point to be remembered is that in this study, when the term *experimentalism* is used, it refers to the general body of philosophic thought associated with the names of Peirce, James, and Dewey. More particularly, when the educational implications of experimentalism are under consideration, it is to be understood that the reference is always to what has come to be called the "Dewey school" in the educational field.

The general plan of the study is as follows: Chapter II, following this introductory chapter, considers factors in American social life which seem to have favored the development of this philosophic outlook. It is believed that this material may serve a two-fold purpose. In addition to describing certain influences in American life which have contributed to the development of this point of view, the writer also hopes that by thus showing connections between these ideas and our social experience, he may cause the ideas themselves to gain in concreteness and in significance.

The third chapter inquires into what, if any, metaphysical positions are affirmed or implied in experimentalism. It is a fundamental thesis of this book that experimentalism is more than a mere contribution to methodology. In other words, that it does include, in broad outlines at least, a definite picture of the nature of the world in which man lives. Its educational emphasis on "creative intelligence," "purposeful activity," and "no fixed goals" can only be understood in its deeper significance when this world view is taken into account.

A discussion of the experimentalist's view of man and the nature of experience is then undertaken in order to show the bearing of these conceptions on certain of his most basic educational views. In this, as in the preceding chapter, the aim is to set forth in positive form the central educational principles found in the philosophy of experimentalism.

The remaining chapters—the major portion of the book—are devoted to a critical evaluation of the philosophic and correlative educational positions of the experimentalist in the light of major criticisms which are now directed against these positions by various leaders in the field of education.

CHAPTER II

THE AMERICAN SCENE AND EXPERIMENTALISM

"America is not simply a young country with an old mentality; it is a country with two mentalities, one a survival of the beliefs and standards of the fathers, the other an expression of the instincts, practice, and discoveries of the younger generations."

SANTAYANA.

"There never was a philosopher who has merited the name for the simple reason that he glorified the tendencies and characteristics of his social environment; just as it is also true that there never has been a philosopher who has not seized upon certain aspects of the life of his time and idealized them."

DEWEY.

1. Experience and Philosophy

THE experimentalist believes that ideas always arise in and through experience. They are not spontaneously generated. In his opinion, all ideas, beliefs, and ideals grow out of, and relate to, concrete experiences. And *experience* as here used means primarily an active process of interaction between the human organism and its natural and social environment. Hence the entire ideational life of man is considered by the experimentalist literally to derive its substance from the "doings and undergoings" of what is called "primary experience."

This not only holds true of our ideas, it appears to be equally true of the very structure of mind itself. This radically objective view of mind is one of the distinguishing features of the philosophy of experimentalism. Mind is not believed to be a transcendental faculty; nor is it considered to be an inherited, ready-made psychic structure which only

8

requires formal exercise to discipline it for its varied intellectual tasks. Rather, mind itself is something built in the very process of experiencing. Since experience is in and of the world of men and things, our minds are also continuous with these objective materials. Had our environments been different, our experiences would have been different. Had our experiences been different, our minds also would have been different. In short, to live differently is to think differently.

As our later discussions will show, in taking this view of mind the experimentalist does not deny the uniqueness of the individual. Neither does he consider the individual to be a passive agent who merely absorbs sensations and ideas from his environment. The individual is a product of his own activity just as truly as he is a product of the social influences which nurture his mind. The uniqueness of the individual and the creative activity of the individual are both foundational principles in the philosophy of experimentalism. Nevertheless, the experimentalist believes it is wholly true that each individual derives his meanings—actually builds his mind—out of his concrete dealings with the particular materials found in his natural and social environment. Group attitudes, beliefs, customs, and institutions play a fundamental rôle in this process of creating minds in individuals.

"The stuff of belief and proposition is not originated by us. It comes to us from others, by education, tradition, and the suggestion of the environment. Our intelligence is bound up, so far as its materials are concerned, with the community life of which we are a part. We know what it communicates to us, and know according to the habits it forms in us. Science is an affair of civilization, not of individual intellect." [1] *

* The numbers used following quotations refer to the numbered references at the end of the chapter.

So also for philosophies. Critical analytical studies seem to reveal that even the most imposing systems of philosophy and of theology are not the sheer products of some disembodied reason unconditioned by factors of time and place. Non-empirical means of achieving understanding are no more to be found in philosophy than in other realms of human thought. The experimentalist has not found it difficult to show that the most pretentious philosophical systems are significantly connected with the social mediums in which they were produced.

For example, he suggests that the traditional dualism in philosophy between thought and activity, between theory and practice, is a dualism which has more than an incidental connection with the social dualism of a feudal society. Such a feudal society, with its cultured leisure class at the top and its mass of slave workers at the bottom, could easily accept the conclusion that intellectual activity and physical activity have nothing in common. It is also intimated that historically the problem of a mind-body dualism gained much of its strength from this same social dualism of a feudal order. The idle thinkers had the minds, the supposedly non-thinking slave workers had the physical bodies. In the belief in eternal patterns and divine essences the experimentalist finds a survival of the earlier conception of a hierarchical natural economy in which the various species were held to be immutable. On closer inspection, the "absolute" of German idealism seems to have something in common with the autocratic form of government found in the former Prussian system. And it is at least possible that the unquestioning obedience which some variants of this same philosophy insist should be granted by everybody to the immediately apprehended moral law reflects something of a national habit of paying docile attention to the orders of Prussian police officers.

It is easy, however, to draw a false conclusion from illustrations such as these. To show that systems of philosophy are the achievements of human minds whose habits of thought and standards of value are conditioned by the "intellectual climate" and the prevailing social organization of particular times and places does not necessarily lessen their importance. As a matter of fact, thus to place them in their social context helps us to understand them better, and enables us to evaluate them more intelligently. To perceive that these philosophies have gathered their intellectual materials from the ordinary world of human experience conceivably might lead to an appreciative approach to much that has hitherto been difficult, if not repellent in them. Significant insights may be contained in even the most "transcendental" philosophies, just because these philosophies, like all others, are the products of emotional and intellectual reactions to concrete conditions of one sort or another. To suppose that a philosophy is insignificant because it has been distilled from experience is to reach a conclusion far removed from that of the experimentalist, who believes that respect for experience is the beginning of wisdom.

Following, then, the lead of the experimentalist, we may well begin our study of his philosophy by surveying the physical and the social environment in which it developed. An understanding of the surroundings out of which it came and to which it is a response should throw some light on the character of this philosophy. Both friends and critics of experimentalism seem to agree that it has achieved a new outlook of large significance. If this be true, it would seem reasonable to assume that clues to some of the forces which shaped the minds of those who formulated this philosophy would be discovered in an examination of the social history of the American people. This assumes, of course, that the philosophy is an indigenous product of American life. As has already been indicated, this seems to be the fact. It may be said to be American in a double sense. First, because the men who have made the most original contributions to the development of this point of view—Peirce, James, and Dewey —are all Americans. Secondly, because of the profound influence which it exerts in the contemporary life of the American people. Its wide acceptance in the United States as contrasted with its lesser influence in Europe suggests that those who formulated this philosophy were possibly giving intellectual expression to tendencies already implicit in American social life.

2. Experimentalism and European Thought

At this point we must be on our guard against exaggeration. For while experimentalism may indeed mark a new start in philosophy, it is of course not new in the sense that it has no important connections with the wider movement of human thought. Undoubtedly many of the materials which went into the making of the mind of the experimentalist were secured from other than American sources. Probably as time passes these connections with European philosophic thought will be found to be relatively more significant than they are now considered to be by many experimentalists.

From the outset Peirce and James were conscious of continuities between their thought and that of earlier European philosophers. In an article on "The Development of American Pragmatism," Dewey says:

"The term 'pragmatic,' contrary to the opinion of those who regard pragmatism as an exclusively American conception, was suggested to him (Peirce) by the study of Kant. . . . The essay in which Peirce developed his theory bears the title: 'How to Make Our Ideas Clear.' There is a remarkable similarity to Kant's doctrine in the efforts which he made to interpret the universality of concepts in the domain of experience in the same way in which Kant established the law of practical reason in the domain of the *a priori*." [2]

In order to call attention to connections between his own thought and that of the English empiricists, William James dedicated his book *Pragmatism* to John Stuart Mill:

"To the memory of John Stuart Mill, from whom I first learned the pragmatic openness of mind and whom my fancy likes to picture as our leader were he alive today." [3]

In the celebrated lecture which formally introduced pragmatism to the general public, delivered before the Philosophical Union of the University of California on August 26, 1898, James makes specific mention of the English antecedents of this philosophy:

"I am happy to say that it is the English-speaking philosophers who first introduced the custom of interpreting the meaning of conceptions by asking what difference they make for life. Mr. Peirce has only expressed in the form of explicit maxim what their sense for reality led them instinctively to do. The great English way of investigating a conception is to ask yourself right off, 'What is it *known as?* In what facts does it result? What is its *cash-value* in terms of particular experience? and what special difference would come to the world according as it were true or false?'" [4]

From the standpoint of technical philosophy, at least one other factor in European thought should be mentioned in connection with the development of experimentalism. In this instance, however, the influence was negative in that it led to a reaction which culminated in the development of the logic of instrumentalism. The reference is to the influence of neo-Kantian idealism. Dewey apparently began by being a neo-Kantian, and according to his own statement his instrumentalism was developed as "a critique of knowledge and of logic which has resulted from the theory proposed by neo-Kantian idealism and expounded in the logical writings of such philosophers as Lotze, Bosanquet, and F. H. Bradley." [5]

Two other general influences, both European in origin, contributed significantly to the development of the philosophy of experimentalism. One of these was the rise and spread of modern science with its experimental method. Peirce says that the inspiration for his writings in logic came from his having developed "the laboratory habit of mind." While it is the contention of this book that experimentalism is more than a method, nevertheless experimentalism is a philosophy which has placed primary emphasis on its method. As will be brought out later, this method is essentially an extension of the method of experimental inquiry into all realms of human experience.

Finally, the theory of evolution as formulated by Darwin has made a profound contribution to the thought of the experimentalist. The contribution here is fundamentally important. It is perhaps not too much to say that without the Darwinian influence experimentalism as a philosophy could not have been. Its conceptions have operated in two fundamental ways to influence the mind of the experimentalist. First, in demanding that we change from a static to a dynamic conception of the universe:

"That the publication of the 'Origin of Species' marked an epoch in the development of the natural sciences is well known to the layman. That the combination of the very words origin and species embodied an intellectual revolt and introduced a new intellectual temper is easily overlooked by the expert. The conceptions that had reigned in the philosophy of nature and knowledge for two thousand years, the conceptions that had become the familiar furniture of the mind, rested on the assumption of the superiority of the fixed and final; they rested upon treating change and origins as signs of defect and unreality. In laying hands upon the sacred ark of absolute permanency, in treating the forms that had been regarded as types of fixity and perfection as originating and passing away, the 'Origin of Species' introduced a mode of thinking that in the end was bound to transform the logic of knowledge, and hence the treatment of morals, politics, and religion." [6]

In the second place, the theory of organic evolution made possible a new conception of human behavior. It was found that "wherever there is life, there is behavior, activity." Important similarities were discovered to be present in the behavior of all living organisms. It was seen that the life of the organism depends upon its ability to maintain a supporting equilibrium with the energies of the environment. As changes in both the organism and the environment were always taking place, constantly new adjustments were required to maintain the equilibrium. These adjustments could be achieved by changing either the organism or the environment. Typically an interaction between the two—which, on the human level, is what is meant by primary experience—resulted in both a modified organism and a modified environment. Interaction was thus declared to be the basic category. Those movements, efforts, which helped the organism achieve its equilibrium tended to become fixed in its structure as habits of response. Hence habits were regarded as functions of this adjustive tendency. So also for the thought life of man. Knowledge was "not something separate and self-sufficing," but was "included in the process by which life is sustained and evolved." Ideas were imaginative projections of possible lines of action. They were boldly declared to be instruments which aided the individual to guide his behavior and to control his environment more effectively. In short, the experimentalists found indispensable materials in the biological principles of Darwin for forging both a new psychology and a new logic of experience.

3. American Conditioning Factors

As the brief and inadequate sketch just given of the European elements in the philosophy of experimentalism reveals, the debt of the American experimentalists to foreign influences is very great indeed. It may truthfully be said that many of the most important materials of experimentalism were appropriated from abroad. How, then, did it come to be that this philosophy based so largely on foreign contributions should have been formulated by a group of American thinkers, and should have met with such wide acceptance among the American people? Apparently novel social forces were operating in the civilization of the New World, and these forces must be at least partially responsible for this result.

A number of superficial explanations of these social forces have been given which are complimentary neither to the culture of the American people, nor to the quality of thought exhibited by the experimentalist philosophers. These so-called explanations are based on such gross misunderstanding of both American life and the theories of the experimentalists that they merit little serious attention. The experimentalist's answer to the most persistent of these erroneous interpretations is given in the following quotation from Dewey:

"These statements of Peirce are quite conclusive with respect to two errors which are commonly committed in regard to the ideas of the founder of pragmatism. It is often said of pragmatism that it makes action the end of life. It is also said of pragmatism that it subordinates thought and rational activity to particular ends of interest and profit. It is true that the theory according to Peirce's conception implies essentially a certain relation to action, to human conduct. But the rôle of action is that of an intermediary. In order to be able to attribute a meaning to concepts, one must be able to apply them to existence. Now it is by means of action that this application is made possible. And the modification of existence which results from this application constitutes the true meaning of concepts.

"Pragmatism is, therefore, far from being that glorification of action for its own sake which is regarded as the peculiar characteristic of American life. It is also to be noted that there is a scale of possible applications of concepts to existence, and hence a diversity of meanings. The greater the extension of the concepts, the more they are freed from the restrictions which limit them to particular cases, the more it is possible for us to attribute the most general meaning to a term. Thus the theory of Peirce is opposed to every restriction of the meaning of a concept to the achievement of a particular end, and still more to a personal aim. It is still more strongly opposed to the idea that reason or thought should be reduced to being a servant of any interest which is pecuniary or too narrow. This theory was American in its origin insofar as it insisted on the necessity of human conduct and the fulfillment of some aim in order to clarify thought. But at the same time, it disapproves of those aspects of American life which make action an end in itself, and which conceive ends too narrowly and too practically." [7]

"William James said in a happy metaphor, that they (ideas) must be 'cashed in', by producing specific consequences. This expression means that they must be able to become concrete facts. But for those who are not familiar with American idioms, James' formula was taken to mean that the consequences themselves of our rational conceptions must be narrowly limited by their pecuniary value. Thus Mr. Bertrand Russell wrote just recently that pragmatism is merely a manifestation of American commercialism." [8]

Whatever may be our final judgment as to the worth of the philosophy of experimentalism, its position in the modern world is such as to warrant that its critics take pains to try to understand it before they dismiss it with assertions to the effect that it is merely a rationalization of what is assumed to be the American's tendency to make activity a substitute for thought, or that it is a mere glorification of his chase for the almighty dollar. It may be doubted whether the American people are more avaricious than other nationalities, and in any case few more trenchant criticisms have been made of the narrowly commercialist spirit than those which have come from the pens of James and Dewey.

It may be concluded, then, that neither interest in pecuniary gain, nor absorption in the practical narrowly conceived, nor the human tendency to seek intellectual support for views emotionally comforting are the important American roots of experimentalism. To recognize this, however, does not point to the conclusion that there are no characteristic phases of our social experience which have been incorporated into its formulations.

The four following aspects of American life are suggested as possible social factors which, in varying degree, may have conditioned the thought of the experimentalists:

(1) The absence of a rigidly fixed system of ancient traditions, customs, and institutions such as tends to orient the life of a people toward the past rather than toward the future. Certainly since the founding of the Republic the "weight of the centuries" has lain less heavily on the American than on the European people.

(2) The primitive quality of life on the frontier where modern trained men were obliged to live in an uncultivated

environment. The biological conception of human behavior as a continuous process of "interactive adaptation" between an organism and its environment was more clearly exhibited in the struggle of the pioneer with primitive conditions on the frontier than it was in the more prosaic life of the settled regions of Europe. Moreover, frontier life was also fluid in character. The frontier was a rapidly changing world. Institutions were made and remade within the life-span of individuals. As compared to older regions there was little that was fixed in either the natural or the social environment of the pioneer.

(3) The reality given to ideas of social democracy and human progress in a new world where natural resources were abundant and men were relatively scarce. American democracy owes much to the existence of free land on the frontier.

(4) The more recent extensive industrial development of the United States, and the unparalleled use made of the machine in serving human ends. Our technology of this later period put scientific processes into the ordinary affairs of everyday life. The logic of experimental science, and "the metaphysics of the instrument," came more naturally to a people who had witnessed man and his tools subduing a continent.

Each of these four social influences will be briefly treated in the following pages. The aim is not to prove that the philosophy of experimentalism is a mere rationalization of tendencies in American life. This is far from being the case. On the other hand, it is hoped that even this brief review of American social experience will suggest important reasons why an experimental philosophy found more friendly soil in the New World than it did in the Old.

4. The Absence of Fixed Traditions

The people who discovered and settled America were Europeans. They landed at Jamestown, at Plymouth, and on the island of Manhattan carrying in their heads pictures of European life and society. For many years colonial America faced toward Europe. In other words, it faced toward the past from which it had come. The commercial, financial, intellectual, esthetic, and religious ties which bound the colonies to the mother-country were as important as were the more formal relations of government. Many of the leading figures in the early colonies were mere sojourners who planned later to return to live in the homeland. Those who came to stay tried to build new Londons, new Yorks, and new Amsterdams in the new territory. The institutions they established and the culture which they enjoyed were derived from European sources. Speaking more precisely, the main source of the colonial civilization was England. For although Scotch-Irish, Dutch, Swedes, French, Germans, Irish, and Jews were numbered among the colonists, the dominant influence was undoubtedly English. In his description of provincial America Beard is most emphatic on this point:

"When the last word is said for all the diverse elements in provincial life, certain indubitable facts obtrude themselves upon the view like giant boulders on a plain. Beyond question, the overwhelming majority of the white people in the colonies were of English descent; the arrangement of classes was English; the law which held together the whole social order was English in essence, modified, of course, but primarily English; the dominant religious institutions and modes of theology were English adaptations of Christianity; the types of formal education, the amusements, furniture, fashions, art, and domestic codes were all fundamentally English too. The language of bench and bar, pulpit and press, was English. . . . Whether for praise, blame, or merriment, colonial America was basically English." [9]

For the most part, colonial America was a reproduction, with such modifications as the circumstances required, of the civilization of the mother-country, England. Contrary to views based on certain school-book fictions, the Englishmen who came as colonists fortunately did not drop all of their European habits of thought and of action into the sea during the course of their stormy passage to America. Even the social hierarchy of the stratified English society was reproduced to a certain extent in the colonial social order.

And yet there was a most important difference. The colonists were indeed Europeans, but they were uprooted, transplanted Europeans. The economic, political, and religious institutions were English in pattern in the main, but they were institutions torn out of their ancient setting, rebuilt in a new environment, and continuously in process of adaptation to meet altered conditions. Now these institutions were radically changed in this process, changed somewhat in form and substance, but more in the way they came to be viewed by the colonists who had undergone this new experience. Out from under the shadow of the palaces, the castles, and the cathedrals of Europe—symbols of an ancient social order with its values enhanced and hallowed by history—the common man began to lose his peasant mind. These social and political institutions, removed from the soil in which they had grown, were not so powerful after transplantation in communicating the mystical impression that, in spite of social injustices which they perpetuated, they were expressions of a divine order inherent in the very nature of things. To uprooted Europeans in a new and rapidly changing environment these transplanted institutions came to look like ordinary human arrangements devised to meet certain social ends. Even that section of the colonial population who served as indentured servants, and were for the time literally economic slaves, found in the abundance of free land an ever-present invitation to break out of their lowly status.

The process by which the American colonies achieved their independent nationhood was the process of revolution. As has been well said, the American Revolution was more than a war with England. It was also a movement for profound social reconstruction. Under the progressive leadership of Jefferson, Paine, Franklin, and many others, the colonists enunciated and proceeded to act upon the principle of John Locke to the effect that governments are to be tested by their social consequences, and that when the majority living under a given government judge that government to be radically unworthy, they have the right to change it, by armed revolution if necessary. In other words, the idea of the "instrumental" value of institutions was written into the very story by which the United States became a nation.

The successful outcome of the Revolution marked the permanent passing from the American scene of the monarchical form of government with all of its royal trappings, and it also marked the overthrow of the ideal of a special class of leisured "gentlemen rulers." Nor did the new mental outlook find its exclusive expression in these political changes. Shortly following the close of the Revolutionary War the churches were disestablished by the governments of the various States, and the false prestige which each had conferred upon the other by virtue of this alliance was removed. The new national government was completely secular in character. Finally a budding land-aristocracy was struck a mortal blow by the abolition of the system of entail and primogeniture, and the removal of the restrictions relating to the occupation of the unsettled areas beyond the Alleghenies. In these and various other ways did the newly founded nation move to wipe out of its social inheritance many characteristic traces of an outmoded feudal order. Such changes in the social structure gave new impetus to the tendency of the American people to find the justification for their activities primarily in the intrinsic value and meaning of these activities rather than in their agreement with an inherited fabric of customs, habits, histories, and institutions. Thus did American life grow more experimental. The American Republic was born in a revolution that broke the political control of England over the colonies. The American mind was born in a parallel revolution that partially broke the control of Old World institutions and ideas over American thought. This revolution and the new institutions which grew out of it tended to place many of the directive forces of our national life within its immediate ongoing social processes.

Fortunately for the young nation, the break with the colonial-European culture was not as abrupt nor as complete as this brief account would seem to indicate. Much that had been developed in the years of the colonial period was of inestimable value in this era of national development. Parts of the earlier inheritance which were not so useful also continued to exist. In religion and morals the dogmatic control of the Calvinist and the Puritan continued powerful. A religion centered in other-worldly ideas continued to flourish, particularly on the frontier. What Santayana has called "the genteel tradition" lingered on in the schools and colleges, and in the art, literature, and academic philosophy of the Republic. This tended to produce a dualism between the so-called cultural influences and the basic economic and social tendencies in American life. But while all this was true, the vital movement of life was such that its most fundamental controls were not located in this inherited tradition. As Mead points out, a new pioneer force was at work:

"I have indicated what seems to me the important character-istic of American life, the freedom, within certain rather rigid but very wide boundaries, to work out immediate politics and business with no reverential sense of a pre-existing social order within which they must take their place and whose values they must preserve." [10]

5. *The Frontier and Continuous Reconstruction*

The close of the Revolutionary War was closely followed by a new interest in the West. The nation soon ceased to look primarily to Europe and turned its face instead toward its own undeveloped territories. It found in the natural re-sources of land, timber, and minerals in that vast area a chal-lenge to its youthful strength and the opportunity for an unparalleled expansion. No precedents existed for the tasks the United States was now about to undertake. The guiding principles for this new adventure had to be created experi-mentally in the actual struggle with novel and changing con-ditions on the frontier. He who would understand the spirit of the philosophy of experimentalism would do well to study the story of this great migration into the Mississippi valley and out into the regions of the Far West.

As has already been indicated, experimentalism character-izes experience as the active process of interaction between man and his environment. The very continuance of life itself demands that the individual succeed in adapting himself to his environment and in deriving from it support for his own vital functions. Now in the highly complex society of mod-ern industrialism with its minute division of labor this con-ception of experience frequently seems remote. Many men have little contact with nature in the raw to-day. They work for employers in large factories. They are paid in money, not in foodstuffs, clothing, etc. Money is not viewed as a mere means of exchange, it comes to be regarded as wealth itself.

Moreover, the individual laborer appears to be lost. His initiative and inventive ingenuity are not much in evidence. The person who tends a machine, repeating automatically one operation day after day, may indeed have to adapt himself to the machine, but his experience too frequently exhausts itself in this mechanical habituation. This is particularly true of the individual confronted with our urban and industrial civilization. He may learn something of this civilization by observing it and studying how its various parts operate and articulate one with another, but the average individual does not see himself as one who actively participates in the control of its processes. In other words, modern life conceals its basic processes in the complexity of its organization, and tends to make the individual a mere spectator whose experience is largely that of passive adaptation and whose knowledge seems to be gained through observing and making mental copies of what is already in his environment. His own desires and purposes seem to be in the main irrelevant to this gigantic structure. Its very size and complexity give it a certain finality, if not fatality.

That grave social problems inhere in the present industrial system, with its tendency to destroy community life and to rob the individual of significant creative participation in its important procedures, is all too apparent. However, this is not the place for the discussion of such problems. Modern industrialism has been referred to merely to sharpen the contrast between it and the primitive life of the frontier. On the frontier the elemental aspects of experience stand revealed. The biological description of organic behavior in general is seen also to be true of human behavior. Human experience in its primary forms is found to be exactly this active process of interaction between an organism and its environment of which the experimentalist speaks. At first, the pioneer must largely adapt himself to what is given in order to survive. But he does not stop with passive acceptance. He studies his natural environment, not as an outside spectator, but as one who is implicated in it, and in order to find out what difficulties and resources it offers for the realization of his purposes. His aim is to reconstruct that which is brutely given in the raw environment in order to make it more adequately serve his needs. He needs to know in order to control. His ideas are not mere copies of what is given, but are suggestions of how what is given may be changed to serve his interests. He tests his ideas in activity: by the conditions they produce; by the consequences to which they lead. Of necessity he modifies them in the light of those consequences. In his important book *The Frontier in American History,* Turner gives a vivid picture of this movement of life on the frontier:

"The wilderness masters the colonist. It finds him a European in dress, industries, tools, modes of travel, and thought. It takes him from the railroad car and puts him in the birch canoe. It strips off the garments of civilization and arrays him in the hunting shirt and the moccasin. It puts him in the log cabin of the Cherokee and Iroquois and runs an Indian palisade around him. Before long he has gone to planting Indian corn and plowing with a sharp stick; he shouts the war cry and takes the scalp in orthodox fashion. In short at the frontier the environment is at first too strong for the man. He must accept the conditions which it furnishes, or perish, and so he fits himself into the Indian clearings and follows the Indian trails. Little by little he transforms the wilderness, but the outcome is not the old Europe, not simply the development of Germanic germs, any more than the first phenomenon was a case of reversion to Germanic mark. The fact is that here is a new product that is American." [11]

Life on the frontier shows existence to be a matter of concrete particulars. If the pioneer were to survive, he had to pay attention to such concrete matters as hunting, fishing, providing shelter, securing protection, tilling the soil, caring for the sick and countless similar specific affairs. His life and that of the members of his family depended upon his ability to manage these concerns. The practical bearing of reality on his existence could not be forgotten. There was "a certain compulsion in the run of events." No doubt there was much of superstition in his beliefs, but the immediately felt precarious character of existence made it imperative that he should seek his security primarily in practical activity guided by intelligent understanding.

It was a life that called for inventive capacity. There was nothing final or finished about the world in which the pioneer lived. He was close to nature, and he found that nature as met in her most primitive mode could not be trusted to take care of him. The possibilities—the raw materials—for life were there, but they had to be developed and utilized. He had to bring order out of disorder. His life depended upon his ability to learn the meanings of things. In other words, he had to find out what things were good for; and how he should behave with reference to them. Will, purpose, activity were constantly called for. Their expression indubitably made a difference in the way things happened. His environment was quick to penalize his wrong inferences and his failures to see the connections between events; it also rewarded those judgments and inferences which were in line with "the grain of circumstance."

The frontier environment taught man that there were some things he could not do. Control he had; but it was within limits. The frontier life was intolerant of ends that could not be translated into effective means. It made repeated demonstrations of how inevitably ends are modified by the means available for their realization. It was, however, a life that gave a career to ideas and ideals. The actual could be, in fact had to be, reorganized to make it more nearly correspond to the ideal. The reconstructive activity of the early settlers daily contradicted the philosophical assumption that "the actual is the rational." That which was given had to be changed into something better if man were to enjoy a humane existence.

"Creative intelligence" was a fact on the frontier. Wildernesses were cleared, swamps were drained, deserts were irrigated, canals were dug, railroads were built, mountains were tunneled, mines were opened, water-power was harnessed, industries were started, towns were founded, and communities were organized. Changes such as these were telescoped almost within a single life-span. It is not to be wondered that American experimentalists believe that novelty and change are naturalized in the world. Nor is it strange that Dewey should define *growth—education*—as that process of "continuous reconstruction of experience which adds to the meaning of experience and which increases ability to direct the course of subsequent experience." He had lived in a nation where this continuous reconstruction of experience—individual and institutional—had been proceeding with an unprecedented momentum. To quote Turner again:

"Behind institutions, behind constitutional forms and modifications, lie the vital forces that call these organs into life and shape them to meet changing conditions. The peculiarity of American institutions is, the fact that they have been compelled to adapt themselves to the changes of an expanding people——to the changes involved in crossing a continent, in winning a wilderness, and in developing at each area of this progress out of the primitive economic and political conditions of the frontier into the complexity of city life. Said Calhoun in 1817, 'We are great, and rapidly—I was about to say fearfully—growing.' So saying, he touched the distinguishing feature of American life." [12]

"Thus American development has exhibited not merely advance along a single line, but a return to primitive conditions on a continually advancing frontier line, and a new development for that area. American social development has been continually beginning over again on the frontier. This perennial rebirth, this fluidity of American life, this expansion westward with its new opportunities, its continuous touch with the simplicity of primitive society, furnish the forces dominating American character." [13]

One need not subscribe to Turner's extreme view that the frontier movement is the determining force in all of American history to recognize its profound influence in shaping our social experience. Implicit in the adventurous life of the pioneers of the westward migration were elements of a new philosophy of man and nature. The experimentalist, in developing "the idea of a universe which is not all closed and settled, which is still in some respects indeterminate and in the making, which is adventurous and which implicates all who share in it, whether by acting or believing, in its own perils," [14] was giving philosophic formulation to traits exhibited in pioneer experience. Furthermore, "the fundamental idea of an open universe in which uncertainty, choice, hypotheses, novelties and possibilities are naturalized" [15] may be said to be literally a description of what Americans found existence to be in the century or more that they lived on the growing edge of civilization on the frontier. Something of that adventure has entered into the mind and soul of the American people. The experimentalists have caught something of its spirit in their philosophy.

6. *Freedom and Democracy*

The most fundamental value in the experimentalist philosophy is its method. This method is the method of experience. It is radically empirical. It boldly takes the things of ordinary experience as evidential of the nature of reality. The doings and undergoings of men, the things men suffer and enjoy— everyday human experience—is said to be just as evidential of the nature of nature as is an electron or a star. Reality is not considered to be something back of, ulterior to, essentially different in kind from, this world of man's experience; but is held to be precisely this world of common experience in all of the myriad forms that experience takes. What is true of reality is also true of values. Values are not values because they are the ideal patterns and ends of some transcendental order; the kingdom of values is within human experience. In thus giving primary emphasis to its method— the method of experience—experimentalism places the democratic principle at the heart of its philosophy. It may be objected that there is no inherent connection between empirical method and democratic principles. It is interesting to note in this connection that scientific method and democratic institutions did actually develop at about the same time and in the same places. Some see more than a mere coincidence in this. But no matter how we may think about the relations

of the two in general, there can be no question about the relation of democratic principles and the experimental method
of experience in the thought of the experimentalist philosophers. Some of the experimentalists have even declared
democracy and experimental method to be two names for one
process. In *Experience and Nature,* Dewey concludes the
opening chapter on philosophic method with the following
sentences:

"Hence it may be asserted that the final issue of empirical
method is whether the guide and standard of beliefs and conduct
lies within or without the *shareable* situations of life. The ultimate accusation levelled against professedly non-empirical
philosophies is that in casting aspersion upon the events and
objects of experience, *they deny the power of common life to
develop its own regulative methods and to furnish from within
itself adequate goals, ideals, and criteria.** Thus in effect they
claim a private access to truth and deprive the things of common
experience of the enlightenment and guidance that philosophy
might otherwise derive from them. The transcendentalist has
conspired with his arch-enemy, the sensualist, to narrow the
acknowledged subject-matter of experience and to lessen its po-
tencies for a wider and directed reflective choice. Respect for
experience is respect for its possibilities in thought and knowledge as well as an enforced attention to its joys and sorrows.
Intellectual piety toward experience is a precondition of the
direction of life and of tolerant and generous coöperation among
men. Respect for the things of experience alone brings with it
such a respect for others, the centres of experience, as is free
from patronage, domination and the will to impose." [16]

Now this radical faith in the "power of common life to
develop its own regulative standards and to furnish from
within itself adequate goals, ideals, and criteria" could
hardly have been evolved in a feudal society. Its obvious connection with a social environment in which some evidence
was to be found of man's ability thus to manage his own

* Italics mine.

affairs need not be emphasized. Apart from a social order in which the common man had achieved, at least for a time, some such significance, it is improbable that this ideal could have been fashioned. In the vast areas of free land of the young Republic was found the indispensable material foundation on which such a society might be constructed. Out of the social ideals and the reconstructed social and political institutions of the Revolutionary period came the social forces which made possible the development of such a democratic society—something new under the sun. Whether it was but a passing episode—the accidental result of fortuitous circumstances—the development of events will tell; but after all discounts are made, the sober judgment of competent observers seem to be that, for a time at least, such a democratic society did prevail. Charles Beard, who has done much to deflate romantic traditions of American history and false idealizations of American democracy, speaks in *The Rise of American Civilization* in these measured words:

"The economy of the new West, essentially agricultural, rested mainly upon a system of freehold farms. . . . In this immense domain sprang up a social order without marked class or caste, a society of people substantially equal in worldly goods, deriving their livelihood from one prime source—labor with their own hands on the soil.

"For many decades, an overwhelming majority of the white men in the West were land-owning farmers. The unit of their society was the family on the isolated holding engaged in an unremitting battle with nature for its living. No benevolent government surrounded it with safeguards; no army of officials inspected its processes of life and labor. In a thousand emergencies it was thrown upon its own resources; it produced its own foodstuffs, manufactured most of its own clothing, warded off diseases with homemade remedies inherited from primitive women, and often walked in the valley of the shadow of death without priestly ministrations.

"In the folkways and mores there was a rugged freedom—
the freedom of hardy men and women, taut of muscle and
bronzed by sun and rain and wind, working with their hands in
abundant materials, shaping oak from their own forests and
flax from their own fields to the plain use of a plain life, content with little and rejoicing in it." [17]

The experimentalist does not assert that social ideals and
ideas were the exclusive forces in bringing this democratic
society into being. They played a part, but an abundance of
free land, and a new industrial economy, were probably more
influential. The fact that property qualifications for voting
were only removed in the older Atlantic coast States after
their labor supply was threatened by the westward movement
is symptomatic of the powerful contribution the free land
of the frontier made to the development of democratic institutions. Now that the free land of the frontier is gone, the
task of maintaining a democratic society grows more difficult. It is apparent that the social habits and philosophy of
the earlier individualism of the simpler agricultural civilization are tragically inadequate to meet the challenge of the
corporate life of the present industrial society. What the
experimentalist hopes is that, once having had the experience of a society based on democratic principles, the intelligence and good-will of men will be adequate to conserve its
essential goods in the midst of changing conditions. In any
event, the ideal of a people collectively directing their entire
experience through the use of experimental procedures is
enshrined in the philosophy of Experimentalism. The democratic principle runs through all of its formulations.

7. Industrialism and Human Control

With the development of industrial society we reach the
modern era in the social evolution of American life. The

industrial revolution caused by the introduction of power machinery began in England but rapidly spread throughout the entire world. There is nothing peculiarly American about it. However, synchronizing as it did with the great migration to the virgin lands of the West, its effects were revolutionary in the economic life of the United States. Schlesinger speaks of these changes in *New Viewpoints in American History* as follows:

"So rapid and comprehensive were the changes that occurred in the two decades following Lincoln's inauguration that no less a term than 'economic revolution' is required to describe them. Referring particularly to American industrial development, the United States Industrial Commission declared in 1902 that the changes and the progress since 1865 have been greater in many directions than during the whole history of the world before. In contrast to the industrial revolution in England, however, the economic revolution was not merely a revolution in manufacturing processes. In just as significant a sense it was an agricultural revolution and also a revolution in transportation." [18]

"The unprecedented activity along all lines of economic endeavor imposed fresh demands upon American inventive genius to which it responded with countless new appliances and machines for farm and factory." [19]

"The records of the Patent office throw some light on the matter. In the entire period before 1860, something less than 36,000 patents had been granted; in the remaining years of the century the number of patents issued reached the astonishing total of almost 640,000." [20]

It is not relevant to our purpose in this discussion to attempt an evaluation of this new industrial order. Machine civilization and its correlated capitalistic culture are dominating forces in contemporary American life. It is inconceivable that a philosophy could have developed during this period and not have been influenced one way or another by these primary social facts. The philosophy of experimentalism does not pretend not to have been so influenced. The fact that the name *instrumentalism* has been used to describe this philosophy is public recognition of this connection. More than any other modern philosophy it has sought to understand this technological civilization and to uncover its implications for man and his understanding of his world.

The experimentalist finds in the machine convincing evidence of the creative character of human thought. The machine is a human invention. In order to invent a machine the inventor must pay attention to the characters of the materials with which he is dealing. He pays attention to these raw materials; he studies their possibilities, and by so doing he gets suggestions for such reorganization of these materials as will eventuate in a new device—something previously not in existence. Here thought is not a mere reproduction of what is antecedently given. Nor is it to be tested by how faithfully it yields a sort of photographic reproduction of these antecedent elements. Hence thinking may be said to be a kind of inventing. As such it is a reconstructive process, and is to be tested by the character of the reconstruction achieved. The reconstruction, if successful, brings something new into the world and is genuinely creative.

The machine is an instrument for getting things done. As Sidney Hook has pointed out in his discussion of *The Metaphysics of Pragmatism,* the existence of the instrument—the machine—is testimony to a lack found in nature. The fact of the machine also witnesses to the indeterminate character of the world in which we live. Were our world complete and finished, machines would not be invented, for there would be nothing they could do. Thus experimentalism finds further evidence for its view of a contingent, unfinished world in the fact that throughout history man has been concerned to improve and multiply his tools.

While one may have many doubts about the narrow ends to which our existing machine civilization is devoted, he can have no doubt about the fact that the machine has immensely expanded man's power of control over natural energies. The experimentalist believes that the new technology offers hope of a society that will have a material foundation adequate to provide a decent life for all. It deepens his confidence in the outlook for social democracy.

> "The recognition that natural energy can be systematically applied through experimental observation, to the satisfaction and multiplication of concrete wants is doubtless the greatest single discovery ever imported into the life of man—save perhaps the discovery of language. Science, borrowing from industry, repaid the debt with interest, and has made the control of natural forces for the aims of life so inevitable that for the first time man is relieved from overhanging fear, with its wolflike scramble to possess and accumulate, and is freed to consider the more gracious question of securing to all an ample and liberal life." [21]

Machines are developed through experimental procedures. They are constantly adapted, modified, improved as they are used. It is the faith of the experimentalist that experimental procedures similar to those which have so extended man's control over the natural environment could, if utilized in the social and moral realm, produce a similar liberation and expansion.

In fact, the experimentalist believes that, without some such development of the experimental method and disposition in the social field, the outlook for man's ability to adjust to the society of the machine is far from reassuring. The strange paradox is that while the machine gives added control and security, it at the same time seems to increase uncertainty and instability in human affairs. The world without the machine was a changing, dynamic world; with the machine the rate of its changes has been accelerated. Our present industrial civilization is inherently a dynamic civilization. Experimental procedures have produced this technological civilization with both its promise of finer things and its threat to human values already achieved. The experimentalist believes we shall be able to control industrialism so as to realize its promise and to remove its threat only as we learn to proceed in this same experimental manner in all realms of our experience.

8. The Two Mentalities

In conclusion it may be said that the experimentalist finds two mentalities existing side by side in present-day America. Not infrequently these two minds keep house together in the life of the same individual.

One is the mind which is reflected in our technological civilization. Within limits it is the scientific manner of mind. For our technology does incorporate scientific principles and procedures. "Modern industry is so much applied science." The American who uses machinery to plow his fields, to harvest his crops, and to manufacture his endless variety of goods; who travels in the automobile, the railroad train, and the airplane; who telephones across the continent; who builds steel bridges and erects sky-scrapers; who utilizes electricity to light his home, to clean his rugs, to iron his clothes, to toast his bread; who tunes in to enjoy his radio program— this American has habits of thought and action which possess something of the quality of science. When one of his many machines won't work, he knows there is some specific cause for the difficulty, and he searches to find out what is wrong. On the farm, in the shop, in his business, and in his laboratories he assumes that if he is to realize his ends he must find the appropriate means. For in these aspects of his experience he has learned to think in terms of regular sequences. In experimental procedures and techniques he has a method for finding hidden continuities and causal relationships. By means of these, natural events are utilized and controlled for his purposes.

This first type of mind also has respect for experience. It is a resourceful mind that trusts its own procedures. It gives due heed to what has been already tested in experience, but it is not afraid of innovations. It finds its directions, its ultimate sanctions, within the situations with which it has to deal. It is experimental. It is also a social mind. It has learned how to coöperate with others in common researches in commerce and labor, and to a lesser degree in projects of government and other public affairs. The adventure in democratic institutions which American society represents, the independence and neighborly feeling which the frontier experiences encouraged, and the exploits of the modern industrial era have all contributed to the formulation of this mentality.

The second mentality found in America has its characteristic forms of expression. It is exhibited in sky-scrapers that omit the thirteenth floor; in the thousands who rush to a grave at Malden to find in magic a cure for their diseases; in the sects that oppose the distribution of birth-control literature because they believe all use of contraceptives to be contrary to Divine commands; in fundamentalists whose belief in an infallible book prompts them to pass laws prohibiting the teaching of scientific theories about the origin of man; in modernists who attempt to dispose of complex social problems by telling us what an earlier religious leader would do were he now here; in all of those who cling to rigid moral codes regardless of consequences; in the "Red" hysteria; in censorship laws of all kinds; in the tenacious manner in which humanist leaders cling to the belief in a golden age in the past and would have us return to it in order to find there the norms and values for present experience; in those who would follow immediate impulse and passing desire rather than be guided by consequences critically evaluated; in short, this mentality is found in all of those who for one reason or another, in one realm or another, do not believe in the use of the experimental method—"the method of observation, of experiment, of framing and following working hypotheses."

In the existence of these two mentalities the experimentalist finds the heart of the modern problem. "The ulterior issue is the possibility that actual experience in its concrete content and movement may furnish those ideals, meanings and values whose lack and uncertainty in experience as actually lived by most persons has supplied the motive force for recourse to some reality beyond experience: a lack and uncertainty that account for the continued hold of traditional philosophical and religious notions which are not consonant with the main tenor of modern life." [22]

The belief of the experimentalist that in the existence of these two mentalities is found the deepest problem of our day may partly account for his absorbing interest in education. He believes that education properly conceived might do much to unify an American mind which is now divided against itself.

REFERENCES

1. JOHN DEWEY, *Human Nature and Conduct* (Henry Holt and Company, 1922), p. 314.
2. JOHN DEWEY, "A Sketch of the Development of Pragmatism," *Studies in the History of Ideas* (Columbia University Press, 1925), II, 432–433.
3. WILLIAM JAMES, *Pragmatism* (Longmans, Green & Co., 1908).
4. WILLIAM JAMES, *Collected Essays and Reviews* (Longmans, Green & Co., 1920), p. 434.
5. JOHN DEWEY, "A Sketch of the Development of Pragmatism," *Studies in the History of Ideas* (Columbia University Press, 1925), II, 367–368.
6. JOHN DEWEY, *Influence of Darwin on Philosophy* (Henry Holt and Company, 1920), pp. 1–2.
7. JOHN DEWEY, "A Sketch of the Development of Pragmatism," *Studies in the History of Ideas* (Columbia University Press, 1925), II, 355–356.
8. *Ibid.,* p. 336 (foot-note).
9. CHARLES BEARD, *The Rise of American Civilization* (The Macmillan Company, 1927), p. 125.
10. *John Dewey, the Man and His Philosophy* (Harvard University Press, 1930), p. 104.
11. F. J. TURNER, *The Frontier in American History* (Henry Holt and Company, 1930), p. 4.
12. *Ibid.,* p. 2.
13. *Ibid.,* pp. 2–3.
14. JOHN DEWEY, in the *New Republic,* Jan. 5, 1927. (Reprinted in *Characters and Events* [Henry Holt and Company, 1929], II, 439.)
15. *Ibid.,* p. 440.
16. JOHN DEWEY, *Experience and Nature* (The Open Court Publishing Co., 1929), pp. 38–39.
17. CHARLES BEARD, *The Rise of American Civilization* (The Macmillan Company, 1927), pp. 534–535.
18. A. M. SCHLESINGER, *New Viewpoints in American History* (The Macmillan Company, 1922), pp. 248–249.
19. *Ibid.,* p. 248.
20. *Ibid.,* p. 256.

21. JOHN DEWEY, *Influence of Darwin on Philosophy* (Henry
    Holt and Company, 1920), p. 58.
22. JOHN DEWEY, *Quest for Certainty* (Minton, Balch & Com-
    pany, 1929), p. 107.

CHAPTER III

HAS EXPERIMENTALISM A METAPHYSIC?

"... 'Method' is dogged by a pack of metaphysical consequences;
... a 'pure' method which does not involve reference to a theory of
existence is as devoid of meaning as a proposition which does not imply
other propositions."

HOOK.

1. Experimentalism and Education

IT IS reported that Professor Dewey accepted the headship
of the department of philosophy at the University of Chicago
on the condition that it should include the department of
education. A few years ago Professor Bode transferred
from the field of general philosophy to the department of
education at Ohio State University. These incidents illustrate
the close connection that has always prevailed between the
philosophy of experimentalism and education. This connection is all the more striking when one considers how remote
much of the subject-matter of present-day technical philosophy is from the vital interests of educators. Nor is the close
relation between experimentalism and education simply due
to the fact that leading experimentalists, such as James and
Dewey, were men who also happened to have an interest in
the schools. The situation indicates that the connection is
more fundamental. The underlying conceptions of experience and knowledge and the social implications of the philosophy of experimentalism are such that they naturally lead

to an interest in education. The experimentalist believes that life should be a continuous process of growth through learning from experience. He desires our schools to be so conducted that habits and attitudes favorable to such a tendency to learn constantly from experience would be developed early in the character of each child.

Nor is the traffic between experimentalism and education a one-way traffic. While philosophic interests have moved experimentalists to work in the schools, educators, faced with the task of developing a public system of education suited to the needs of a democratic society, have also found important resources in the philosophy of experimentalism. Particularly have teachers in daily face-to-face contact with children gained help from the new tools of understanding which the experimentalists have contributed. The aim of this and the following chapter will be to consider some of the central implications of experimentalism for education. We shall begin by considering certain of the more general positions of the philosophy, particularly those which have a bearing on its understanding of the nature of the world in which we live.

2. Wider Implications of Method

Were we to accept certain statements of the experimentalists at full face value, we would be led to conclude that as a philosophy it has no interest in a general world view and is directed exclusively to the development of a philosophic method. In *Creative Intelligence,* Dewey, writing on the theme "The Need for A Recovery of Philosophy," says,

"It is often said that pragmatism, unless it is content to be a contribution to mere methodology, must develop a theory of Reality. But the chief characteristic trait of the pragmatic notion of reality is precisely that no theory of Reality in general, *uber-haupt*, is possible or needed. It occupies the position of an eman-cipated emipiricism or a thoroughgoing naïve realism. It finds that 'reality' is a *denotative* term, a word used to designate in-differently everything that happens." [1]

In an article in the *New Republic* on "Fundamentals," which appeared at the time of the fundamentalist-modernist controversy, the same writer declares that there is only one fundamental, namely, method:

". . . there are a steadily increasing number of persons who find security in *methods* of inquiry, of observation, experiment, of forming and following working hypotheses. Such persons are not unsettled by the upsetting of any special belief, because they retain security of procedure. They can say, borrowing lan-guage from another context, though this method slay my most cherished belief, yet will I trust it. The growth of this sense, even if only half-consciously, is the cause of the increased in-difference of large numbers of persons to organized religion. It is not that they are especially excited about this or that doctrine, but that the guardianship of truth seems to them to have passed over to the *method* of attaining and testing beliefs. In this latter fundamental they rest in intellectual and emotional peace." [2]

The import of these two statements is much the same. The first asserts that experimentalism believes that a theory of Reality in general is not only not needed, but is, in fact, impos-sible. The second states that particular beliefs about the na-ture and meaning of the world in which we live are to be held tentatively, as hypotheses. All such beliefs are subject to revision in the light of further knowledge. Our funda-mental trust, therefore, should not be placed in these neces-sarily partial beliefs, but rather in the methods of procedure by which we arrive at all of our beliefs. As thus understood, philosophy is a spirit and method with which we approach the various subject-matters of experience. To be philosophical is to approach experience in the manner of critical, experimental inquiry; to be unphilosophical is to be uncritical, or non-experimental in thought and action.

However, as we examine these two propositions more closely, certain questions arise. What is implied when it is said that our world is such that "no theory of Reality in general is possible or needed"? Apparently one implication is that the future is not a mere word, but is something that must always be taken into consideration; for as time passes situations change—one thing grows into another thing. This points to the conclusion that the ongoing nature of existence is such that it is impossible to deal with it wholesale or exhaustively. Hence thought and activity to be fruitful must relate to concrete events or situations.

Regardless of whether we do or do not accept this conclusion, can it be said to be devoid of assumptions about the nature of reality in general? It would seem to include several such general assumptions. One of these is to the effect that all things are in such a process of change that no final description of reality is possible. But does not this negative conclusion also involve a positive assertion about the nature of the world in general? Apparently it affirms that we live in a world which is characterized throughout by process and change. Our concern here is not with the truth or falsity of this generalization about existence, but merely to point out that, in any event, it is an inclusive generalization of the largest significance.

Again, does not the above view also assume that all one need know about any given situation in order adequately to orient himself to it can be known without first taking the whole nature of all reality into account? To this extent, at least, it would seem that the pluralistic character of existence is held to be true.

Moreover, if one proclaims that the experimental method is the all-inclusive method, does he not in so doing express a belief that the general nature of the world is such that this one method is adequate to discover all important meanings discoverable by any valid method? Is this not equivalent to saying that experimental procedures are our ultimate resource in each and every realm where we are concerned to gain knowledge of and control of experience? Does not this position also tend to imply that there is no trans-empirical Reality? That supernaturalisms of all sorts are untenable? That it is both useless and unnecessary to appeal for support to something above and beyond experience? Is it not also implied that no matter how emotionally invigorating immediate mystical experience may be, it can contribute nothing to be taken reliably as knowledge about the nature of existence?

Apparently the method and test of experimentalism is not as innocent of metaphysical consequences as some of its advocates have at times assumed. The writer believes in the fundamental value of this philosophy. Because he believes it is important, he is unwilling to see it robbed of its larger significance by an obscurantism which says it is merely a method that is equally hospitable to every conceivable sort of world view. We are committed to a good deal if we accept whole-heartedly the pragmatic test of significance as formulated by Peirce:

"Our idea of anything is our idea of its sensible effects. . . . Consider what effects that might conceivably have practical bearings, we conceive the object of our conception to have. Then, our conception of these effects is the whole of our conception of the object." [3]

James stated the same principle as follows:

"What difference would it practically make to anyone if this notion rather than that notion were true? If no practical difference whatever can be traced, then the alternatives mean practically the same thing, and all dispute is idle." [4]

The view that in experimentalism we have a philosophy which has kept entirely out of the field of metaphysics is increasingly challenged. Professor Lewis in a recent article on "Pragmatism and Current Thought" discusses this question:

"Pragmatism is, as James indicated, not a doctrine but a method: viewed logically, it can be regarded as the consequence of a single principle of procedure. But this principle, though by itself it says nothing material in the field of metaphysics or epistemology, and though its application is by no means confined to philosophy, has nevertheless a wealth of philosophic consequences. It implies at least the outline of a theory of knowledge; and if it dictates no metaphysical theses, at least it rules out a good deal which has been put forward under that caption, and it operates as a principle of orientation in the search for positive conclusions." [5]

In even more emphatic language Sidney Hook opens his book on *The Metaphysics of Pragmatism* with the following statement:

"The title of this study has been selected with malice prepense. It conjoins two terms whose connotations are generally regarded as opposite in order to make more emphatic the belief that 'method' is dogged by a pack of metaphysical consequences; that a 'pure' method which does not involve reference to a theory of existence is as devoid of meaning as a proposition which does not imply other propositions. 'Pragmatism' has become a debased word in the linguistic exchange of contemporary philosophy. Its one indisputable signification is that of a militant method of approaching and settling philosophic problems—some say by ignoring them, others say by calling familiar assumptions into question. But unless pragmatism is to experience the same fate which has befallen the positivism of Comte and the phenomenalism of Mach—philosophies proudly and avowedly anti-metaphysical— it must analyze the implications of what it means to have a method and examine the generic traits of existence which make that method a fruitful one in revealing them." [6]

Apparently Dewey is not opposed to the view expressed in the above quotation, for he has written a foreword to the book in which he gives approval to its central thesis. In certain of his writings Dewey seems to recognize frankly that experimentalism is not only a philosophy of method, but is also a philosophy with a world view. In his *Experience and Nature* mention is made of a "naturalistic metaphysics." It would appear that one of the important aims of the entire book is to set forth the more general implications of experimentalism in contrast with what is spoken of as the "classical philosophical position." In reply to an article by Lewis Mumford which charges James with not having developed a *Weltanschauung,* Dewey affirms "that James brought with him not only a *Weltanschauung,* but a revolutionary one." [7] It is obvious from this article that Dewey fully recognizes that experimentalism does possess a novel world view. Since both Peirce and James also seemed to believe this to be true, it may be concluded that all three of the pioneer leaders of experimentalism recognize it to be a philosophy not only with a method but also with a world view.

Emphasis has been given here to the fact that a world view is contained in the philosophy of experimentalism because of its important bearing on matters in the field of education. To grasp the genuine significance of the philosophy of experimentalism for education, it is important to try to apprehend how the experimentalist understands his world. It should be candidly admitted that many of his educational ideas are not equally hospitable to all current philosophical and theological views. Much of the confusion now apparent in the effort to work out the ideas of experimentalism in education arises from the effort to combine these *newer methods* in education with *older outlooks* which are the correlatives of a world view which experimentalism has repudiated. We shall now proceed to examine more in detail some of the philosophical conceptions included in the view of the experimentalist.

3. Findings of Naïve Experience

The world view of the experimentalist is revolutionary partly because it is so naïve. Now a naïve view is not necessarily one easy to achieve. In philosophy the direct, naïve approach to the various subject-matters of experience is probably the most difficult of all to attain. No one can wholly succeed in achieving it. Our world has been the subject-matter for philosophizing for many centuries. In Athens some of the greatest minds in the history of human thought worked out their philosophies centuries before the dawn of the Christian era. So important were their contributions that even to-day there are those who say that all of the significant varieties of philosophic method and viewpoint were achieved by these early Greek thinkers. Some of these Greek points of view and habits of thought—developed long before the modern scientific era—have so imbedded themselves in the intellectual inheritance of the Western world that the very structure of our minds has been molded by them. Not only so, but much of Greek and medieval philosophy was incorporated into the religious tradition of the West and through the influence of the church was widely disseminated among the rank and file of the people, whose sense of values and conceptions of reality have been profoundly influenced thereby. As a consequence often the so-called "common-sense" views of the man in the street do not at all reveal the pure findings of naive experience. Very frequently they are but the unconscious reflections of influences from the classical tradition in both philosophy and theology. These traditions have so saturated our minds that many views which otherwise might seem strange and farfetched now seem eminently reasonable and "natural." For example, the divisions between the natural and the supernatural, the real and the ideal, reality and appearance, subject and object, mind and body, thought and activity, all seem to many to be obviously "natural" dualisms. Our moral bias also makes it "natural" to believe that in the last analysis the good is the permanent and real, while the evil is transient and illusory. Thus it comes also to be a matter of mere "common sense" to perceive that confusion, ambiguity, uncertainty, and indeterminateness have their exclusive locus in man, and that nature is without any such irregularities, for nature is an orderly, fixed, and rational system. In other words it becomes "natural" for us to think that things actually are not what they are experienced to be. Experience is good enough for managing everyday affairs, but if we desire to get a description of things as they really are, we must resort to something other than the common things of ordinary experience.

At this point the experimentalist enters his objection. He asserts unqualifiedly that experience is all that we have or can ever hope to have. It is "the ultimate universe of discourse." In more homely language, "it is anything that any-body can talk about." As such it has the first word and the last word. Experience "sets our problems," and it "tests our solutions." Hence if human experience cannot give us an adequate account of realities, then man has no possibility of gaining such an account.

Detailed consideration of the important educational impli-cations of this radical use of the method of experience need not detain us here. Obviously it involves a shift in the basis of authority. On this basis institutions and customs, religious creeds, moral codes, the specialized findings of the particular sciences, and the pronouncements of both prophets and ex-perts are all to be tested by the consequences to which they lead in ordinary life experience. They are to be judged in terms of their "instrumental" value. "The world which is lived, suffered and enjoyed as well as logically thought of, has the last word in all human inquiries and surmises." [8] Since experience is an ongoing process, this view also means that finality and absolute certainty are impossible. Absolute dogmas must give place to hypotheses. These hypotheses must be modified as experience alters. This puts the issue squarely before education. Can education so equip men and women that they can achieve a satisfying experience on this experimental basis? Can the schools lead in achieving a new and unifying view of nature and of man which is consonant with science and our knowledge of social affairs?

4. The Precariousness of Existence

The naïve, yet critical, use of experience in philosophy is well illustrated by the unique approach the experimentalist makes to the problem of learning to know the nature of the world in which we live. He begins by making a study of the earliest human materials, the proverbs and sayings of folklore. He considers it significant that the proverbs of primitive peoples are filled with references to "luck" and the factor of "chance" in human experience. Clearly they found existence to be precarious. Observation of present-day events seems to confirm the view that we, too, live in a precarious world. Things do not always turn out as planned, not even when considerable care has gone into the planning. Results achieved are not always commensurate with effort expended. "We always build better or worse than we can foretell." The longer the time-span between the initial and the final stage in any project, the greater the possibility that unexpected things will intervene. From the consideration of simple facts such as these the experimentalist formulates the hypothesis that in all of our thinking about the nature of nature, due regard must be given to the element of time, and the unanticipated changes which the passing of time brings.

The experimentalist also accepts at face value the implications of the theory of organic evolution. Thus man is believed to be included in, and to be continuous with, the natural process. Now man has acquired the ability to think. Nature in man is nature grown intelligent. The experimentalist ponders on the fact that man, one natural event in interaction with other natural events, has found it useful to learn how to think. Perhaps the occurrence of thinking in the world may give us an important clue to the nature of that world itself. For the experimentalist, human beings with their habits of thinking are just as evidential of the nature of nature as are "the happenings of suns, radioactivity, thunderstorms or any other natural event." [9] Does examination of an act of thought show that it possesses any structure of its own, or is thought a formless, shifting sort of thing that has no specifiable traits? If it is of the latter sort, manifestly it can tell us nothing about our world.

A careful analysis of typical acts of thought is undertaken. The analysis reveals that thinking does have its characteristic features. One of these traits common to all thinking is that it originates in the problematic, the indeterminate, the uncertain, and the ambiguous. In fact, its very function may be said to be the resolution of the problematic and the uncertain into the clear and definite. From this the experimentalist infers that we live in an incomplete and indeterminate world. Thinking occurs. This is evidence that "the world must actually be such as to generate ignorance and inquiry, doubt and hypothesis, trial and temporal conclusions." [10] A philosophy that treats the subject-matter of experience seriously finds important proof of the indeterminate character of nature in the fact that thinking man developed in nature. To the objection that the uncertainty and ambiguity which call thinking into existence are merely subjective and located exclusively in the mind of the thinker, the obvious reply is that this is to employ once more the old dualism which separates subject and object and which cuts man off from nature, whereas experience in its primary integrity reveals no such division, but rather discloses organism and environment in an integral relationship.

Of course these are not the only considerations that lead the experimentalist to the conclusion that we live in an unfinished, changing world, in which novelty and variety are naturalized—in a contingent world of plural possibilities. The physical sciences, which for several centuries under the Newtonian influence considered nature to be a vast machine working in perfect order and harmony according to immutable laws, are now also contributing their evidence to the effect that indeterminacy is a basic fact. Biology has accustomed us to the conception of a dynamic universe in which the unprecedented, the novel, constantly appears. From a variety of sources evidence pours in to support the experimentalists in their contention that:

"The stablest thing we can speak of is not free from conditions set to it by other things. That even the solid earth mountains, the emblems of constancy, appear and disappear like the clouds is an old theme of moralists and poets. The fixed and the unchanged being of the Democritean atom is now reported by inquirers to possess some of the traits of his non-being, and to embody a temporary equilibrium in the economy of nature's compromises and adjustments. A thing may endure *secula seculorum* and yet not be everlasting; it will crumble before the gnawing tooth of time, as it exceeds a certain measure. Every existence is an event." [11]

James and Dewey unite in stressing the precarious, contingent character of existence. This does not mean, of course, that the world has no determinate characters. On the contrary, it is the very mixture of the stable and the unstable, the recurrent and the novel, which lends "poignancy to all existence." Therefore in the metaphysics of the experimentalist "incompleteness and precariousness is a trait that must be given footing of the same rank as the finished and the fixed." [12] The complaint of the experimentalist against the classical tradition in philosophy is that it has been unwilling to grant such equal footing to the uncertain and changing in its formulations. The permanent and the unchanging have been said to be the real; the uncertain and changing have been held to be mere appearance. He believes that it has been this preference and insistent search for the "immutable" which has led philosophy into many of its abstractions and confusions.

However that may be, it is apparent that he who is interested in the educational conceptions of an experimentalist must realize how much his thought is conditioned by this view of the adventurous character of all existence. It is the initial premise that permeates all of his subsequent thought about life and education.

"The conjunction of problematic and determinate characters in nature renders every existence, as well as every idea and human act, an experiment in fact, even though not in design. To be intelligently experimental is but to be conscious of this intersection of natural conditions so as to profit by it instead of being at its mercy." [13]

Existence in its ultimate character is thus seen to be changing, uncertain. Hence life itself is inherently experimental. A fundamental aim of education is to enable men and women to make that experiment—which is life—more intelligent.

5. Man and Nature

The time was, and not long since, when the physical scientists were picturing the world as a vast, uniform, closed and determined system, the mechanism of which operated according to universal and necessary laws, constituting a mechanical order from which all chance and uncertainty were forever barred. Even while the physicists spoke consistently of this one view, the experimentalist appealed from their conclusions to the neglected facts of organic life, and in particular to the facts revealed in man's ordinary experience of his world as "lived, suffered, and enjoyed." The protest was not

in vain. Later researches have given astonishing proof that
the earlier scientific view was partial and framed in terms
of falsifying abstractions. It had been a conception fruitful
in carrying forward certain types of research, but as White-
head has pointed out, such a view of nature also hinders research, particularly in those fields most closely associated with
human affairs.

To-day the declaration of William James to the effect that
we live in a "universe with the lid off" has attained distinguished scientific support. Physicists unite with the experimentalist philosophers in affirming that every existence
is an event. Nature is no longer thought of as merely "a
homogeneous mass differentiated by differences of homogeneous motion in a homogeneous space." The present
tendency in science is "to substitute qualitative events, marked
by certain similar properties and by recurrences, for the older
notion of fixed substances." As a result the findings of naïve
experience and scientific research are once more in general
agreement. The experimental outlook is accepted.

Now events are particular affairs. As has been well said,
a thing is the thing it is and not some other thing. If an event
is to be noted as an existence, it must have its own distinctive qualities—its inherent "irreducible isness." These qualitative differences in events as actually experienced prompt
the experimentalist to assert that no matter how many connections an individual event may have with other events, it
is grossly misconceived when it is thought to be merely a
relational element in some absolute whole which devours all
particular qualities. Empirically, the universe is a qualitative
affair. Sound and color, sweet and sour, hot and cold, hard
and soft, smooth and rough, wet and dry, light and heavy,
and all similar qualities have full objective standing in

nature's economy. Such qualities are not mere subjective phantoms exclusively located in the human mind. They are actual characters of the existential world.

Moreover, the experimentalist does not stop at this point. Experience is characterized by immediate enjoyment and suffering. Now what is denoted by the fact that primary experience reveals that man literally suffers and enjoys in an endless variety of ways the world in which he lives? Supporting the standpoint of naïve realism, the experimentalist believes it indicates that "things are poignant, tragic, beautiful, humorous, settled, disturbed, comfortable, annoying, barren, harsh, consoling, splendid, fearful; are such immediately and in their own right and behalf." [14] Nor is this all. Since experience is in and of the world of things and events, the experimentalist believes that the "things characteristic of practical life, such things as lack and need, conflict and clash, desire and effort, loss and satisfaction," may be "frankly referred to reality." [15] In other words, meanings possess objective character. Hence reality may also be said to possess "practical character." And finally, "if experienced things are valid evidence, then nature in having qualities within itself has what in the literal sense must be called ends, terminals, arrests, enclosures." [16]

What is meant when the experimentalist states that nature literally may be said to have ends? Does this imply that he sees all of nature as a rational moral order striving to achieve moral and esthetic values? In certain of his writings James seems to say that a belief in a striving moral purpose immanent in the universe might be a tenable one. Whether he accepted it for himself is not so clear. In any case it was a finite purpose, trans-human, perhaps, but far from all-powerful. Man, by taking active part in the process, might help the moral forces of existence achieve a final triumph. However it may have been with James, apparently Dewey does not subscribe to such an optimistic belief in the value-conserving tendency of the universal cosmic scheme. On the whole his position on this point may be said to be shared by most of the experimentalists to-day.

Ends are naturalized in nature. But ends are endings. They are the termini of events. As such they are just the sort of endings they may happen to be, for nature is a scene of all sorts of beginnings and endings. Reality is precisely this succession of events. Each event has its own quality. It is what it is.

"To insist that nature is an affair of beginnings is to assert that there is no one single and all-at-once beginning of everything. It is but another way of saying nature is an affair *of* affairs, wherein each one, no matter how linked up it may be with others, has its *own* quality. It does not imply that every beginning marks an advance or improvement; as we sadly know accidents, diseases, wars, lies and errors, begin. Clearly the fact and idea of beginning is neutral, not eulogistic; temporal, not absolute. And since wherever one thing begins something else ends, what is true of beginnings is true of endings. Popular fiction and drama show the bias of human nature in favor of happy endings, but by being fiction and drama they show with even greater assurance that unhappy endings are natural events." [17]

Nature is "a scene of incessant beginnings and endings." Natural processes start and stop. One event merges into another. Nature has its continuities; but there are also pulses in the movement of events, and natural happenings are qualitatively of all sorts. Man's life is implicated in these manifold happenings. Some are favorable to his interests; others are not. Some support and carry forward his activities; others are hostile and harmful in their effect. The actual world was not built for man, but as Santayana has aptly said, "It is the place in which he happened to grow." Since man's life is a development—an event—in that natural world, his organic structures are, for the most part, congruent with it. On the other hand, man, least of all the animals, can rely blindly on his native equipment. As an infant he is greatly inferior to the young of the lower animals. At first he is utterly dependent on the care of others. His own native stock of responses is too indefinite and undeveloped to take care of him. In order to continue to live, he has to learn. He has to learn to distinguish between those processes whose outcomes meet his needs and through intelligent control can be made more surely available, and those events which end in frustration and loss.

In other words, he lives in a world in which discriminative choice is inherently demanded. His very life depends upon his ability to secure at least a degree of control. Fortunately he lives in a world in which intelligent foresight and purposeful activity do make a difference. Natural processes are sufficiently indeterminate and flexible so that by learning to anticipate consequences and by paying attention to natural resources, man can devise means which enable him to make more secure and stable those events whose endings are counted as good and to avoid or eliminate many of those other events whose final outcomes are regarded as bad. The experimentalist believes that in this intelligent reorganization and reconstruction of affairs man is literally a creative agent remaking his world. In this sense the experimentalist is an idealist. He believes that what now exists, the real, can be so changed as to make it include more of the ideal. The "ideal" is that which better serves the life of man. This profound faith in the ultimate significance of intelligent human participation in the movement of events is fundamental in the philosophy of experimentalism, as the following statement so forcibly shows:

"Intelligence is, indeed, as you say, discrimination, distinction. But why? Because we have to *act* in order to keep secure amid the moving flux of circumstances, some slight but precious good that Nature has bestowed; and because, in order to act successfully, we must act after conscious selection—after discrimination of means and ends. Of course, all goods arrive . . . as natural results, but so do all bads, and all grades of good and bad. To label the results that occur culminations, achievements, and then argue to a quasi-moral constitution of Nature because she effects such results, is to employ a logic which applies to the life-cycle of the germ that, in achieving itself, kills man with malaria, as well as to the process of human life that in reaching its fullness cuts short the germ-fulfilment. It is putting the cart before the horse to say that because nature is so constituted as to produce results of all types of value, therefore Nature is actuated by regard for differences of value. Nature, till it produces a being who strives and who thinks in order that he may strive more effectively, does not know whether it cares more for justice or for cruelty, more for the ravenous wolf-like competition of the struggle for existence, or for the improvements incidentally introduced through that struggle. Literally it has no mind of its own. Nor would the mere introduction of a consciousness that pictured indifferently the scene out of which consciousness developed add one iota of reason for attributing eulogistically to Nature regard for value. But when the sentient organism, having experienced natural values, good and bad, begins to select, to prefer, and to make battle for its preference; and in order that it may make the most gallant fight possible picks out and gathers together in perception and thought what is favorable to its aims and what hostile, then and there Nature has at last achieved significant regard for good. And this is the same thing as the birth of intelligence. For the holding of an end in view and the selecting and organizing out of the natural flux, on the basis of this end, conditions that are means, *is* intelligence. . . .

"It is indeed true that problems are solved only where they

arise—namely, in action, in the adjustments of behavior. But, for good or for evil, they can be solved there only with method; and ultimately method is intelligence, and intelligence is method." [18]

To summarize: Man lives in a world where all sorts of things are happening; some of these happenings are friendly, others are hostile to his interests. No vague trust in the goodness of the world in general can substitute for specific, intelligent effort. In man mind has appeared in nature, but that does not justify the conclusion that all nature is therefore mind, or the product of mind. Man does live in a world, however, in which things are not all fixed, but in a world in which he can do something to make the goods of experience more secure and the evils less menacing. He wins his freedom by developing the ability to anticipate consequences and to devise means which give him effective control over particular outcomes. Participate he must in the movement of natural and social affairs. A basic aim of education is to help him to develop the attitudes and habits, and to gain the mastery of the techniques which will serve to make that participation progressively more intelligent. The task of education within the school and in society at large is viewed from the perspective of a world order in which the mixture of the stable and the precarious makes "creative intelligence" in man the supreme essential.

6. Education and Social Change

Certain questions may be raised about these primary conceptions in the philosophy of experimentalism because they are based so largely on biological foundations and also because they make such generous use of materials derived from primitive experience. It is often affirmed that the value of anything is to be measured by what it has become, by its possibilities, and that it is not to be discounted because its genesis is found in simple beginnings. Above all, it is said, educators should be chiefly interested in eventual outcomes and future possibilities rather than in taking their standards from primitive origins. Early man, living without tools, largely as an animal among other animals, may have found his life to be an unstable and precarious affair of continuous adjustment to shifting and threatening conditions, but with the advance of the arts, and the expansion of scientific knowledge and means of control, has not this uncertain and hazardous factor been largely eliminated from existence? People to-day living ordered, sheltered lives in our modern communities do not find life to be "uncannily unstable." If anything, it is too fixed and monotonous. The restless search for artificial thrills and excitement during leisure hours is merely a symptom of the dull and uneventful character of modern life. In order to find adventure, people deliberately undertake perilous flights across oceans, seek constantly to establish new records for speed, go on difficult explorations to the polar regions, or organize parties to climb the few dangerous mountain peaks which have not as yet been conquered by man.

With some of these contentions the experimentalist is in agreement. He heartily endorses the view that wonderful and beautiful things do come from very humble beginnings. He also believes that the whole is more than a mere aggregation of its parts. It is an integrated functioning unity which until it actually came to be, could scarcely if at all have been predicted from the simpler elements which conditioned its development. "Organization is so characteristic of the nature of some events in their sequential linkages that no theory about it can be as speculative or absurd as those which ignore or deny its genuine existence." [19] He also protests against so-called explanations that end by explaining out of existence the indubitable thing that originally initiated the inquiry. Nevertheless the experimentalist believes the genetic approach rightly employed can throw much light on difficult problems. The very simplicity of the more primitive forms may reveal vital processes which are present and equally important, although hidden, in more complex organizations and behaviors. Also in following continuous processes through various stages of complexity, a better sense of the direction of the process may be gained. Often by this method a perspective is gained which gives insight that could not otherwise be had.

But to return to the original question, the experimentalist is not so sure that the development of science has actually reduced the uncertain, hazardous factors in human existence. There is much that can be pointed to which indicates that it has had such an effect. It has given man a better understanding of his world and in so doing has removed much of fear from his life. Science through its practical applications has also so greatly extended control over nature that, at least for large sections of the population, life is not the precarious struggle for a bare subsistence it once was. This greater security in economic matters is merely one illustration of how science by giving more control to man has added to his practical security.

But this is not the whole story. Science can give this control because it has brought something genuinely new into human experience. Undoubtedly this new factor has a twofold influence. By one and the same process it extends both security and insecurity in human affairs. Lippmann describes this new factor as follows:

"Men have not merely invented the modern machines. There have been machines invented since the earliest days, incalculably important, like the wheel, like sailing ships, like the windmill and the watermill. But in modern times men have invented a method of inventing, they have discovered a method of discovery. Mechanical progress has ceased to be casual and accidental and has become systematic and cumulative." [20]

Probably no one living in our present technological civilization would deny that the invention of a *method* of inventing has operated to accelerate the rate of change in our material culture. Most competent students of social history would agree with the following statement from Beard:

"Though machine civilization has here been treated as if it were an order, it in fact differs from all others in that it is highly dynamic, containing within itself the seeds of constant reconstruction. Everywhere agricultural civilizations of the pre-machine age have changed only slowly with the fluctuations of markets, the fortunes of government, and the vicissitudes of knowledge, keeping their basic institutions intact from century to century. Pre-machine urban civilizations have likewise retained their essential characteristics through long lapses of time. But machine civilization based on technology, science, invention, and expanding markets must of necessity change—and rapidly." [21]

It is not always so clearly perceived, however, that technological changes occasioned by new inventions often call for the most radical readjustments in the whole cultural life of man. Ogburn has made an important contribution in his discovery of the intimate connection between the technological and the social aspects of our culture:

"But a good many of the ways of using the material objects of culture involve rather larger usages and adjustments, such as customs, beliefs, philosophies, laws, government. . . . These ways of adjustment may be called for purposes of this particular analysis, the adaptive culture. The adaptive culture is therefore that portion of the non-material culture which is adjusted or adapted to the material conditions. . . . When the material conditions change, changes are occasioned in the adaptive culture. But these changes in the adaptive culture do not synchronize exactly with the changes in the material culture. There is a lag which may last for varying lengths of time, sometimes indeed, for many years." [22]

Hence the following logic of events leads the experimentalist to conclude that present society is the most dynamic and uncertain of all human history. Modern man has invented a method of making inventions. This means an ever-expanding number of inventions. These inventions constantly alter our material culture. Our organized social life is continuous with this material culture and in consequence should change with it if social health is to be maintained. The fact is, however, that changes in the material culture are proceeding at a more rapid rate than constructive adjustments are being made in other parts of our culture. As a result cultural lag and social maladjustments occur. These social maladjustments are impressive testimony to the changing, uncertain, precarious character of modern civilization. The experimentalist believes that this highly dynamic character of civilization is apt to continue indefinitely. One of the leading experimentalists in the field of education writes of the significance of this for education:

"Education therefore must consciously face its highly unknown future. Our situation, while shifting, is, however, flexible and within limits amenable to our control. The factors which must mainly guide us are suggested by such terms as change, increasingly rapid change, unknown future, thought, control within limits, experimental method, testing thought by results, methods approved by test. As we recall the uneven cultural advance, our emphasis must be upon social-moral outlook and effective grasp in order to bring and keep these abreast of the rapidly moving 'material' aspects of our civilization." [23]

Much the same position is taken by Lippmann in his discussion of present moral difficulties. He believes society today to be so unstable and changing that man can rely no longer on authoritative moral codes and fixed principles. Written with no thought of the experimentalists' educational program in mind, it is interesting to see how closely his analysis agrees with theirs:

"An authoritative code of morals has force and effect when it expresses the settled customs of a stable society: the pharisee can impose upon the minority only such conventions as the majority find appropriate and necessary. But when customs are unsettled, as they are in the modern world, by continual change in the circumstances of life, the pharisee is helpless. He cannot command with authority because his commands no longer imply the usages of the community: they express the prejudices of the moralist rather than the practices of men." [24]

In conclusion it may be said that, in the opinion of the experimentalist, study of contemporary society reinforces his belief in the precarious character of all existence. Man's raw experience of nature reveals existence to be inherently an affair of change and uncertainty. A critical analysis of modern civilization shows that rapid change is one of its most outstanding features. To live successfully in such a changing world requires the continuous exercise of intelligent choice. Hence thinking is not a luxury but a necessity for all who are other than institutional charges in the modern world. From his conviction that change and uncertainty are ultimate traits of existence arises the belief of the experimentalist that "thinking is the method of an educative experience." [25] "All which the school can or need do for pupils, so far as their *minds* are concerned . . . is to develop their ability to think." [26]

As the experimentalist understands his world, there is no substitute for the exercise of "creative intelligence" on the part of man. His intense interest in schools in which children are encouraged to engage in purposeful activities through which they learn at first hand from their own experiences is inherently connected with his conviction that we live in a changing natural and social world. In such a changing, precarious existence, intelligent, creative reconstruction of experience is required of all if we are to maintain and extend human values.

REFERENCES

1. JOHN DEWEY, *Creative Intelligence* (Henry Holt and Company, 1917), p. 55.
2. JOHN DEWEY, in the *New Republic,* Feb. 6, 1924. (Reprinted in *Characters and Events* [Henry Holt and Company, 1929], II, 457.)
3. MORRIS R. COHEN, *Chance, Love and Logic* (Harcourt, Brace and Company, 1927), p. 45.
4. WILLIAM JAMES, *Pragmatism* (Longmans, Green & Co., 1908), p. 45.
5. C. I. LEWIS, "Pragmatism and Current Thought," *Journal of Philosophy,* Apr. 24, 1930, Vol. 27, p. 239.
6. SIDNEY HOOK, *The Metaphysics of Pragmatism* (The Open Court Publishing Co., 1927), p. 6.
7. JOHN DEWEY, in the *New Republic,* Jan. 5, 1927. (Reprinted in *Characters and Events* [Henry Holt and Company, 1929], II, 439).
8. JOHN DEWEY, *Experience and Nature* (The Open Court Publishing Co., 1929), p. 12.
9. *Ibid.,* p. 68.

10. *Ibid.,* p. 69.
11. *Ibid.,* pp. 70–71
12. *Ibid.,* p. 51.
13. *Ibid.,* p. 70.
14. *Ibid.,* p. 96.
15. *Essays in Honor of William James* (Longmans, Green & Co., 1908), p. 54.
16. JOHN DEWEY, *Experience and Nature* (The Open Court Publishing Co., 1929), pp. 96–97.
17. *Ibid.,* pp. 97–98.
18. JOHN DEWEY, *Influence of Darwin on Philosophy* (Henry Holt and Company, 1920), pp. 42–44.
19. JOHN DEWEY, *Experience and Nature* (The Open Court Publishing Co., 1929), p. 255.
20. WALTER LIPPMANN, *A Preface to Morals* (The Macmillan Company, 1929), p. 235.
21. CHARLES BEARD, *Whither Mankind* (Longmans, Green & Co., 1928), p. 15.
22. W. F. OGBURN, *Social Change* (B. W. Huebsch, Inc., 1928), pp. 202–203.
23. W. H. KILPATRICK, *Education for a Changing Civilization* (The Macmillan Company, 1926), pp. 84–85.
24. WALTER LIPPMANN, *A Preface to Morals* (The Macmillan Company, 1929), p. 317.
25. JOHN DEWEY, *Democracy and Education* (The Macmillan Company, 1916), p. 192.
26. *Ibid.,* p. 179.

CHAPTER IV

EXPERIMENTALISM AND THE NATURE OF MAN

"If we are willing to conceive education as the process of forming fundamental dispositions, intellectual and emotional, toward nature and fellow men, philosophy may even be defined *as the general theory of education.*"

DEWEY.

I. The Biological Approach

It has been said that the most penetrating question one can ask of any philosopher is, "What does he see when he sees a man?" It becomes a doubly important question to ask when one is interested in discovering the educational implications of a particular philosophy. Many of the most important disagreements in educational theory and practice are rooted in underlying different ways of thinking about the individual. The fact that often these more basic conceptions of the nature of the individual are not explicitly formulated does not make their influence in education any the less powerful.

Since the experimentalist has something very definite in mind when he thinks of an individual, it will probably help us better to understand his educational aims if we are able to see what he sees "when he sees a man." At the outset, however, it is important to notice that his perspectives are plural, for he finds it important to see the individual from several points of view. The same individual is under observation throughout, but he is studied from different angles of approach and with different purposes in mind. The failure of

some to apprehend that the perspectives of the experimentalist are various causes them to condemn experimentalism as
a philosophy, because, in their opinion, it tends to see man
as a mere animal. Now the experimentalist does see man
as a biological organism, but he also sees man as a human
being capable of all that which makes a refined, humane
experience possible. Nor does he believe these two views are
antithetical.

It is true, however, that the experimentalist does consider
it useful to view man through the eyes of the biologist. He
never ceases to marvel that so many people readily accept
the theory of organic evolution and then immediately proceed to ignore many of its most important implications for
human behavior.

From the standpoint of the biologist, the experimentalist
sees man as an organism in continuous interaction with its
environment. At times he almost seems to see man as that
environment individualized into an unique, concrete character. In any case, man and nature are seen as continuous.
For purposes of discourse it is convenient to distinguish between the organism and the environment. But such discriminations are logical in character, and the underlying,
primary fact is the unity of organism and environment. Jennings's recent suggestion that heredity and environment "are
not mutually exclusive categories" [1] is in line with his way
of thinking.

Man is seen as a living organism, and the most characteristic thing about life is behavior, activity. The analysis of any
organic activity shows that it is as much a function of the
environment as it is a function of the organism. Breathing,
for example, is an affair of the air as well as of the lungs;
eating involves both the food that is eaten and the organs

that digest the food. Acquired responses, habits, may also be said to belong to the environment just as truly as they do to the organism. Swimming implies the water in which we swim just as surely as it does the movements of legs and arms by which we swim. So also for our basic aversions and likings, our fundamental dispositions. We do not fear fear; we fear fearful things. We are not loyal to loyalty; we are loyal to objective causes, to institutions, to people. "In truth, attitudes, dispositions and their kin, while capable of being distinguished and made concrete intellectual objects, are never separate existences. They are always *of, from, toward,* situations and things." [2]

The experimentalist believes that the adequate recognition of this primary continuity of organism and environment would be sufficient in itself to challenge many of our current educational procedures. How much of our school procedure assumes that the individual child is an isolated unit so completely self-enclosed that he can be treated entirely apart from the environment which actually penetrates his every act and thought! Thus to understand behavior is actually to misunderstand it.

"We cannot change habit directly: that notion is magic. But we can change it indirectly by modifying conditions, by an intelligent selecting and weighting of the objects which engage attention and which influence the fulfilment of desires." [3]

For the experimentalist, the very beginning of intelligent understanding of the individual and his behavior is to grasp "that living as an empirical affair is not something which goes on below the skin-surface of an organism: it is always an inclusive affair involving connection, interaction of what is within the organic body and what lies outside in space and time." [4] Such interaction is the primary fact in all experience. Nor is the activity of the organism any mere random affair. While the very life of the organism itself is derived from natural energies, not all of these energies are friendly to the growth of the organism. "Growth and decay, health and disease, are alike ·continuous with the activities of the natural surroundings."

Hence the organism continues its life by maintaining a life-sustaining equilibrium with these surrounding forces. This optimum state of equilibrium Raup has termed "complacency." [5] The effort to maintain the state of "complacency" is considered to be foundational in all behavior. Now as changes are constantly taking place in both the organism and the environment, the maintenance of this equilibrium is a precarious affair. The organism must constantly act so as to bring about adjustments which are favorable to its own interests. These adjustments necessary to maintain the equilibrium may be effected by changes made either in the organism or in the environment or in both. The higher the organism, the more it seeks to control and reconstruct the environment, so as to make it better serve the organism's own needs. Biologically a need is seen in that redistribution of energies which upsets the equilibrium of the organism-environment relationship and results in a vital tension. When such a disturbance occurs, the organism acts to reduce the strain. If its efforts succeed, the need is met and the equilibrium is reëstablished, possibly at a different level. Such a restored equilibrium produces a state of well-being, of satisfaction. Sooner or later responses which are successful in reducing recurring difficulties tend to get built into the structure of the organism as habits. Those means, processes, materials which satisfy the needs of the organism are counted as goods.

A typical unit of experience would include the various phases of an activity, which starts with the need occasioned by a disturbance in the equilibrium relationship, which continues through the various efforts made by the organism in overcoming the disturbance, and which ends with the restoration of the state of complacency. Such an experience is a developing affair. The control of the organism is generally indirect. The activities of the organism have to modify the direction of independent changes taking place in the environment. To secure such redirection takes time. Hence the reference of activities of the organism is always toward future outcomes. It acts to modify things in the given present so as to bring about an eventual situation which will yield satisfaction. Thus, life may be said ever to "live forward." Activity projects itself into the future. In fact, experience may be described as "a future implicated in a present." As has already been said, it is inherently experimental in character, because "all invasion of the future is a risk, an adventure." Experience is primarily an active affair. It is "a process of undergoing: a process of standing something; of suffering and passion, of affection, in the literal sense of these words. The organism has to endure, to undergo, the consequences of its own actions." [6] By its very structure experience is adjustive in character, even if not always intelligently purposeful.

The educational implications of this way of conceiving experience will be dealt with later. We pause here simply to indicate that it has an important bearing on psychology. One of the conflicts in psychology to-day is about method and what should be taken as the elemental unit for psychology. Some consider states of consciousness and sense data to be the ultimate units; others suggest that organic drives or instincts are the fundamental elements; still others seem to believe in the omnipotence of the environment and the all-dominating influence of the external stimulus in controlling behavior. The suggestion of the experimentalist is that the more fruitful approach is to take a complete unit of experience as the foundational element. Behavior is seen as a function of the organism and environment in a total condition of need. Once the two are torn apart and either the organism or the environment is treated as the determining factor in behavior, a misleading abstraction has taken place which inevitably leads to confusion.

But while the experimentalist sees man as an organism interacting with an environment, he also sees that man's activity has its uniquely important characteristics. For the most part sub-human animals do not use tools, although certain experiments with apes indicate that at least a rudimentary use of tools may be achieved. Apparently man alone has acquired the use of that tool of tools, language, which makes communication and the sharing of experience possible. It thus becomes possible for man to preserve his past experiences. "He lives not in a world of merely physical things but in a world of signs and symbols." Through these various means man's interaction with his environment comes to possess distinctive intellectual quality. When is behavior intellectual? The simple answer of the experimentalist is, when "it knows what it is about"—when it knows what can be expected of things and what can be done with them. As we have already seen, the organism acts in the present to start influences moving which will bring about an eventual state of affairs more in harmony with its vital interests. When such activity is not a mere blind trial-and-error process; when it is more than mere mechanical reaction to immediate stimulus; in short, when present behavior is guided by anticipation of consequences, it is intelligent behavior. When that which is given is used as a basis for making inferences about that which is yet to happen, thinking is in process. When an organism can respond to meanings—can see the connection between "the thing signifying and the thing signified"— when it grasps the connections between its own acts and the consequences which flow from those acts, it behaves intelligently. It is important to note the use of the adverb *intelligently*. Intelligence is not a substantive thing back of the activity of an organism which makes that activity intellectual; intelligence *is* behavior that is guided by anticipated consequences. In other words, we behave intelligently when we participate in the movement of events in such a way as to shape the direction of present happenings so that they terminate in outcomes favorable to growth and expansion. Every tool which man has invented in order better to achieve his ends is an evidence of behavior marked by this quality of mind.

Now this type of behavior which is intelligence did emerge in the natural development of events. Man, thinking man, is wholly naturalized within nature. Mind is not some immaterial entity outside of the course of natural existence and antithetical to it. Man is not part body and part mind, as a centaur is half man and half horse. Repeatedly the experimentalist opposes this dualism of mind and body, of subject and object. The following quotation from Dewey is typical of the general position of the experimentalist on this point:

"The realization that the observation necessary to knowledge enters into the natural object known cancels this separation of knowing and doing. It makes possible and it demands a theory in which knowing and doing are intimately connected with each other. Hence, as we have said, it domesticates the exercise of intelligence within nature. This is part and parcel of nature's own continuing interactions. Interactions go on anyway and produce changes. Apart from intelligence, those changes are not directed. They are effects but not consequences, for consequences imply means deliberately employed. When an interaction intervenes which directs the course of change, the scene of natural interaction has a new quality and dimension. This added type of interaction *is* intelligence. The intelligent activity of man is not something brought to bear upon nature from without; it is nature realizing its own potentialities in behalf of a fuller and richer issue of events. Intelligence within nature means liberation and expansion, as reason outside of nature means fixation and restriction." [7]

On the one hand the experimentalist maintains, as the above quotation indicates, that intelligence is wholly naturalized in nature. It does not represent a supernatural intrusion into the natural scene. He believes that the dualism of mind and body has been the source of that pernicious abstract intellectualism which has so dominated educational thought and practice. He protests against the unhappy separation of thought and activity. This separation tends to make thinking unreal and irresponsible, and it also tends to make action a blind and routine following of fixed patterns.

On the other hand, the experimentalist is equally insistent that intelligent behavior is a fact. The intelligent behavior of man is something qualitatively different from the external pushing and pulling of inanimate objects on one another. Nor is it to be equated with the behavior of an animal which has not the capacity for achieving ideas. Finally, much as he believes that knowing and thinking are intimately associated with language, the experimentalist does not believe that intelligent behavior is mere word-reaction:

"Take speech as behavioristically as you will, including the elimination of all private mental states, and it remains true that it is markedly distinguished from the signaling acts of animals. Meaning is not indeed a psychic existence; it is primarily a property of behavior, and secondarily a property of objects. But the behavior of which it is a quality is a distinctive behavior; coöperative, in that response to another's act involves contemporaneous response to a thing as entering into the other's behavior, and this upon both sides." [8]

Intelligent behavior turns reaction into response. Intelligent activity is purposeful; that is, it is guided by meanings. The experimentalist points out that the condition which evokes reflective behavior is a situation which is so confused that it is inadequate to produce a response. The business of reflection is to remake the situation so that ambiguity is resolved into meaning. Thinking is the active seeking of an adequate stimulus, the remaking of the problematic situation into a situation with meanings so clarified that behavior can go forward. The experimentalist even suggests that *means* and *consequences* may be better terms to apply to such reflective behavior than are *stimulus* and *response* as now frequently interpreted in present-day psychology. Nor is he content with a psychology that eliminates conscious activity. We act consciously whenever activity requires the immediate integration of conflicting meanings in order to proceed. In the opinion of the experimentalist, denial of the unique quality of such conscious behavior is a disregarding of empirical fact.

2. Some Educational Implications

Although the preceding discussion of the biological approach to human behavior is much abbreviated, it is hoped that it will aid in an understanding of what the experimentalist from one point of view conceives experience to be. An understanding of what the experience process denotes for the experimentalist is indispensable for an appreciation of both his philosophical point of view and his basic approach to the problems of education. Certain important conclusions are derived from this conception of behavior.

In the first place, experience is considered to be an active process of doing and undergoing and not primarily a cognitive affair. The knowledge experience is only one form of experience. The position of knowledge is secondary and derived in origin, no matter how important it may be in its actual contribution to life. Primary experience is not an affair of knowing; it is esthetic in quality, a matter of "being and having," of "doing and undergoing," of "suffering and enjoying." The function of knowledge is instrumental. We seek to know in order to regulate the happenings of primary experience; in order to multiply and render more secure the experienced goods, and in order to eliminate and avoid those happenings that bring suffering.

As such, knowledge is not an affair of a spectator trying to copy reality as it antecedently exists. So also do "the senses lose their place as gateways of knowing to take their rightful place as stimuli to action. . . . Sensations are not parts of *any* knowledge, good or bad, superior or inferior, imperfect or complete. They are rather provocations, incitements, challenges to an act of inquiry which is to *terminate* in knowledge." [9] "The true 'stuff' of experience is recognized to be adaptive courses of action, habits, active functions, connections of doing and undergoing; sensori-motor coördinations." [10] In short, knowing is linked with activity. It is controlled participation in the movement of events so as to learn of their conditions and consequences. Knowledge is not that which produces a change; it *is* a change. When things are known, they are different things. They become objects. Now an object is an event with its possible consequences in experience telescoped into it. These anticipated consequences become a part of the stimulus; response that is directed by anticipated consequences is behavior controlled by meanings. The more adequate the stock of meanings, the more reliable is the behavior.

Thinking is inquiring. Logic is a study of the conditions which lead to success and failure in conducting inquiry. All thinking originates in some specific affair. It is a piecemeal, not a wholesale, activity. It starts in a situation of ambiguity; its business is to get rid of that ambiguity. Problematic situations which occasion thinking are of all sorts. A *situation* has been defined by one experimentalist as "anything that needs attention." Concrete particulars are the ends; ideas, conceptions, general principles are means which help us to explore these perplexing particulars of experience. As such they are hypotheses, tools of analysis and discovery. Their function is also instrumental. Ideas, conceptions, are possible modes of response to situations of difficulty. They are tested by the consequences to which they lead. The true is the verified. Not *truth* but *truths* is the concern of the experimentalist. Truths are the opinions, the beliefs, the hypotheses which have been verified in experience. Since experience is ongoing in nature and conditions do change, absolute finality is not to be had. Present working, not past prestige, is the criterion by which principles are evaluated.

A knowledge experience is a longitudinal affair. As has already been said, it is something that requires time. One situation matures into another situation. Thinking is a series of controlled operations which seeks to discover the hidden continuities and to control the movement in such a developing situation. The experimentalist finds it useful to think of science as a perfected art of guiding "processes of change."

As thus understood, thinking is not something which goes on exclusively in the head of the thinker. It begins in an existential situation of difficulty. "Desire, purpose, planning, choice, have no meaning save in conditions where something is at stake, and where action in one direction rather than another may eventuate in bringing into existence a new situation which fulfills a need." [11] Observation and the gathering of data are required if one is to deal constructively with such problematic situations. Proposed solutions can in the last analysis only be tested by objective reference to the particular situation of difficulty. Thinking literally is experimenting. It is an active operation in which we "both discover and test" in the same process. In short, thinking is "learning through experience."

Obviously the foregoing conceptions of experience, knowledge, thinking, and learning have fundamental significance for education. The implications of these conceptions is such that the experimentalist inevitably tends to think of life as education, and of education as life. As he views it, the experience process and the educative process are essentially one. He measures society and its various institutions in terms of their total effect in experience, which is their educative effect. The society which so orders its affairs that it produces an undesirable type of person is a defective society no matter how efficient it may be in getting certain things done. So also the worth of the school is measured in terms of the quality of its interaction with the wider social life of which it is a part. For the experimentalist the only justification for the existence of a school is that it can through intentional effort produce an environment in which the experiences of youth will be more truly educative than they otherwise would be. Since experience and education are inherently linked, any school which is not a place where childern have varied and vital experiences calculated to give them an understanding of themselves and of their natural and social environment is not adequately organized to accomplish educational ends.

Thus two basic conceptions in the philosophy of experimentalism point alike to the same general conclusion for education. As we have already seen, the experimentalist sees man living in a world that is a mixture of the regular and the changing, of the fixed and the uncertain, of the stable and the precarious. In short, man lives in a world in which the character of existence is such that intelligent, purposeful activity is demanded if he is to achieve a satisfying experience. In the second place, the experimentalist also believes that the nature of experience is such that the necessary condition for learning to behave intelligently is the freedom to engage in purposeful activity. By purposeful activity is not meant mere random activity in response to fleeting impulse. Purposeful activity is controlled, experimental activity. But the primary controls inhere in the subject-matter of the situation of concern rather than in externally imposed influences. Purposeful activity is activity freely initiated by the agent in response to a situation whose difficulties have a challenging grip in his present experience. He frames his ends in the light of the resources and difficulties found in the actual problematical situation. Normally the motivation and the interest are intrinsic in the process itself, because the person dealing with the situation is awake to its bearing on his experience. In purposeful activity the learning is more sure because the whole individual is attending to what is developing. He is alert to see connections between transitive events, and between his acts and the consequences that flow from those acts.

In attempting to introduce the principle of purposeful activity into the school, the experimentalist is not concerned merely to add one more technique by which children can be induced to learn desired subject-matter. Purposeful activity as the foundation for school procedures is the natural outgrowth of his whole philosophical position. It is the educational correlative of his understanding of the world in which we live, and of the nature of the process by which experience grows intelligent. As such it is the fundamental principle in his entire program for education.

3. Nature and Nurture

Not only does the experimentalist see man as a biological organism interacting with a physical environment, but he also sees him as a human being living in an organized society. In the philosophy of experimentalism the social is just as final as the physical. One may be taken to be as truly indicative of the nature of nature as the other. Indeed, if any choice were to be made between the two, the preference would be given to the social rather than to the physical.

"While the theory that life, feeling and thought are never independent of physical events may be deemed materialism, it may also be considered just the opposite. For it is reasonable to believe that the most adequate definition of the basic traits of natural existence can be had only when its properties are most fully displayed—a condition which is met in the degree of the scope and intimacy of interactions realized." [12]

As we have already noted, the experimentalist makes large use of the findings of the biologist in his interpretation of life and experience. From the study of the biological organism and its relation to the environment he has learned much that throws light on the nature of the individual and the primary character of human behavior. He does not believe, however, that any exclusively physiological study is at all adequate for an understanding of human experience. In a discussion of new methods used in the Russian schools Dewey says, "this social behaviorism seems to me much more promising intellectually than any exclusively physiological behaviorism can ever prove to be." [13] For the individual living in modern society the most significant part of his environment is the social aspect. It is in the facts of human association, language communication, customs, tools, and institutions that we find the influences that nurture minds and that make a humane experience possible. The experimentalist believes that to overlook the part played by communication in developing mind and moral sensitivity in the individual is to fail to see the natural bridge that joins the world of mind, of meanings, with the rest of existence. In the simple fact that people talk to one another the experimentalist finds the clue to that which makes the life of the mind possible.

"Of all affairs, communication is the most wonderful, . . . When communication occurs, all natural events are subject to reconsideration and revision; they are re-adapted to meet the requirements of conversation, whether it be public discourse or that preliminary discourse termed thinking. Events turn into objects, things with a meaning." [14] Communication "is a fact of such distinction that its occurrence changed dumb creatures— as we so significantly call them—into thinking and knowing animals and created the realm of meanings. . . . Language makes the difference between brute and man." [15] Too often "the office of signs in creating reflection, foresight and recollection is passed by." [16]

"Mother and nurse, father and older children, determine what experiences the child shall have; they constantly instruct him as to the meaning of what he does and undergoes. The conceptions that are socially current and important become the child's principles of interpretation and estimation long before he attains to personal and deliberate control of conduct. Things come to him clothed in language, not in physical nakedness, and this garb of communication makes him a sharer in the beliefs of those about him. These beliefs coming to him as so many facts form his mind; they furnish the centres about which his own personal expeditions and perceptions are ordered." [17]

"An individual usually acquires the morality as he inherits the speech of his social group." [18] "So with conscience. When a child acts, those about him re-act. They shower encouragement upon him, visit him with approval, or they bestow frowns and rebuke. What others do to us when we act is as natural a consequence of our action as what the fire does to us when we plunge our hands in it. The social environment may be as artificial as you please. But its action in response to ours is natural, not artificial. In language and imagination we rehearse the responses of others just as we dramatically enact other consequences. We foreknow how others will act, and the foreknowledge is the beginning of judgment passed on action. We know *with* them; there is conscience." [19]

The whole discussion may be epitomized by saying that the experimentalist sees man becoming a human being through his interaction with a social environment. The individual is inherently social in nature. Through his membership in a human society he learns that which makes a humane existence possible. "Prior human efforts have made over natural conditions." The dependent child forms his habits of thought and action in response to "weighted stimuli." As a result he is "able to traverse in a short lifetime what the race has needed slow, tortured ages to attain." His plastic organic tendencies with their marvelous capacity to modify themselves through experience give the raw materials for mind. But these native tendencies of the individual are not mind and would not become mind in any very significant sense were they not directed and organized by participation in the activities of others who have minds. By responding to the "weighted stimuli" of his group the child weaves his responses into the pattern of the group activities. His habits, his manners and morals, his ways of feeling, believing, and thinking are fashioned by this sharing in the experience of the group. Through shared experience he becomes a person. Important implications for education are contained in this view of the social nature of the self.

Through the process of experiencing, the child literally becomes a self. Individuality is not an original datum, it is an achievement. Education is the directing of the responses that children make. In reality all such direction is a redirection. Such redirection is accomplished through the control of the medium in which, and to which, the child responds. By controlling this environment we can within limits modify the acting, feeling, and thinking of the child. Moreover, his responses are never single. The whole individual is implicated in behavior. Emotional and intellectual attitudes are revealed in, and develop simultaneously with, the overt responses of the child. His present behavior is as much a function of his previous history as it is of the immediate situation. It can only be understood and fairly appraised in the light of that history. Any educator worthy of the name must be sensitive to the various responses the child is now making and should also see his present behavior as an expression of a longitudinal self with many previous specific experiences incorporated into that self and coloring what it now does and feels.

For the experimentalist education is the process of sharing experience. Through such shared experience selves come to be. The primary concern, however, is with the manner in which this sharing of experience is carried out. Important as the experimentalist believes the task of transmitting the social capital to be, he does not consider that the chief aim of the school is to fill the young with the things adults already know. An individual with a certain kind of mind may be secured that way. But it is apt to be a passive mind and is not the type of mind the experimentalist wants to build. He desires an inquiring mind, one that has "learned to learn," one that not only knows how to do many things but has also learned the reason for doing those things and is equipped to alter the way of doing them should situations change. He wants the type of mind that can continue its own education on through life—the experimental mind that is equipped to live in a changing, uncertain world. He sees that with the advance of civilization, the growth of things already known, and the development of many intrenched beliefs, there is danger that schools may become so absorbed in transmitting this body of knowledge and belief they will fail to develop individuals who can think. *Mind in the individual* and *an individual mind* denote two different realities to him. The first points to a person who has been trained to purpose, feel, and react in accordance with the pattern of his group. The group has formed its mind in him, but it has not developed individuality in the process. On the other hand, *individual mind* denotes an individual socially conditioned, nourished on the group tradition to be sure, but also so educated that he has become a conscious center of experience, and in the light of consequences as experienced can critically evaluate existing institutions and initiate reconstructive processes in the very social medium that has conditioned his own growth.

Growth is seen as an individual-social process by the experimentalist. It is a process that is accomplished through a continuous "reconstruction of experience" that begets new meanings and yields further power of control over subsequent experience. Such reconstruction will include reconstruction of social processes and institutions because the life of the individual incorporates these social influences and is conditioned by them. Growth through reconstruction of experience by the gaining of knowledge is a creative process. It can only be carried on by a mind that has learned to think and to inquire into all of the varied aspects of its experience.

4. Pupils as Ends

Looking at man through the eyes of the biologist, the experimentalist sees an organism characterized by preferential activity maintaining its life and providing for its growth through purposeful interaction with its environment. Looking at man through the eyes of the social psychologist, the experimentalist sees the biological organism developing mind and becoming a human individual through responses guided by the "weighted stimuli" of an environment which has become social and incorporates developed meanings in its language, customs, institutions, beliefs, and social habits. If we think the experimentalist is indifferent to the worth of this social milieu, we have not properly understood him. He views it literally as the means by which animals of a certain complex structure grow into human beings.

"Loyalty to whatever in the established environment makes a life of excellence possible is the beginning of all progress. The best we can accomplish for posterity is to transmit unimpaired and with some increment of meaning the environment that makes it possible to maintain the habits of decent and refined life." [20]

As this quotation from Dewey indicates, the experimentalist holds in high regard the social factors which make a human life possible. He recognizes that one of the basic functions of education is the continuance of the social inheritance. But it is also clear that it is not in the responsibility for passing on the social inheritance that he finds his foundational principle for education. We have already seen how his philosophy reverses the traditional arrangement by making particulars the ends, and universals the means. This same principle holds for the relation of the individual to society. The individual, the particular, is the end; society, the universal, is the means. The supreme aim of education is the enrichment of the life of the individual, and the social inheritance is only a means to that end. To be sure, his conception of the correlative nature of ends and means is such that he would consider it a mere travesty to stress the value of the individual, and at the same time be careless about the social means through which these individuals are developed. There is no antagonistic dualism in his thought between the individual and the social. Individuals are individuals by virtue of the fact that they are born into a social environment and achieve individuality through its nurturing influence.

On the other hand, he is too much of a radical empiricist not to recognize that society in general is an intellectual abstraction. Actually each person lives in many overlapping societies. These societies are of all sorts. Often most serious conflicts can and do develop between existing institutions and traditions and the ongoing life of a people. In all such cases of conflict, the very purpose of intelligent action is to see how the influences which hinder and frustrate the growth of individuals can be removed. Hence his basic educational aim is to develop individuals who through critical experimental procedures come to possess the resources needed to carry on this responsible work of social reconstruction. While Bertrand Russell is at some points far removed from the position of the experimentalist, he well states their view on this matter when he says:

"No man is fit to educate unless he feels each pupil an end in himself, with his own rights and his own personality, not merely a piece in a jig-saw puzzle, or a soldier in a regiment or a citizen in a State. Reverence for human personality is the beginning of wisdom, in every social question, but above all in education." [21]

It is from this ethical perspective that we reach our final answer to the question, "What does the experimentalist see when he sees a man?" He sees man as an object of consideration, the individual as the final value. He has extended this ethical principle by asserting that children are persons to be treated as ends just as truly as are adults. Child life is not viewed primarily as a time for preparation; it has its own inherent value, and the aim of education should be to recognize and utilize the intrinsic worth of the activities and interests of children. Maximum meaningful living in the present is the best preparation for the future.

It is because of his interest in individuals as ends that he has so consistently opposed the effort to make education and life serve fixed, external ends. He has boldly asserted that growth is its own end, and that there is nothing to which education should be subordinated save to more education—which is growth. In order to grow, individuals must be given freedom to share in determining the ends for which they are to spend their energies. These ends or purposes must be rooted in present experiences if they are to be charged with meaning. The aim of education is to assist the individual to be more intelligent about the bearings of his own activities. It is the faith of the experimentalist that in proportion as individuals and groups become intelligent about their own purposes and have insight into the social means required to realize them, so also will social welfare be better conserved. In other words, the social process provides its own regulative principles within itself and does not have to be controlled by external standards or outside authorities.

The principle of the moral autonomy of each individual throws further light on the insistence of the experimentalist that education should be continuous with life. He is concerned that the school may be in vital interaction with problems and conflicts of present society, because it is only through such first-hand contact that social intelligence can be developed. If the individual is to have effective control over his own experience, he must understand the society in which he lives and moves and has his being. No amount of absorption in the records of the past or creative activity in the fine arts in and of themselves alone will equip a person to share in the direction of our contemporary urban and industrial civilization. If the individual is not to be helpless in this corporate age, he must have had experiences with it that have given him insight into underlying causes. He must be learning how to coöperate with others in maintaining a social environment in which individual choices and acts count for something.

5. Experimentalism and Democracy

Finally, to say that the experimentalist believes in treating each individual as an end is merely another way of saying that he believes in the democratic ideal. Bode, for example, declares:

"A system is not democratic simply because it is made available to everybody or because it is administered without distinction of persons. . . . To be truly democratic, education must treat the individual himself as the end and set itself the task of preparing him for that intellectual and emotional sharing in the life and affairs of men which embodies the spirit of the Golden Rule." [22]

Apparently without exception the experimentalists have this faith in the democratic ideal. Kilpatrick defines it as "that respect for men which we call democracy. . . . Each individual shall count as a person and be so treated." [23] In concluding this chapter, therefore, we may well examine into what, if any, connections are to be found between the experimental method and the democratic ideal. Were both of these factors present in modern society, and were they therefore simply appropriated by the experimentalists, or is there some deeper connection between the experimental principle and the democratic principle? With no thought of the philosophy of experimentalism in mind, Beard discusses the same question in *The Rise of American Civilization:*

"It is one of the significant phases of history that the development of political democracy during three revolutionary centuries was accompanied by the rise and growth of science and invention. Students have been baffled in their efforts to establish causal relations, to explain why the world had to wait thousands of years for the steam engine and the formula of atomic weights, why Rousseau was working on his Social Contract at the very time that Watt was bringing the steam engine to an operating basis.

"Yet the fact remains that political democracy and natural science rose and flourished together. Whether in their inception there were deep connections, researches have not yet disclosed but beyond question their influence upon each other has been reciprocal. Democracy arrested the attention of idle curiosity and demanded that the man of microscope and test tube come into the street to invent, relieve, and serve. Science, on the other hand, helped to determine the course of democratic development. It was itself democratic in that it spurned nothing low or common-place in its researches—the mold on decayed vegetables, the composition of the dirt in the field, the nature of curds in sour milk. Nothing was sacred to its relentless inquiry. Before it there was neither prerogative nor privilege.

"More than that, science pointed the way to progressive democracy in its warfare against starvation, poverty, disease, and ignorance, indicating how classes and nations long engaged in strife among themselves might unite to wring from nature the secret of security and the good life. It was science, not paper declarations relating to the idea of progress, that at last made patent the practical methods by which democracy could raise the standard of living for the great masses of people. Finally science gave to man revolutionary concepts of the world and of his place in the great scheme of nature, feeding the streams of thought which wore down ancient institutions of church and state." [24]

When we come more specifically to examine the philosophy of experimentalism and the democratic ideal, the following possible connections are worthy of consideration:

(1) Experimentalism is a philosophy of experience. It frankly views the world from the standpoint of its bearing on man's welfare. While it does not construe the world so as to make it appear that it was all planned for man's benefit, it does place its emphasis on examining the world as *our* world. Things are said to be what they are experienced to be. Common experience is not discounted in the name of some superior reality. It is valued for what it is.

(2) Experimentalism sees man as a creative agent. It believes that through intelligent participation in the movement of events man changes the nature of outcomes. Within

limits he can remake his world. Experimentalism, by thus giving human thought and action a genuine career, dignifies and renders more significant man's position in the world.

(3) Moreover, experimentalism is a philosophy which challenges external authorities and fixed ends of all sorts. Ideals are based on consequences as actually experienced. The realm of values is said to be within, not outside, human experience.

(4) Finally and most important of all, it believes that in the experimental method experience has a means for developing its own regulative standards from within its own process. The emphasis of experimentalism on this fundamental method is essentially an emphasis on the democratic process. Life is deemed adequate to find its own solutions through coöperative research and activity. So also is life its own sanction.

Hence the ultimate educational aim of experimentalism is to develop individuals who can intelligently manage their own affairs, at times "alone," more usually in shared or joint enterprise. It believes this ideal will be achieved as children are given opportunity to practise it under intelligent guidance in the schools. As the experimentalist conceives it, education is the social process by which human beings are created.

In the last two chapters we have stated in some detail philosophical positions underlying what is called the progressive movement in education. This has been done for two reasons, in the first place, in order to show that the progressive movement in education is inherently linked with a philosophy of life. To be an intelligent friend or critic of the educational ideas of this movement, it is fundamentally important to see that these ideas are an outgrowth of a philosophy about the nature of our world and about the nature of man. To consider the educational movement apart from this larger view is to tear things apart which should be kept together.

Second, in the chapters that follow, certain current criticisms both of these philosophical ideas and of their correlative educational program are to be reviewed. To provide a background for the intelligent discussion of these criticisms it seemed necessary to give first a somewhat systematic outline of these major positions of experimentalism.

REFERENCES

1. H. S. JENNINGS, *Biological Basis of Human Nature* (W. W. Norton and Company, 1930), p. 135.

2. JOHN DEWEY, *Experience and Nature* (The Open Court Publishing Co., 1929), p. 238.

3. JOHN DEWEY, *Human Nature and Conduct* (Henry Holt and Company, 1922), p. 20.

4. JOHN DEWEY, *Experience and Nature* (The Open Court Publishing Co., 1929), p. 282.

5. R. B. RAUP, *Complacency* (The Macmillan Company, 1926), Ch. I.

6. JOHN DEWEY, *Creative Intelligence* (Henry Holt and Company, 1917), pp. 10–11.

7. JOHN DEWEY, *Quest for Certainty* (Minton, Balch & Company, 1929), pp. 214–215.

8. JOHN DEWEY, *Experience and Nature* (The Open Court Publishing Co., 1929), p. 179.

9. JOHN DEWEY, *Reconstruction in Philosophy* (Henry Holt and Company, 1920), pp. 87, 89.

10. *Ibid.*, p. 91.

11. JOHN DEWEY, *Quest for Certainty* (Minton, Balch & Company, 1929), p. 226.

12. JOHN DEWEY, *Experience and Nature* (The Open Court Publishing Co., 1929), p. 262.

13. JOHN DEWEY, *Impressions of Soviet Russia* (The New Republic, Inc., 1929), p. 75.

14. JOHN DEWEY, *Experience and Nature* (The Open Court Publishing Co., 1929), p. 166.

15. *Ibid.*, p. 168.

16. *Ibid.,* p. 169.
17. JOHN DEWEY, *Reconstruction in Philosophy* (Henry Holt and Company, 1920), p. 92.
18. JOHN DEWEY, *Human Nature and Conduct* (Henry Holt and Company, 1922), p. 58.
19. *Ibid.,* pp. 314–315.
20. JOHN DEWEY, *Human Nature and Conduct* (Henry Holt and Company, 1922), p. 21.
21. BERTRAND RUSSELL, *Sceptical Essays* (W. W. Norton and Company, 1928), p. 205.
22. BOYD BODE, *Fundamentals of Education* (The Macmillan Company, 1921), pp. 61–62.
23. W. H. KILPATRICK, *Education for a Changing Civilization* (The Macmillan Company, 1926), p. 27.
24. CHARLES BEARD, *The Rise of American Civilization* (The Macmillan Company, 1927), I, 737–738.

CHAPTER V

EXPERIENCE, HYPOTHESES, AND EDUCATION

"We cannot sacrifice experience to the requirements of any system."
BERGSON.

"A third significant change that would issue from carrying over experimental method from physics to man concerns the import of standards, principles, rules. With the transfer, these, and all tenets and creeds about good and goods, would be recognized to be hypotheses."
DEWEY.

1. Life Its Own Sanction

EXPERIMENTALISM is a radically empirical philosophy. It maintains that the ultimate source, authority, and criterion for all belief and conduct are to be found in ordinary human experience. Experience stands on its own bottom. Life is its own sanction. Whatever of guidance and inspiration man requires to meet the exigencies of his life is to be sought from the resources within experience and not from some supra-empirical source. The very corner-stone of experimentalism is the faith that experience is able to develop from within its own processes all necessary regulative standards and ideals. This interpretation of experience has significant implications for both philosophy and education. Some of the more important of these will be considered in this chapter. It may be stated at the outset that the radical emphasis given to experience in the philosophy of the experimentalist is not without its far-reaching consequences. It is an emphasis which carries a fundamental challenge to many traditional notions.

2. Experience and Knowledge

On the constructive side, the experimentalist believes that his interpretation of experience saves us from the paralyzing effect of wholesale skepticism. For the experimentalist, as Dewey frankly states, "a problem of knowledge in general is, to speak brutally, nonsense." [1] And yet much of modern philosophy has been centered on the discussion of precisely this problem. Nothing in the field of technical philosophy grieves the experimentalist more than the time and ingenuity which have been spent on the discussion of the general question of the possibility of knowledge. For him the irony of the situation is found in the fact that this problem of knowledge has come to the front exactly during the period which has witnessed the largest development of the use of the scientific method. In other words, at the same time that man has been making such an astounding display of his ability to gain knowledge and control, many technical philosophers have been skeptical about the possibility of man's achieving any worth-while knowledge at all.

In dealing with this subject the experimentalist once again attains a fresh approach to a vexing problem in philosophy by assuming the naïve standpoint. In connection with the problems of knowledge and the nature of truth, the naïve view is particularly difficult to achieve because of an inherited notion deeply imbedded in men's minds to the effect that existence is divided into two realms: one that of true being; the other that of imperfect being. According to this traditional view, in *ordinary experience* we deal only with the objects found in the realm of inferior being, and as a result all such intercourse is with a world of mere appearances and shadows. Consequently, unless man can discover some means of getting beyond this inferior realm of *ordinary experience* into the realm of pure thought and ultimate reality, he has no means of gaining a knowledge of things as they actually are. This view that knowledge of reality would involve a grasp of the ultimate structures of the universe in their true being, and as such is finally impossible to attain, is often reinforced by the psychological theory of sensationism. According to this theory, knowing is the process of receiving impressions and sensations from things located in the "external" environment, and consequently one can never be sure that the mental pictures his mind constructs out of these sensations and images are true copies of the original "external" objects.

As has been indicated earlier, the experimentalist believes that if we accept the dualisms found in the premises of the above positions, we do have an insoluble problem of knowledge on our hands. His view of the nature of experience and the function of knowledge in experience starts, therefore, with the basic principle of the continuity between man and nature. Man is in the world, not outside of it. Experience is an active participation in the actual affairs of the real world. A fresh attack is made on the problem of knowledge by indicating that if we are to be in a position to discuss intelligently the question of whether it is *possible to know,* we must first have some understanding of what it *means to know.* What, then, does it mean to know? This is a problem set by experience; and the experimentalist believes that it is also to experience that we must look for the answer. What does naïve life have to tell us about the process of thinking and the nature of knowledge?

"If we were to ask the thinking of naïve life to present, with a minimum of theoretical elaboration, its conception of its own practice, we should get an answer running not unlike this: Thinking is a kind of activity which we perform at specific need, just as at other need we engage in other sorts of activity: as converse with a friend; draw a plan for a house; take a walk; eat a dinner; purchase a suit of clothes; etc., etc. In general, its material is anything in the wide universe which seems to be relevant to this need—anything which may serve as a resource in defining the difficulty or in suggesting modes of dealing effectively with it. The measure of its success, the standard of its validity, is precisely the degree in which the thinking actually disposes of the difficulty and allows us to proceed with more direct modes of experiencing, that are forthwith possessed of more assured and deepened value." [2]

In other words, the desire to gain knowledge "comes after something and out of something, and for the sake of something. . . . The antecedents of thought are our universe of life and love; of appreciation and struggle." [3] We think because we find it necessary to think. Problems do emerge in the course of our "doing and undergoing." Thinking is instrumental to the resolution of such specific problematic situations. Its typical function is thereby defined. Knowing, then, is not to be thought of as the mere beholding of a spectator. It is an active process. Knowledge is a necessity for an individual living within the world and participating in its activities. We need to know in order to deal effectively with the difficulties of one sort or another that arise in our experience. To know anything we have to do something. We do not learn to know about an object by merely looking at it. Knowledge relates primarily to its conditions and consequences. We learn to know these as we search into the wider connections of the occurrence which initiated the inquiry.

"If the living, experiencing being is an intimate participant in the activities of the world to which it belongs, then knowledge is a mode of participation, valuable in the degree in which it is effective. It cannot be the idle view of an unconcerned spectator." [4]

Once knowledge is thus defined, there can be no wholesale problem about it. The indubitable fact is that man does have knowledge. Difficulties have been met. Means have been found of overcoming these difficulties and ambiguities. Since means of inquiry have been improved through the development of experimental procedures, man's ability to gain knowledge has been vastly extended. His control over the events in which he participates is increased because he has learned to know the consequences of many of these happenings and also the conditions on which they depend. As a result his activity is informed and guided by meanings. These meanings are relevant to the characters of the actual world. He believes they constitute "objective" knowledge because they give him objects that reliably tell him what to expect and what to do. They work when put to the test of actual experience. In *Experience and Nature* this objective character of man's knowledge of the world is discussed by Dewey:

"The new introductory chapter accordingly takes up the question of method, especially with respect to the relation that exists between experience and nature. It points to faith in experience when intelligently used as a means of disclosing the realities of nature. It finds that nature and experience are not enemies or alien. Experience is not a veil that shuts man off from nature; it is a means of penetrating continually further into the heart of nature. There is in the character of human experience no index-hand pointing to agnostic conclusions, but rather a growing progressive self-disclosure of nature itself. The failures of philosophy have come from lack of confidence in the directive powers that inhere in experience, if men have but the wit and courage to follow them." [5]

But the objection may be raised that this answer of the experimentalist does not meet the heart of the difficulty. It is not denied that man can get a certain practical knowledge for purposes of control. But such knowledge is related to particular affairs. However far the particular sciences may develop their researches, they can never give us knowledge of reality as a whole. Such findings are particular, and what man needs for the guidance of his life is an interpretation of the meaning and significance of existence as a whole. The experimentalist makes two answers to this criticism. Empirically he finds that existence is just this succession of specific events. To be sure, these concrete events have sufficient continuity and interrelatedness to enable us to go from one thing to another, and there is enough stability to make prediction, generalization, and human control possible within limits. Why, then, he asks, should we assume that reality is something other than this stream of events? These particulars are the reals of existence. The realm of ends is precisely this realm of particulars. Moreover, has not man steadily made progress in gaining more adequate understanding as he has substituted piecemeal activity for efforts to get knowledge wholesale?

Finally, if there were any higher synthesis of these particulars, how should we discover it? There is only one way in which man can get more inclusive meanings, and that is by following out the leads that his particular experiences give

him. "If there be a synthesis in ultimate Being of the realities which can be cognitively substantiated and of meanings
which should command our highest admiration and approval,
then concrete phenomena . . . ought to be capable of being
exhibited as definite manifestations of the eternal union of
the real-ideal." [6] Actually, however, many experimentalists
tend to be suspicious of generalizations that grow too inclusive. They believe that such generalizations constantly run
the danger of glossing over the intractable events which do
not happen to fit well with the particular unity which the individual desires to substantiate. Thus the desire for certainty
and the stable may prompt one to neglect the uncertain and
changing factors in experience; the approval of the beautiful
and the good may lead to a denial of the full reality of the
ugly and the evil; the demand for unity and simplicity may
override the variety and plurality of things as they are actually experienced. In particular, there is danger that imaginative reconstructions will come to compensate for the more
difficult and prosaic task of making the certainties and experienced goods of actual existence prevail more widely.

"Attainment of the relatively secure and settled takes place,
however, only with respect to *specified* problematic situations;
quest for certainty that is universal, applying to everything, is
a compensatory perversion. One question is disposed of: another
offers itself and thought is kept alive." [7]

The experimentalist avoids wholesale skepticism because
he does not demand that he have wholesale knowledge. His
skepticism is specific. It relates to the validity of particular
beliefs and theories. As such it stimulates further efforts
to find out rather than resulting in a general doubt about the
value of trying to know anything. Such specific doubts as he

has encourage further inquiry and more patient and thorough experimentation. The experimentalist points to the fruits which have progressively come from the use of the experimental method in the field of the physical sciences. While scientific theories are constantly revised, a growing body of concrete knowledge is achieved. He asks that this method be extended to the moral and social realm. It is his faith that it will be equally productive in this area. Experimentally controlled experience is an adequate means for guiding and regulating human affairs provided men develop the attitudes and the dispositions which the critical, constructive use of this method demands. Once the burden of mistaken traditional views of the nature of experience and of knowledge is removed, he has confidence in the ability of men through coöperative endeavor to gain the knowledge needed to guide human affairs. It is from this background that he views the opportunity of the schools.

3. "Intellectualism" and the Schools

The experimentalist also finds that a revised conception of experience keeps him from the errors of abstract intellectualism. The cognitive experience is not the only form of experience. As a matter of fact, as already indicated, cognitive experience is a secondary and derived experience, no matter how important its function may be in the ordering of man's affairs. In its primary form experience is a matter of "being and having," an affair of "feeling and doing." In this mode experience may be said to be more esthetic than intellectual in character. It is literally a "doing and undergoing," a "suffering and enjoying." Man has developed mind, but he had an affectional and volitional nature before

he came to possess mind. He is still far from being a mere
passionless reason. Desire, preference, active seeking and
avoiding are basic qualities in all experience. Thinking grows
out of this primary experience instinct with its propulsive af-
fectivities. It gets its relevance and significance in relation to
these primary "beings and havings" of macroscopic experience.

Holding this view of that form of experience called thinking, the experimentalist is not seriously disturbed that clinical
psychology shows thought to be often largely a rationalization
of desire. Originally it was the radical error of abstract intellectualism to suppose that thought and desire were antithetical.
It is probably inevitable that the fresh discovery that thought
and desire are intimately connected should lead many to react
to the other extreme, causing them to assume that thought is
the mere servant of already existing desires. The business of
thought is not to oppose our desires, but to reconstruct and
reorganize them. What is wanted is that desire, preference,
bias may become more intelligent. As related to desire,
thinking has this instrumental function to perform. It may
be said to be the process by which competing desires find
some more inclusive, unified manner of expression.

The same logic holds in the field of moral experience.
Moral values do not exist in some realm outside the life of
impulse and emotion. Such values are also immanent in the
doings and the undergoings of primary experience. Moral
judgments are directed to such reorganization of this primary experience as eliminates conflicts, and by thus liber-
ating impulse adds to the values of life. In short, *feeling* and *thought* are inherently connected in every realm of
experience.

"The separation of warm emotion and cool intelligence is the great moral tragedy. This division is perpetuated by those who deprecate science and foresight in behalf of affection as it is by those who in the name of an idol labeled reason would quench passion. The intellect is always inspired by some impulse." [8]

The experimentalist believes that much of philosophy is weakened by an arbitrary intellectualism. Intellectualism is defined as the false assumption that all experience is a mode of knowing.

"The assumption of 'intellectualism' goes contrary to the facts of what is primarily experienced. For things are objects to be treated, used, acted upon and with, enjoyed and endured, even more than things to be known. They are things *had* before they are things cognized." [9]

That this vice of intellectualism has not been confined to philosophy is evidenced by the curriculum of the conventional school. This curriculum is the typical counterpart in education of the philosophical doctrine that all significant experience is a form of knowing. Too often the bodies of children have been ignored, and it has been assumed that minds could know apart from all physical activity. Not only so, but this dualism of mind and body with its correlative bifurcation of experience into purely intellectual activities, on the one hand, and merely physical activities, on the other, is by no means absent from many of our more progressive schools with their enriched offerings. Although expressional activities have been given a much larger place in these schools, too often the intellectual possibilities of these activities are not apprehended. We still have a long way to go before the deeper implications of the experimentalist's revised notion of experience gets fully incorporated into our educational thought and activity. The failure to realize that objects are "things *had* before they are things cognized" has been, and continues to be, the source of untold evil practice in school procedures.

4. Knowledge and Verification

The insistence that all experience is not a mode of knowing makes clearer certain false assumptions inherent in the various forms of *intuitionism,* while at the same time it opens the way for the experimentalist to give due recognition to the fact of immediate experience. The protest of the intuitionists against the intellectualistic tendency to absorb all experience to the type of the analytical, cognitive form is well grounded. "A large part of our life is carried on in the realm of meanings to which truth and falsity as such are irrelevant. . . . The realm of meanings is wider than that of true-and-false meanings; it is more urgent and more fertile." [10]

"It is well to emphasize this non-thought basis of thinking itself; for upon this plane of experiencing lies most of the content of our living. Here are included our loves and hates, our eating and our sleeping, our friendships and our animosities, our illness and our health; here too are the fine arts; here the dumb gladness that welcomes the dawn, the quiet contemplation of the sun's trailing glory at eventide, and the silent watching of the passing night. This is the primal and ever the larger aspect of human life. It is the good-in-itself, from which reflection arises and for the sake of which reflection exists as an instrument." [11]

As the above quotations indicate, experimentalists give generous recognition to the primacy of the life of immediate experience. They believe that the findings of the poet, the

moral leader, and the artist are just as relevant to our sense
of the realities of existence as are the findings of the scientist in his laboratory. But the experimentalist does not stop
with these. He asserts that fancies, dreams, illusions, lies, and
errors are also inherent parts of reality as *immediately* experienced. Each of these things is just the real sort of thing it
is. Macroscopic experience includes all possible varieties of
"being and having," of "feeling and doing." There is the fact
of direct awareness—of sheer immediacy. Life is replete with
such uniquely final experiences. The instrumental theory
of the experimentalist is not to be understood as implying
that all of experience is instrumental. On the contrary, by
emphasizing that the instrumental knowledge experience is
only one form of experience, it makes possible the recognition that other forms of experience are immediate and final.

Experimentalism is not concerned to deny either the existence or the significance of such immediate, qualitative experiences. Its concern is with the tendency to assume that
such immediate experiences are *noetic* experiences. To be
sure, William James recognized that such experiences might
be said to possess a certain knowledge value. He took pains,
however, to discriminate two forms of knowledge: one the
knowledge of immediate acquaintance; the other the knowledge of and about things. More recently, however, in order
to avoid confusion, experimentalists are inclined to reserve
the term *knowledge* for our understanding of the conditions
and consequences of events. Immediate acquaintance is said
to be esthetic, not cognitive, in character. *Knowledge* is that
which has a significant opposite—*ignorance* or more positively, *error*. *Truth* and *falsity* are terms that apply exclusively to our ideas about things. Experience as such cannot
be said to be either true or false. It is whatever it happens to

be. It is our judgments about that experience, our active interpretations of it that are either true or false. Knowing involves the process of judging, of making inferences, of anticipating the consequences to which our thoughts would lead if carried out. Any complete act of thought involves overt operations, and, as already indicated, to find out anything we have to do something. Knowledge is never gained by an immediate consciousness of things, no matter how vivid that consciousness may be. To assume that such immediate awareness gives knowledge that requires no further testing is the root error of all forms of intuitionism. As Lewis declares in a recent book on *Mind and the World-Order:*

"It is the first thesis of this chapter that there is no knowledge merely by acquaintance; that knowledge *always* transcends the immediately given. The merely contemplated or enjoyed may possess esthetic significance, but if it is to have cognitive meaning this immediacy must become the subject of an interpretation which transcends it; we must take toward the given some attitude which serves practical action and relates it to what is not given." [12]

This holds just as truly for our moral ideas as it does for our ideas about the connection of things in the physical world. Several considerations lead the experimentalist to the conclusion that moral intuitions are no more to be accepted as final than any other form of immediate awareness. As has already been explained, the experimentalist finds an essential unity in experience. There is no specific moral realm except in so far as we, for purposes of convenience or emphasis, choose to classify certain types of behavior as preeminently "moral." The desirability of thus classifying some acts as moral and others as non-moral or amoral is challenged by the experimentalist. He believes that whenever a significant choice has to be made between a better and a worse in experience, we face a genuine moral situation. It follows then that, potentially at least, moral conduct is co-extensive with all of conduct. If this be true, morals do not constitute a realm apart from ordinary experience. The questions of what diet to give a baby, of how one is to invest his money, may on occasion be moral questions as full-fledged as are questions of truth-telling and sex behavior. The moral factor in any choice-situation is proportional to the significance of the various sets of value consequences which follow from the alternative courses of action. To discriminate and anticipate such consequences is an intellectual act of the highest quality. Decisions that are thus related to all aspects of our complex social experience cannot be safely taken merely on the basis of what "feels right" in the situation as immediately experienced.

This is particularly seen to be true when one recalls how these inner feelings of what is right and wrong are socially conditioned during infancy. As has been frequently pointed out, the "inner voice" speaks a different language with different people in different ages and in different places. Each individual conscience tends to reflect the "goods" and the "bads" of the particular social approvals and disapprovals that have trained its development. To follow obediently its promptings without careful examination of the consequences which result from the behavior it inspires is to be guilty of a "blindfolded morality," blindfolded because it is a morality that cannot progressively reconstruct itself by gaining the instruction that observation of consequences alone can give. Hence the voice of conscience in moral matters is no more infallible than is the voice of intuition in scientific matters. Just as the experimentalist believes that there is no special agent or knower in general, so also does he believe there is no special moral faculty that can be trusted to give intelligent moral guidance.

"If it is recognized that knowing is carried on through the medium of natural factors, the assumption of special agencies for moral knowing becomes outlawed and incredible." [13]

This is all so obvious that one would hesitate to dwell upon it were it not for the fact that even to-day so many are unready to accept the full implications of the foregoing without discount. This confusion is particularly manifest in current educational programs in the moral field. Even professed empirical thinkers hesitate to accept whole-heartedly the experimental rather than the *a priori* basis for morals. In his recent book *Our Changing Civilization,* Randall seems to illustrate this tendency of present-day liberal thinkers who strive to be empirical and experimental while at the same time they continue to search for some non-experimental sanction for the moral life of man. As there is danger that a short quotation considered apart from its wider context may not do justice to the writer a rather long selection is herewith given:

"This is the critical, experimental spirit that science itself employs. It accepts the best hypothesis to test, not the easiest. It employs the most rigorous standards of verification, not the laxest. It seeks out that principle which will organize the richest body of facts, not the most meager and simple. And in its formulations it constantly embodies new truth.

"Yet even a rightly understood experimental attitude is not enough on which to build our supreme loyalties. All human living rests ultimately on some faith,—the faith that certain things are of transcendent importance. Such final values cannot be touched by scientific verification. They are exempt from experiment. The scientist himself has such a faith,—the faith in science. His ultimate conviction the laboratory can neither prove nor disprove, for it is the faith in laboratory proof itself. Such supreme allegiances can find no other verification than that men do and will live by them.

"It is these final goods that are enshrined in a great moral tradition. They are handed on from generation to generation, for they do not grow spontaneously in every childish heart. It has taken centuries for civilization to attain their ethical wisdom. Those who can contribute to it are rare, far rarer than scientists or artists, so rare that men have looked on them as divine and on their messages as revelation. When such prophets arise, they do not beseech men to listen, offering signs and tests that they bring truth. They speak with authority, and some few follow in their train. Slowly their insight wins its way among their people, knowing no other test than that men cannot deny.

"Our own moral heritage has been rich in such ethical geniuses. The Hebrew prophets thundered, 'Thou shalt not violate thy brother's soul,' and something in their fierce zeal won the entire Mediterranean world. The man of Nazareth added, 'Thou shalt love thy neighbor as thyself,' and even Christians have never been able entirely to forget. The revolutionists of the 18th century set forth, 'All men are created equal,' and for all our despair and bravado, for all our little theories and our bitter experience, we know that somehow it is true. These convictions are not the fruits of experiment, they are its premises. They are touchstones by which we ultimately judge." [14]

Before proceeding to the discussion of the more central issue of the nature of general principles raised by this quotation, some attention should be given the brief that it makes for the *a priori*. For example it is asserted that "final values can not be touched by scientific verification. They are exempt from experiment. The scientist himself has such a faith,— the faith in science." The experimentalist does not so understand the case for science. He believes that in so far as science has a certain authority in modern life, it is because it has earned that authority. Men have made a wide variety of experiments in their efforts to get knowledge and truth.

These various adventures have been subjected to many centuries of testing in human experience. For a long time popular opinion was not in favor of the experimental method of science. The methods of revelation, of intuition, of rationalistic dialectic were once all held in greater esteem. Why has the prestige of experimental procedures grown greater while the prestige of many other methods has declined? Precisely because of the fruits which have come from the intelligent use of the experimental method. It has won its way because it has demonstrated its power to make good in an expanding number of life's activities.

Nor does the experimentalist believe that the scientist's faith in laboratory method should be exempt from continuous scrutiny. For example, statistical procedures have shown a great variety of usefulness. Their important position in physical and social investigations has been earned by the results they have achieved. On the other hand, it by no means follows that on purely *a priori* grounds we should accept statistical devices as adequate to deal with all types of problems. Some of the bad effects in education which have followed from this blind faith in the exclusive value of analytical and quantitative procedures have led many who are friendly to the "scientific movement in education" to challenge certain tendencies now present in that movement. When the scientist in education announces his faith "that everything that exists, exists in some amount and therefore can be measured," experimentalist philosophers are at least inclined to reserve judgment and to evaluate critically this zeal for measurement by the actual consequences it produces. In short, dogmatism is not altogether foreign to science. In actual practice both the claims and the techniques of individual scientists do need constant critical attention.

It is also stated in the above quotation that prophets do not offer "signs and tests that they bring truth." It may be the privilege of the prophet to proclaim his vision without regard for the consequences which his policies, if acted upon, would produce. But surely those who elect to follow a prophet will inescapably suffer or enjoy those consequences. They will, therefore, do well to evaluate the probabilities in the situation before committing themselves to a line of action with regard to it, no matter how strongly that line of action may be recommended by some eminent prophet. False prophets as well as true prophets speak with assurance. Those whose names have endured in the memory of the race have been on the whole those whose teachings have led to consequences which have verified their insights.

But to come to the main issue. What about general principles? What is their nature and function? Are ethical principles "the fruits of experiment," or are they "its premises"? Are they the "touchstones by which we ultimately judge," or do they also grow, and change, and get reconstructed in the process of being used? * Consider, for example, the conviction of the Hebrew prophets quoted by Randall, "Thou shalt not violate thy brother's soul." The critical study of the ethical experiences of the Hebrew people seems to indicate that this principle was not immaculately conceived in the mind of some individual prophet. There was a long cultural experience back of it. Moreover, the national and racial restrictions which the earlier ethical insight of the Hebrew prophets placed upon that principle now have been largely

---

* In fairness to Randall's position it should be said that at other places he seems to be in accord with the view here taken of the nature and function of principles. It is the apparent desire to introduce a transcendental factor in a philosophy otherwise empirical and experimental which is under examination.

removed. Ethical theory has grown until the soul of the alien is considered to have rights just as inviolate as the soul of one's fellow-national. A new content has also been put into the meaning of the term "violate thy brother's soul." It would have scarcely occurred to one of the earlier prophets to question his solemn right and duty to persuade all others to believe as he believed. His missionary zeal would not have been tempered as is that of many a present-day missionary with the conviction that there are things to be learned from the "heathen" as well as some things to be shared with them. It would have been difficult for an Old Testament prophet to believe that to impose his faith on another might be to "violate his soul."

But let us consider the question more broadly. The experimentalist believes that all our decisions should relate to determinate situations. He recognizes that there is much of continuity between these situations. A thing learned in one situation can be abstracted and used in another. Were this not so, we could not get far in the development of intellectual or ethical procedures. We can profit both by our own experiences and by those of others. Man has achieved a fund of knowledge and general principles that greatly aid him in controlling the course of subsequent experience. All of this is fully recognized by the experimentalist. It is of the essence of his educational ideas. But he also insists on the ongoing character of experience. Conditions do change. One situation is not just a repetition of an earlier one. We do not measure concrete situations by these abstracted general principles. On the contrary, we use these principles as tools to help us explore the difficulties and the possibilities of the particular situations which now confront us. If tradition, habit, rules were sufficient, we would not have a "situation"

on our hands. A "situation" is something that needs attention. It needs attention because old ways of responding to
it are in conflict. Values are at stake. Our problem is how to
act in the light of conflicting goods. Such conflicts do occur.
This fact of conflict between rival goods seems often to be
ignored by ethical theorists who demand a complete hierarchy
of values arranged in a final system. Every ethical decision
is a concrete decision. We do not have to solve problems in
general, we have to find a way of dealing with individualized
situations which now are ambiguous in meaning. Our ethical
task is to create a way of dealing with such novel situations
that will most adequately care for all of the interests in conflict. The past operates through old habits and principles that
should help us discover just what this situation is with which
we now have to do. Ideas, hypotheses, are evolved out of the
interaction of the old with the new. They are not tested by
their agreement with the habits and standards of the past.
Nor are they tested by what we "feel" we "know" on *a
priori* grounds to be true. When the contents of the *a priori*
are turned inside out, they are apt to be found to be the
things that habit, training, and repeated response have made
familiar. Now the old and familiar has its rightful prestige,
but it lands us in endless difficulty if we use it to coerce and
constrain our ongoing experience.

In sum, for the experimentalist all ideas are hypotheses.
They are possible ways of responding to the problematic as
such. The test of hypotheses is their adequacy to resolve
the confusion and ambiguity of the situation now in conflict.
In other words, the ultimate test of all ideas, principles, and
ethical intuitions is in their ability *to make* good. They are
judged by the concrete, public consequences to which they
lead. This brings us to the central problem of this chapter;

how adequate are hypotheses and an attitude of tentativeness to meet the complete demands of individual and collective experience?

5. The Case for Hypotheses

Many of the same considerations which lead the experimentalist to reject immediate acquaintance as a sufficient ground for reliable knowledge, also lead him to oppose all absolutes, final ends, and fixed principles. He believes the ongoing nature of experience is such that it precludes such finality as these presuppose. As we have already noted, the experimentalist sees nature as a moving complex scene of individualized, qualitative events. Each event is linked up with other events in a variety of ways, but it has its own distinctive pattern. Continuity and discreteness are both characters of existence. Existence is not all of one piece—it is an affair of affairs. Our experience is in, and of, this world of qualitative particulars. Hence our problems relate to specific, concrete life-situations.

Moreover, for any thing to exist at all, it must be in process, in change. Man is changing, and the situations with which he has to deal are also changing. The rate of change is by no means even. Some events are fleeting and evanescent; others are relatively permanent and stable. Our world is not a world of sheer chaos, it is characterized by structure as well as process. In fact, some sort of structure is essential to process. But these are relative terms, and what from one perspective may be taken as stable structure, may, from another point of view, be just as truly seen as process.

"Thus if an engineer were studying Niagara as a water-power, he would count the banks and bed as structure and conditions. But if he were asking whether the falls will not in time cease, banks and bed become movements and he studies them accordingly as results of other things as conditions. In like manner if we are studying curiosity we take eye and ear and fingers as structure and conditions of expression; but at another time we may ask how eye or ear or fingers were developed during the long ages and these then become movements and processes and are studied accordingly." [15]

In the field of the physical sciences the immutable has been banished. The whole physical world is seen to be in process. Conceptions of fixed entities and unchanging substances have been replaced by notions of events and processes. The physical sciences have accepted these new conceptions. They do their work with these new tools, and in light of this more adequate understanding. To recognize that all existences are events and that process and change are universal traits has not thrown the physical sciences into chaos. The new insights, instead of making the work of further investigation and generalization seem futile, as some seem to fear must follow if the universality of change be admitted, have had exactly the opposite effect. These more adequate tools of understanding have opened all sorts of new possibilities for study and investigation in the natural sciences.

As we have already seen, the experimentalist believes that the same principle of change and process also characterizes our social life. If anything the factor of change is, for our purposes, more significant in the social field. Institutions, customs, and moral conventions are structural parts of our social order. But these structures must change as conditions change if social disorders are not to occur. In the dynamic civilization created by our scientific technology, the need for a much greater degree of flexibility in these social structures than has prevailed hitherto is imperative if we are not to suffer disastrous consequences. Intelligent direction must be given to this continuous process of social reconstruction. As a preliminary to this undertaking, the experimentalist urges that we abandon all ideas of fixity in the social and moral field just as they have been abandoned in the physical field. Instead of seeing social institutions such as the family, the existing economic order, and our present religious societies as final forms, he asks us to view them as experiments in caring for certain phases of our social experience. As this social experience changes, these social forms should also be changed whenever they cramp human development.

The same dynamic logic also applies to our moral ideals. These ideals have also grown out of experience, and are to be tested by their contributions to a changing experience. Instead of regarding them as final, absolute rules, we are to understand them as working hypotheses. Now hypotheses are tested and reconstructed in their working. Things that have worked well over long periods may not continue to work so well once relevant conditions have changed. We forget, or disregard, this fact of change at our peril. If we recognize the changing, ongoing character of experience, we must also be willing to substitute flexible working hypotheses for fixed moral dogmas.

Sometimes the experimentalist is charged with overemphasizing this factor of change. It is asserted that this insistence on change represents an expression of preference on his part. It is even said that his philosophy seems to be characterized by a complex against permanence and stability. It is not improbable that the amazing degree to which he finds the element of contingency and change neglected in many current philosophic and educational theories does tend to prompt him to dwell more on these factors in his writing and speaking than he otherwise would. But the emphasis is given to these traits of existence because he believes they need to be stressed. It is not that instability is preferred to permanence, nor uncertainty to certainty; these are stubborn factors he finds in experience. They are so important that he believes that any moral theory which omits them is radically deficient and will guide us badly. The way to manage life in an uncertain, changing world is not to seek by some hocus-pocus of dialectic to banish these traits from experience. It is better to recognize them fully for whatever they are found to be, and to shape our thinking and acting accordingly. It is not an arbitrary choice that has put uncertainty and contingency into his philosophy. It is the precarious character of the world as "lived, suffered and enjoyed" that is responsible. Finding these factors in his world, the experimentalist believes that an empirical philosophy must take account of them. For the experimentalist, one obvious corollary is that trust should be placed in experimental procedures rather than in following fixed rules and absolute principles.

6. How Adequate Are Hypotheses?

But is the experimentalist completely consistent at this point? How far does he go in his tentativeness? We have already seen enough of his philosophy to find that it seems to possess many positive convictions. Apparently for the experimentalist the open mind does not denote the empty mind. What, then, is the relation of convictions to hypotheses? For example, the experimentalist believes profoundly in the ability of experience to develop its own regulative standards. Is that an hypothesis or an absolute conviction? He seems also to believe in the principle of democracy, or respect for personality, of treating individuals as ends. How tentative is his belief in this democratic principle? These are important questions, and we have a right to expect an unequivocal answer from the experimentalist.

Apparently if we go back far enough, we do encounter at least one "absolute" in the philosophy of experimentalism. That "absolute" is the conviction that it is imperative that man should face his world with courage and hope and seek to find solutions to his specific problems as they confront him in experience. Even Dewey, who more than other experimentalists has opposed fixed beliefs, absolute ends, unchanging hierarchies of values, seems to recognize that there is something final about the attitude and disposition with which man should approach experience. He condemns as mere compensations and perversions all flights from the responsible task of seeking to understand and to control the events, natural and social, in which our lives are implicated. In the closing chapter of *The Quest for Certainty* he says that we can dispense with all fixed beliefs about values, "save the one value of the worth of discovering the possibilities of the actual and striving to realize them." [16]

To the experimentalist this does not appear to be the arbitrary selection of some preferred value, but rather a recognition of the inherent nature of life itself. He affirms that all normal human life does seek to participate intelligently in the movement of events. Life is caught up in these constant changes which surround it; its only hope of participating in them so as to secure a differential gain is by the exercise of intelligent foresight and control. Physical ill health and the enervating influence of beliefs about the futility of all existence and man's share in it may produce pathological individuals who do not exhibit this active interest in the movement of events, but generally speaking it is the normal reaction to life. The life process itself makes this basic affirmation. Organically man is so constructed that he inevitably engages in activity. In any case, as far as the philosophy of experimentalism is concerned, it is difficult to make sense out of its teachings without recognizing the fundamental character of its faith in intelligent effort. This "sense of the possibilities of existence" and the "devotion to the cause of these possibilities" may even be said to be the religious attitude of experimentalism.

Faith in the value of the experimental method would seem to be on a somewhat different level. As we have already pointed out, experimental procedures have won their way because of repeated demonstrations of their ability to make good. Moreover, experimental method is not a finality. It is rather an *art* in conducting investigations. Its techniques vary greatly with different subject-matters. Its procedures are constantly being modified and improved in the light of growing experience. In a genuine sense the method of observation, of experiment, of forming hypotheses, of submitting results to public inspection, of revising theories in the light of consequences and criticism, of being willing to act on the basis of working hypotheses may be said to be inherent in the activity of "creative intelligence." For the experimentalist this method seems to be the only adequate one to follow. None of the alternatives is a serious rival. Nevertheless, he recognizes that his proposal that experimental method be employed in the social and moral field as it has been in the field of the natural sciences is in the nature of an experiment, as the following quotation indicates:

"It is, once more, a hypothesis rather than a settled fact that extension and transfer of experimental method is generally possible. But like other hypotheses it is to be tried in action, and the future history of mankind is at stake in the trial." [17]

It would seem that the devotion of the experimentalist to the democratic principle is on the same general level as is his faith in experimental method. Democracy is not a cult; it is a principle. It contributes a sense of direction, it affords an indispensable orientation to the social situation, but it is not a fixed goal. It is accepted as an hypothesis. As is the case with all hypotheses, its significance is discovered and tested as it is employed. It takes on new meanings as conditions change. New ends develop as experience moves forward. The individualistic democracy of the pioneer on the frontier is ill adapted to cope effectively with the large-scale problems of a corporate age. As a result, the simple demand that each adult be given a vote changes to a demand for a socialized control of our economic processes. Without a greater degree of economic and industrial democracy, political democracy is seen to be insecure and woefully inadequate. Without social planning and effective communication of specialized expert knowledge, it is also seen that although a certain legal power be in the hands of the people, there is no guarantee that that power will be so used as to be socially advantageous. In short, a variety of complex social problems such as we now face cannot be solved by any automatic application of what we now know the democratic principle to imply. Specific solutions will have to be experimentally discovered for each of these difficulties. The principle of democracy is an important tool of discovery, but a tool is something to be used, and improved as it is used.

But after all of these qualifications are admitted, the fact remains that the devotion of the experimentalist to the democratic idea is a faith. It is an hypothesis, but one in which the attitudes and activities of men help create the facts by which its adequacy is to be tested. By acting on this hypothesis we may create the facts which make it true. If we do not have faith to inspire effort in the general direction of democracy, we may make false that which otherwise might have been made true.

Once again, however, it is not a blind faith. Other experiments in the management of government, of industry, and of our general social life have been tried and are still being tried. The democratic hypothesis has achieved a sufficient verification to justify abundantly the confidence the experimentalist has that it points in the direction of social advance. But it is also obvious that its adequate verification will be a matter of centuries and not decades. What, then, becomes of the character of an hypothesis on which men base their activities, but which will never be verified in any decisive manner in the lifetime of the present generation?

Here we find some divergence in the attitudes of experimentalists. All admit that experimentalism gives ample place for far-reaching directive hypotheses. Its emphasis on the uniqueness of the concrete situation does not imply that general principles do not have their important guiding function. Some of the experimentalists would agree with Dewey that faith in experimental method and the democratic principle of respect for personality are "working hypotheses." Others would say that they have such a fundamental place in the thought and conduct of the experimentalist that they are of the nature of "practical absolutes." By *practical absolute* is meant a belief so verified in experience that its hypothetical character is no longer of sufficient significance to require practical attention. Which of these two positions is most consistent with the theory and the practice of the experimentalist will be for the reader to decide. The important thing for us to remember is that all experimentalists agree that:

"When we take the instance of scientific experience in its own field, we find that experience when it is experimental does not signify the absence of large and far-reaching ideas and purposes. It is dependent upon them at every point. But it generates them within its own procedures and tests them by its own operations." [18]

"There is no limit set to the scope and depth of hypotheses. There are those of short and technical range and there are those as wide as experience." [19]

The bearing of this on education is of crucial significance. The failure to give adequate recognition to the importance of these basic personal attitudes and the necessity for "far-reaching social ideas and purposes" is a weakness in much that is called "progressive" education to-day. Possibly the experimentalist in his constant emphasis on tentativeness and in his sweeping opposition to all finality shares some responsibility for this situation.

7. Does Growth Define Itself?

Philosophic principles may be tested in the laboratory of education. As has been stated, the difference they make for education is an excellent measure of their true significance. From the standpoint of their bearing on education, let us examine some of the conceptions of experimentalism which have been outlined in the previous sections of this chapter. What is signified for education if existence is viewed as a dynamic affair of qualitatively unique events? What are the implications for education in the conclusion of the experimentalist that changing, specific situations are the measure of the adequacy of our concepts and general principles rather than the reverse? If all of our generalizations from previous experience are of the nature of hypotheses what does this denote for educational theory and practice? In sum, what does it mean to educate on the basis of the belief of the experimentalist that the ongoing character of experience is such that all finality of belief is excluded?

The experimentalists have given their own answers to these questions. It would probably be widely admitted that these answers of the experimentalists taken collectively form the most important contribution to educational philosophy and method of our generation. Here we are concerned to consider only one central theme in the educational principles of the experimentalists. It may be summarized somewhat as follows:

We live in a dynamic, changing world. Contingency and uncertainty are ultimate traits of all existence both natural and social. As conditions change, problems change. We cannot with certainty predict what the future will be. Since we face an unknown future, any conception of education that conceives it to be primarily a process by which we hand on already known solutions to existing problems is seriously deficient. No greater disservice can be done the young than to fix in them mechanical habits of response and rigid mental and moral outlooks which cannot be changed when occasion requires. From the standpoint of the experimentalist thus to fix habits of conduct and belief so that they cannot be intelligently reviewed and altered in light of changing situations is to "indoctrinate" rather than to "educate." It is indeed true that adult experience must be shared, but if it is so shared that the child does not intelligently understand and participate in the process as an autonomous individual,

he is not being educated as a human being; he is being
trained as an animal.

In contrast to the conception of education as the transmission of fixed economic, political, moral, and religious
beliefs, and in opposition to the view of education as the
building of habits which so establish certain modes of behavior that these behavior patterns come to possess the individual and dominate all later experience, the experimentalist
sets his ideal of education as "the continuous reconstruction
of experience." This reconstruction of experience is to be so
managed during childhood that the individual child will find
his experience ever expanding in meanings which he appre-
hends. It is also to be so managed that the child constantly
grows in ability to control the course of his experience
because his responses are made with intelligent understanding
of what he is about. The aim is not primarily to tell him
what to do or what to think, but so to equip him that he can
creatively manage his own doing and thinking. It is believed
that if this is achieved, the individual will be in the way
of dealing successfully with changing conditions, because
all along his actual experience has given him confidence in
his own ability to find solutions to his problems as they
occur. From the beginning he has had experience in setting
up plans in the face of concrete difficulties, and in creatively
devising means in the light of actual possibilities to carry out
those plans.

For a world of process and change, the experimentalist
would have education also conceived as a dynamic process.
Education becomes the process of active experiencing. It is
the process by which the individual continually revises his
experience through the knowledge he gains out of his own
"doings and undergoings" and the intelligent connections he

makes between his acts and the consequences that flow from these acts. Education is thus defined as growth. It is not something that is subordinate to fixed external ends; it is its own end.

"Since in reality there is nothing to which growth is relative save more growth, there is nothing to which education is sub-ordinate save more education. . . .

"Since growth is the characteristic of life, education is all one with growing; it has no end beyond itself. The criterion of the value of school education is the extent in which it creates a desire for continued growth and supplies means for making the desire effective in fact." [20]

The positive contributions of such a theory of education are at once apparent. They become all the more significant when one recalls the abstract subject-matter and formal method which for so long dominated the schools. A few of the contributions of this view may be briefly summarized:

(1) In the first place, the conception of "education as its own end" has contributed a powerful weapon to the educa-tor who finds it necessary to oppose agencies of one sort and another which, because of institutional interest or preju-dice, want child life manipulated for external ends. The principle of the experimentalist that "education is its own end" has made it much more difficult to view children as so much raw material to be molded to serve the purposes of industry, the state, the church, or any other institution. On the positive side, it has asserted that children are per-sons, and are to be given the respect in both school and home which is accorded to persons.

(2) The emphasis on the growth of the individual child also has tended to promote respect for the individuality of each child. The significance of individual differences for

education is given philosophic reinforcement by this conception. A uniform, rigid curriculum cannot be easily reconciled with a conception that makes the growth of each individual child with his unique limitations, interests, and capacities the ultimate aim of all education.

(3) Freedom, initiative, and activity for children in the school-rooms are all promoted by this conception of growth as continuous learning from the active process of experiencing. The view of education as the process by which the benevolent teacher pours into reluctant minds all sorts of cut-and-dried subject-matter is compelled to give way to a program of purposeful activities by, of, and for children. Education comes to be thought of less as something that the teacher is to do, and much more in terms of what children are to do. There is still large scope for teacher activity and guidance, but under this ideal it is directed to the enrichment of the activities of children rather than serving as a substitute for such activities. The infallibility and arbitrary authority of the teacher disappear. "The 'teacher' also becomes a learner and the 'learner' also becomes a teacher."

(4) Mechanical drill and compulsory "learning" of studies with little or no present meaning for the child are replaced by the intelligent, whole-hearted participation of children in activities that have a vital grip in present interests and purposes. Education as preparation for a remote future is supplanted by an education which emphasizes rich and vital living *now*. As a rule, important habits and skills are acquired as needed in meeting the varied situations of a growing life.

(5) Education is seen to be continuous with life. Historically it began long before schools were organized; it still begins for each child before he enters school. It does not end when school-days are over. It is an unending process of

experience and growth. The aim of specially organized schools is to facilitate this process for a period of highly influential years in the development of each person. To achieve this aim the activity of the school must be in vital contact with the wider activities of the community of which it is a part.

Even this brief review of some of the reforms in education which the experimentalists' conception of "education as its own end" has helped to accomplish shows that these reforms are of fundamental significance. A conception which has been thus fruitful in the educational world should not be lightly criticized. In the opinion of the writer, however, it needs criticism. This principle as formulated, and certainly as frequently interpreted, seems to be a somewhat ambiguous doctrine. While it has served powerfully in the attack on wrong methods and emphases in education, it has also revealed limitations when it is used to serve as an organizing principle for the new education. It is possible that the ambiguity of this principle is responsible in part for certain undesirable tendencies in "progressive" schools to-day.

Is growth something that defines itself? Is it the inevitable by-product of free activity on the part of children? Apparently the experimentalist does not so believe, because he aggressively attacks the notion of education as a process of "natural" unfolding from within. He believes the original impulses are too vague and chaotic to provide for their own effective development. The experimentalist even asserts that "all that is human has to be learned." He believes in child activity, but in activity under guidance, and activity that progressively develops in a controlled environment.

Now if education involves adult guidance, then that guidance must be of a concrete sort. No one more than the experimentalist has stressed the fact that all behaviors, all choices are specific in character. We do not behave in general, we do not face problems in general. Conduct is always an affair of particulars. If this be true, we cannot give guidance in general. Concrete choices are inevitably present in the process of guiding children. Make as much place as possible for pupil initiative and purposeful activity; also give genuine conscientious adherence to the principle that education is a sharing of experience; emphasize as we will the fact that the teacher learns from her pupils just as truly as they learn from her, and that the teacher must be willing to criticize and to modify old views in the light of the responses of children to them; even place education on a basis of mutuality between children and adults, and yet to do all of this does not relieve the adult teacher from a certain responsibility for final outcomes. Judgments must be made. Decisions, evaluations are constantly called for. The fact that these are made "on the spot" does not make them any the less real choices. *This* sort of behavior is preferred to *that; this* type of conduct is approved, *that* sort is disapproved. The teacher has working standards by which these judgments are made. These standards change and grow, but they operate all the time. The fact of choice is inherent in all education. To paraphrase the statement of an experimentalist framed in another connection: it is not choice that invalidates the process; it is concealed and disguised choice—choice that is unavowed and cannot be critically evaluated either by the one who makes it or by others because it is not admitted that the choice is there.

Now if choice is inherent in all guidance, then the experimentalist as educator has his ends. Not absolute, fixed ends, to be sure, but aims which direct the process. Education, growth, is its own end; but to produce a person who has the habits, dispositions, and insights which are essential if he is effectively to continue his own education through the continuous reconstruction of his experience is a fine and difficult art. The child cannot try out for himself every conceivable sort of experiment in living. The old dilemma of life that "you cannot eat your cake and have it too" still operates. To develop the type of emotional and intellectual dispositions which the experimentalist desires is surely not a hit-or-miss affair. The educator must have a definite sense of the direction in which he wants things to move. He controls and judges the educative process by constant reference to the direction in which he thinks growth lies. If this is not done consciously, critically, then it will be done unconsciously and blindly.

For example, a course of action that is rendering it increasingly difficult for a child to get along with other children will not meet with the approval of an experimentalist. He has as the ideal for each child the achievement of a due regard for other children, and the attainment of the ability to work in sympathy and understanding with them. No more will the experimentalist approve of a developing situation in which children are tending to become increasingly slovenly in their intellectual habits; a situation in which they permit opinion and prejudice to substitute for genuine knowledge of the facts; in which wishful thinking displaces careful observation and concrete attention to conditions and consequences of activity.

Finally, the experimentalist realizes that for an individual to be an effective member of present-day society it is important that he have a genuine understanding of that society. He must know more than mere surface conditions. He needs an appreciation of the strong and weak points of the society in which he lives. He also needs insight into present tendencies in that society, and knowledge of the ünderlying causes for those tendencies. Opposition to a hierarchy of values to be imposed on all is important, but it should not lead to a denial that there is a "hierarchy of problems." In every age "there are some issues which underlie and condition others."

What the future will hold no one can surely foretell, but we know enough about the probable effects of present tendencies to predict what some of the crucial problems that lie ahead are likely to be. Our education is less than adequate if it does not develop individuals equipped with sufficient insight into present social tendencies to enable them to frame far-reaching purposes with regard to those tendencies. No mumbling that "education is its own end" or that we must follow the initiative of children can excuse us, if, through the indulgence of superficial interests of children, we fail to lead them to a realistic understanding of themselves and the nature of the world in which they live. As indicated earlier in this chapter, even the experimentalist believes that there is something final about the attitude with which we should seek to discover and develop the finest possibilities of existence.

Growth is the end. We do not want to fix our creeds or our various social "isms" in the thoughts and habits of the child. Our immediate and ultimate aim is to produce the individual who can manage his own experience, make his own judgments, develop his own beliefs and ideals. To do this he must have freedom in school to initiate and to participate in worth-while activities of sensed present meaning. We are concerned, however, that he do this intelligently and co-operatively. If our analysis is correct, the experimentalist also has such ends in mind when he thinks of the task of education, and he believes that these aims are best achieved under wise adult guidance. Frequently, however, he has not made explicit that which is implicit in his own educational program.

I am not sure that any experimentalist in education would disagree with anything that has been said above. Unfortunately the thought of the experimentalist has been frequently so occupied with the weaknesses and injustices of a formal dogmatic educational program that he has not always made clear and explicit just what his own positive conceptions are. On the whole the principle that "education is its own end" seems to be more effective as an instrument to undermine unsound educational procedures than to serve as a positive ideal to point to the better way.

As was indicated earlier, a thoroughgoing experimentalist may also cherish far-reaching purposes and ideals. Working hypotheses are not antithetical to energizing convictions. A society which is to manage all of its affairs, personal and social on the basis of intelligent understanding and not on the basis of blind adherence to custom, moral codes, or obedience to imposed commands, must be a society composed of people who can creatively find their controlling ideas and ideals in the ongoing process of experience itself. Such a democratic society is utterly dependent on constructive educational efforts in and out of school if it is to succeed in its experiment. More than transcendental philosophies, therefore, experimentalism should be concerned that the schools do not trifle with their responsibilities.

REFERENCES

1. JOHN DEWEY, *Experience and Nature* (The Open Court Publishing Co., 1929), p. 21.

2. JOHN DEWEY, *Studies in Logical Theory* (Chicago University Press, 1930), pp. 2–3.
3. *Ibid.*, p. 1.
4. JOHN DEWEY, *Democracy and Education* (The Macmillan Company, 1922), p. 393.
5. JOHN DEWEY, *Experience and Nature* (W. W. Norton & Co., Inc., 1929), p. iii.
6. *John Dewey, The Man and His Philosophy* (Harvard University Press, 1930), pp. 98–99.
7. JOHN DEWEY, *The Quest for Certainty* (Minton, Balch & Company, 1929), p. 228.
8. JOHN DEWEY, *Human Nature and Conduct* (Henry Holt and Company, 1922), p. 258.
9. JOHN DEWEY, *Experience and Nature* (W. W. Norton & Co., 1929), p. 21.
10. *Ibid.*, pp. 411, 410.
11. T. V. SMITH, *The Philosophic Way of Life* (University of Chicago Press, 1929), p. 118.
12. C. I. LEWIS, *Mind and the World-Order* (Charles Scribner's Sons, 1929) pp. 118–119.
13. JOHN DEWEY, *Human Nature and Conduct* (Henry Holt and Company, 1922), p. 185.
14. J. H. RANDALL, JR., *Our Changing Civilization* (Frederick A. Stokes Company, 1929), pp. 330–331.
15. W. H. KILPATRICK, *Our Educational Task* (University of North Carolina Press, 1930), p. 88.
16. JOHN DEWEY, *The Quest for Certainty* (Minton, Balch & Company, 1929), p. 304.
17. *Ibid.*, p. 194.
18. *Ibid.*, p. 138.
19. *Ibid.*, p. 310.
20. JOHN DEWEY, *Democracy and Education* (The Macmillan Company, 1916), pp. 60–62.

CHAPTER VI

EDUCATION AND FREEDOM

"The pursuance of future ends and the choice of means for their attainment are thus the mark and criterion of the presence of mentality in a phenomenon."

WILLIAM JAMES.

"Freedom or individuality, in short, is not an original possession or gift. It is something to be achieved, to be wrought out. Suggestions as to things which may advantageously be taken, as to skill, as to methods of operation, are indispensable conditions of its achievement. These by the nature of the case must come from a sympathetic and discriminating knowledge of what has been done in the past and how it has been done."

JOHN DEWEY.

1. The Nature of Individuality

FOR the experimentalist education is something other than the process by which an individual gains certain items of useful information. Nor does he interpret education primarily as the procedure by which important skills such as the ability to read and to write are acquired. Fundamentally all education is considered to be in the nature of a moral undertaking. In its broad sense, the experimentalist conceives education to be that total process by which we become individuals. Individuality is not something given at birth; it is an achievement. Intentional, organized education is the conscious effort to guide the process by which individuality is developed. Whether we realize it or not, all education, particularly in childhood, is in the nature of character education. While at

135

no stage in life do we have to accept the self as final, fixed beyond all possibility of further change, nevertheless there is much truth in the following statement from Lippmann:

"Much is learned after puberty, but in childhood education is more than mere learning. There education is the growth of the disposition, the fixing of the prejudices to which all later experience is cumulative. In childhood men acquire the forms of their seeing, the prototypes of their feeling, the style of their character." [1]

To say that individuality is an achievement is not to deny that there is a certain uniqueness about the organic equipment of each person. Nothing here stated is to be understood as challenging the significance of native individual differences. The existence of varying individual capacities and interests has too long been ignored in our educational procedures. The experimentalist recognizes the basic importance of individual differences, both native and acquired. His respect for their significance has led him to oppose all educational procedures which treat children *en masse,* and which by the imposition of a standardized subject-matter and a uniform schedule of activities tend to produce a regimentation which thwarts the development of true individuality. Neither is the demand of the experimentalist for adequate provision for individual differences satisfied by the attempt now often made to provide for these differences by so-called "ability groupings." Individuality is an affair of individuals, not of "superior" and "inferior" classes. The experimentalist's concern for individuality is so thoroughgoing that he desires an educational arrangement which gives individual consideration to each child with his concrete limitations and possibilities. In his opinion, no other educational plan is consistent with the democratic ideal, for this ideal "denotes faith in individuality, in uniquely distinctive qualities in each normal human being; faith in corresponding unique modes of activity that create new ends, with willing acceptance of the modifications of the established order entailed by the release of individualized capacities." [2]

But such organic uniqueness as is given at birth by no means predetermines the sort of a mature individual the child is to become. Innumerable different adult selves are all genuine possibilities in the normal native equipment of any child. Which of these potential selves is actually to be realized depends upon the specific educative experiences to which the organic capacities are subjected. For example, there is nothing in the organic structures that determines what language a child is to speak. As far as the original structures are concerned, any language could become the "native tongue" of any normal child irrespective of the race and nationality of his parents. So also could any variety of manners and morals become for him the "natural" way of behaving and of looking at things. As the previous discussion concerning the social nature of the self indicated, the language, manners, and morals of a person are fashioned by his interaction with a particular cultural environment, and not primarily by the structures of his original endowment.

"Social institutions, the trend of occupations, the pattern of social arrangements, are the finally controlling influences in shaping minds." [3]

The question may be asked, how about intelligence? Is not the intelligence of each individual fixed in the capacities given at birth? Has not the testing movement made abundantly clear that intelligence is largely, if not entirely, a constant factor determined exclusively by inherited capacities? More detailed consideration of the bearing of the findings of the intelligence tests upon the educational program of the experimentalist will be reserved for a later discussion. For present purposes it is sufficient to point out that to which all would probably agree regardless of how much they may differ in their interpretation of the findings of the tests. Suppose an American child with an I.Q. of 175 were to be placed in the exclusive care of a primitive tribe, under whose care he continued to live until adulthood. Undoubtedly at adulthood his "effective intelligence" would be far inferior to that of another child with an I.Q. of only 100 who had had the opportunity to develop in the midst of an advanced society. By *effective intelligence* is meant insight into the behavior of persons and things, and actual ability to guide present activities in the light of foreseen consequences. Intelligent behavior is behavior guided by meanings. Now meanings are primarily group possessions. The individual acquires most of his meanings through communication with the members of his cultural group, and through participation in their established activities. If such activities are rich in the number and variety of meanings they incorporate, the individual with an average capacity to learn will in time probably achieve a valuable equipment of meanings by sharing in the activities of his group. On the other hand, if the activities of one's group afford meager "weighted stimuli," the individual nurtured on these meager stimuli will achieve a meager mind no matter how excellent his native endowments may be. In sum, even effective individual intelligence is achieved through the getting and giving of experience which is education, and it is not something given at birth.

The above analysis, however, is over-simplified. To be an individual in any significant sense means to possess the capacity for intelligent self-determination. Society in a general way recognizes this to be true, for it does not hold children, idiots, and the insane legally responsible for their actions. This is equivalent to recognizing that without the capacity for intelligent self-direction the essential condition for individual responsibility is not present. A clan system of society gives similar recognition to this principle, because in such a society, the family, and not the individual, is the legally responsible unit. There is a certain justice in thus holding the family as a whole responsible, inasmuch as the actual unit of directive control is not the individual, but the family. Plato aptly defined a slave as one who is compelled to take his purposes from others. In short, while individuality includes more than capacity for self-direction, one who is without that capacity does not qualify as an individual in any complete sense. It is certain that the experimentalist is not willing to adopt any lesser standard. The degree of capacity for effective self-direction might be said to be his basic criterion for measuring the quality of individuality a person has achieved.

Now it is entirely possible for a person with more than average native capacity to grow up in a society in a most advanced state of culture and yet not realize a high degree of individuality in the sense herein described. In the first place, there is the fact of early emotional conditioning. Leaving aside certain extreme theories of the psychoanalytical school of psychology, there is sufficient clinical evidence to warrant the conclusion that childhood conditioning does often result in emotional fixations which are so enduring as practically to confiscate the individuality of the person who is controlled by them. Again, there are those who believe that present-day complex society with its immense weight of accumulated knowledge, with its relatively standardized ways of thinking and living, and with its powerful and subtle ways of controlling private opinion through advertising and propaganda, gives the average person little latitude to achieve any conduct which can be truly said to be his own. More specifically, some believe that present tendencies in our machine civilization make for a regimentation of life that carries a most ominous threat to the individual. In our interdependent complex modern world it becomes extremely difficult for an individual to achieve significant control over his own experience. Some are even doubtful whether any kind of education can equip an individual for creative self-expression under modern conditions. At times probably the most hopeful share something of the mood of Randolph Bourne when he wrote:

"The most important fact we can realize about society is that to every one of us that comes into the world it is something given, irreducible. We are as little responsible for it as we are for our own birth. . . . We all enter as individuals into an organized herd-whole in which we are as significant as a drop of water in the ocean, and against which we can about as much prevail. Whether we shall act in the interests of ourselves or of society is, therefore, an entirely academic question. For entering as we do a society which is all prepared for us, so toughly grounded and immalleable that even if we came equipped with weapons to assail it and make good some individual preference, we could not in our puny strength achieve anything against it. But we come entirely helpless." [4]

Of course Bourne's picture of the relation of the individual to modern society is partial and one-sided. It is wholly due to the fact that we are born into an organized society with its functioning institutions and its funded learnings that we do not live as primitive men fighting with other animals for a sheer existence. Bourne's view needs to be balanced by

what others consider to be an extreme statement of the
posite side of the picture:

"When the patterns that form individuality of thought and
desire are in line with actuating social forces, that individuality
will be released for creative effort. Originality and uniqueness
are not opposed to social nurture; they are saved by it from
eccentricity and escape. The positive and constructive energy of
individuals, as manifested in the remaking and redirection of
social forces and conditions, is itself a social necessity." [5]

It is possible, however, to conceive of education so absorbed in the task of transmitting already acquired knowledge; so centered in developing habits and attitudes of loyal
obedience to our existing standards and institutions; and so
devoted to implanting established moral and religious beliefs
in the minds of children, that it would fail utterly to produce
the capacity for individual initiative and independent thinking.
As a matter of fact, it is because so much of education has
been precisely this process of training and indoctrination that
the experimentalist has thought it necessary to fashion a
radically different theory of the basic function of education.
The following statement from T. V. Smith's recent book
The Philosophic Way of Life frankly states what many
experimentalists believe has been the chief interest of traditional education:

"Historically education has not been concerned primarily with
thinking. It has been an instrument to prevent thinking. Thinking breaks new ground. The breaking of new ground endangers
old structures. Institutions that get firmly established, classes
that get strategically placed, unite in agreeing to minimize
change and in monopolizing the fruits of what goes on irrevo-
cably. Education easily becomes under such circumstances an indoctrination of each generation to respect the order which they
find pre-existent. To induct one into the culture created for him,

to generate in him respect for it and for its agents, to reconcile him to his lot in life, and to foreswear him to loyalty for the rights of others, as pre-established as his own lot—this is the story of traditional education." [6]

Opposed to this theory of education as mere transmission and habituation, the experimentalist advances his theory of education for the development of individuality. His concern is to see intentional education so managed that it increases rather than decreases individual freedom. Notwithstanding his full realization of the forces that are hostile to the development of individuality in present society, he believes that a reconstructed educational program is a hopeful means to the above end. No other principle in his philosophy of education has been as subject to persistent attack as has been his radical emphasis on freedom as both process and end in education. It is also fair to say that probably at no other point has he been more seriously misunderstood by both the critics and the friends of his educational ideas. That discussion should have centered around this phase of his program is as it should be, for it is primary in his whole educational outlook. It is not so fortunate, however, that much of the discussion should have been highly controversial in character, and often apparently based on a will to misunderstand what the experimentalist really is concerned about under the name of freedom. The subject is difficult enough at best without having it complicated by imputation to the experimentalist of extreme libertarian views which no responsible person would think of advocating.

Perhaps the experimentalist is not entirely without fault in this matter. He is quite right in showing that much of traditional education has been largely occupied with efforts to fix certain beliefs and habits in the life of the child. The schools of Communistic Russia and of Fascist Italy, and the sectarian schools in our own country are only samples of many contemporary efforts thus to utilize organized education for ulterior purposes. Again, the experimentalist has rendered an important service in reinterpreting the ideal of respect for personality so as to broaden it to include respect for the present capacities, interests, and experiences of the child. An education interested in freedom must use these actual interests of the child as the starting point. Furthermore, his insistence that the best preparation for the future is the most meaningful experiencing in the present is also a contribution of the first rank to educational thought.

On the other hand, the experimentalist has found it difficult to believe that some of those who differ in judgment about the educational methods to be used in the development of individuality and effective freedom are, nevertheless, as much concerned as he is that these values be attained as the final outcomes of the educative process. Possibly he has been too prone to assume that those who oppose certain methods of educating for freedom must be inspired by a desire to manipulate the lives of children for selfish private purposes of their own. That frequently such motives operate cannot be doubted, but this is not always the case. To-day many parents and teachers who genuinely desire only the richest development for their children are seriously troubled by what they understand the proposals of the experimentalist to imply for educational practice. Some of them have experimented faithfully with what they have assumed were the recommended procedures of the experimentalist, and they are doubtful about the outcomes. Recently eminent experimentalists have shown concern about present tendencies in schools supposedly organized on their principles. Probably no one was more astonished than the progressive school teacher to read the following criticism in a recent article of Dewey's:

"In some progressive schools the fear of adult imposition has become a veritable phobia. . . . Schools farthest to the left (and there are many parents who share the fallacy) carry the thing they call freedom nearly to the point of anarchy." [7]

Apparently there is considerable confusion as to just what the principle of freedom really denotes for educational procedure. As a preliminary to the further discussion of the educational implications of the experimentalist's conception of freedom, an attempt will be made to summarize what he considers to be the nature and function of freedom in human experience. To gain an adequate approach to this question, it is necessary to deal with certain general questions in the field of psychology and philosophy. Since freedom and individuality seem to be inherently connected, possibly a better understanding of what the experimentalist considers a person to be, as well as an understanding of the process by which he believes a person becomes a free individual, will throw light on present educational difficulties.

2. An Old Controversy

From the beginning of philosophic thought freedom has been a central problem in philosophy. For a long time all discussion of the problem seemed to end in an impasse. One was apparently forced to make a choice between two equally undesirable possibilities. On the one hand were to be found the advocates of freedom who identified it with *freedom of the will*. It was held that if choice is real, and not a mere fiction, then of necessity it must be equally possible for a

person faced with any choice-situation freely to select any
one of a number of lines of action. It was argued that previous training and experience do not determine our specific
choices. Choice is an act of a "will" essentially undetermined
by habits and preferences which have developed out of earlier
experiences. A free act represents a motive-less choice.
Motive-less choice is choice not dictated by inherited impulse
or acquired habit. It was maintained that the existence of
such motive-less choice is essential if individual responsibility
is not to disappear. If it is just to hold a person responsible
for his acts, then it must always be genuinely open for him to
choose to act in any one of a variety of ways. If there be not
such open possibilities, if one's acts are determined by his
character, and if his character is the product of the twin
forces heredity and environment, it would follow that freedom of choice is an illusion. Without free choice no rational
basis is left for personal responsibility.

On the other side were found the determinists who were
ever ready to point to fatal weaknesses in the argument of
the "free-will" adherents. What is rational, or just, they
asked, about holding a particular individual responsible for
his acts if these acts are not the expression of his own concrete character? If choices do not proceed from the individual's habits, desires, and purposes, but are rather to be
attributed to a mysterious power called "will" which lies
back of his behavior and which arbitrarily determines how
he shall choose to act in utter independence of the actual
character and desires of the person, why, then, should we
hold this particular person responsible? If choice does not
have some more responsible connection with "the actual
make-up of disposition and character" than this theory allows,
it is indeed true that all ground is cut out from under per-

sonal responsibility. Furthermore, this theory of an arbitrary "free-will" flies in the face of all experience. If we know anything, we know that habits and attitudes are formed out of experience, and that they do determine later conduct. If this were not so, both home and school training would be futile. The underlying premise of all educational effort is that character can be formed, and that such acquired preferences, tastes, and underlying dispositions do actually control the concrete choices each individual makes.

However, the "free-will" advocates were not without a disconcerting rejoinder. They asked the determinists to tell in what respects a man differed from a stone or a tree if all of his actions were fixed by his nature, original and acquired? They asserted that we know man's behavior is different from that of such impersonal objects precisely because it is marked by freedom and responsibility. Hence, they said, the position of the determinist, however superficially plausible, is actually untenable. It was maintained that this view also contradicts the findings of everyday experience. The fact that in dealing with others we treat them as free individuals, that we praise and blame, reward and punish them for their conduct shows that common sense rejects the assumptions of the determinists.

As a matter of fact, each side was better able to pick flaws in the position of the other than it was able to develop an adequate philosophy of freedom. Most people soon wearied of the whole argument and were inclined to dismiss it as a metaphysical subtlety. This is always a convenient way to dispose of a problem that obstinately resists efforts to resolve it. Common sense recognized that character formation was a fact. Education was held to be both necessary and desirable. It was also held to be obvious that all normal people are free, at least sufficiently free to be responsible for their acts. To

be sure, it was not exactly clear how these two attitudes were
to be theoretically reconciled. They were justified, however,
by the practical requirements of the situation. Now such an
unresolved dualism in thought is likely to have some undesirable practical effects. Apparently this dualism in our
thinking about freedom and determinism has not been without such evil consequences. It has been accompanied, for
example, by an unintelligent use of praise and blame that
often has produced most unhappy results. It has tended to
justify an irresponsible treatment of criminals and delinquents
which has long been an open scandal. Most serious of all have
been its effects in education. Our practice in home and school
has too frequently alternated between arbitrary disciplinary
procedures, on the one hand, and sentimental indulgence, on
the other. And this because we have not better understood
the nature of freedom, and the significance of choice, and
the defensible function of praise and blame and of a sense
of responsibility in human conduct.

3. A New Approach to an Old Problem

There are those who count the contribution of the philosophy of experimentalism to our thinking about freedom to
be one of its most significant achievements. Experimentalism
has not been content to accept the alternatives of "free-will"
and "determinism" as exhaustive of the possibilities in the
situation. On the one hand, it rejects completely the hypothesis
of motive-less choice. It considers the traditional doctrine of
"free-will" to be both intellectually untenable and practically
undesirable. At the same time, experimentalism is a philosophy that provides a central place for individual freedom and
responsibility. It believes that any philosophy which does

not recognize the rôle of preference and choice in human conduct leaves something out of its formulation which is empirically well grounded. It attributes much of the difficulty in traditional thought about human freedom to an unexamined assumption, in the premises of both the determinists and the "free-will" advocates to the effect that the moral self is essentially an inborn, ready-made psychical entity separate in existence from the natural order.

"The significance of the traditional discussion of free-will is that it reflects precisely a separation of moral activity from nature and the public life of men." [8]

Accepting the better established view that man and nature are continuous, the experimentalist is able to make a new approach to the problem of freedom. He begins with the elemental consideration that all existences are discovered to be in process of change and interaction with other existences. With this as the starting point, he frames the hypothesis that the real issue in freedom is the question of the quality of the individual's interactions with other people and things which constitute what we call experience. Can the individual be said to participate in this interactive process? If so, to what end? What is the nature and quality of his participations? Is he merely pushed and hauled about by the activity of other things, or does he from within the process help to determine its character? What kind of participation on his part would be required if we were to acknowledge it as carrying the marks of genuine freedom? In short, what sort of behavior is the behavior of a free individual? The experimentalist believes that to substitute questions such as these about the quality of behavior for the time-honored puzzles about freedom opens the way for a more meaningful inquiry into the whole subject of freedom.

Attention is called to the fact that even on the inanimate level the inherent constitution of a thing has something to do with the character of its reactions to other things. In accordance with their make-up, all inanimate things manifest selectivity or bias in their reactions. Even atoms and molecules are found to exhibit a certain bias in their behavior. They respond positively to some things, negatively to others, and they are apparently indifferent in the presence of still other things. Without straining language too much, such uniqueness of behavior may be said to indicate that inanimate things possess a certain rudimentary individuality. Furthermore, this individuality counts in the interaction of one thing with another. It helps to determine outcomes. It is a casual factor in the process. The fact that an event is conditioned in no way prevents it from being the condition of other events. That which has been "caused" can and does, in turn, become the "cause" of other things.

It is also important to remember that all individuality involves some sort of limitation. If a thing is to exist at all, it must be something in particular, and not everything in general. Without limitations of some determinate sort, there could be no selective reaction. Thus in a true sense limitation may be said to be the inevitable precondition of individuality because selective reactions are of the essence of individuality. This is as true of persons as it is true of things. To be a person means to be biased. It is a superficial understanding of the nature of a person, and of the nature of freedom, that leads one to assume that to be a free person means to be equally open to all sorts of possibilities. Were all things thus equally desirable and possible, a person would have no important preferences. Without the expression of preference, freedom would be a meaningless term. Under the name of freedom people generally have not been concerned to get rid of preferences; what they have not been concerned to acquire is the necessary ability to give actual realization to their preferences and the capacity to improve their preferences by learning from their experiences. Even passive philosophies which have recommended the elimination of desire have done so largely because of a pessimistic belief that man has little possibility of making his desires prevail in the face of hostile conditions. Moreover, if one sincerely believed that elimination of all desire were the road to freedom, he should also urge the extinction of the entire human race. As long as we remain as individuals, we shall give expression to preference. To be an individual means to have preferences. Hence the aim of education interested in freedom should not be to attempt to eliminate bias, but rather should be to make bias grow "less arbitrary and more significant."

What is denoted when it is said that the expression of preference of an individual is intelligent rather than unintelligent? We do not say that the reactions of inanimate things are intelligent, even though these reactions are characterized by a certain selectivity. One reason among others for this is that while inanimate things display bias in their reactions, they do not manifest any particular bias in favor of continuing their own existence in characteristic form. The principle of equilibration operates on the inanimate level, but the inanimate object is apparently unconcerned if in the process of interaction with other things occasioned by a movement to restore a disturbed equilibrium, it is itself changed into some other thing. Here we find an important difference between living and non-living forms. Every animate thing strives so to control its interactions with its environment that it will insure its own continued existence. It struggles to

maintain itself. It tries to make its preferences prevail. Even
the simplest organism's responses are marked both by
selectivity and discrimination—that is, they are in behalf of
certain outcomes, and they are opposed to certain others.
As we pass from the inanimate to the animate level, simple
bias changes into active *interest*. The organism is implicated
in the changes going on in its environment. As we have
already seen, its very life is at stake in the process of maintaining a supporting equilibrium with the environmental
energies. Now intelligence is a function of the striving of the
organism to achieve a life-sustaining and life-expanding relation to its surrounding medium. Without the presence of
interests, intelligence probably could not be, and it would have
no significance even if it could exist.

The "higher" the organism, the more efficient it is in con-
triving interactive adjustments friendly to its own interests.
The animal with locomotor organs and distance receptors
is especially well equipped to control the course of its experiences. Its distance receptors enable it to respond to things
distant in space, and this becomes equivalent to responding
to events future in time. The activity of such an organism
becomes serial in nature. It is possessed of cumulative character. Earlier activities are preparatory to later consummations.
Such an animal is not merely pushed about by what lies
behind, it is also motivated in its feelings and responses by
that outcome events are moving toward. It is implicated
in what is going on, and, for better or worse, what it does
now will have a contributing share in determining the final
outcome. Such participation in the movement of affairs
comes to be conditioned by both "hindsights" and "foresights." Obviously, as the time-span of a unit of activity is
extended, the possibility of more active manipulation of

affairs on behalf of felt interests is also increased. Thus the active preferences of such an organism gain wider scope in shaping the course of events. With increased possibility of control, desires and preferences can also be enlarged. The rudiments of purposeful activity are present in all such behavior. The ability thus to form purposes is dependent upon the capacity to give such a temporal spread to one's activities. Man is the time-binder. He responds to the immediate situation in the light of what has occurred and what is about to occur. An important meaning of freedom is found in this capacity to purpose intelligently.

As we come to the higher animals, learning also plays its significant part. An animal which can learn modifies its preferences in the light of experienced consequences. For example, a fish feeds on minnows. It has an original impulse to attack and devour minnows when hungry. But it also prefers not to get hurt by bruising its head against hard and unyielding objects. An experiment is reported which shows that a pike kept in a tank divided into two parts by a glass partition learned in time actually to turn away from minnows that were thrown into the protected part of the tank instead of dashing toward them as it at first did. Out of the experience of repeated bumpings against the glass partition a new preference was born. This capacity of an organism to modify its behavior so as to meet the demands of changing situations is one measure of its capacity for practical freedom. Without such ability to alter its behavior in the light of experienced consequences, its possibility of achieving freedom is practically nil. Presumably a moth has a preference not to get burned to death. But it also has a mechanism of balance so fixed in its inherited structure that apparently it is impelled to continue to fly toward a bright flame even though this may lead to its own destruction. The response fixed by the inherited behavior pattern is so inflexible that it cannot yield even to the desire to avoid getting burned to death. Where ability to modify behavior is thus circumscribed by the inflexibility of original structure, the capacity for actual freedom is likewise reduced.

In this respect the human organism has an advantage over other animals because it inherits few, if any, inflexible, specific behavior patterns. To be sure, it has organic needs and impulses, but as originally given most of these are so indeterminate that they can find satisfaction in a wide variety of concrete types of behavior. The very dependence of the human infant, as has been so often pointed out, is an element of strength, because it becomes necessary for the infant to learn most of its responses. On the whole, learned responses are more flexible than are those specific responses given in original structures. They can be more readily adapted to changing situations. The prolonged period of dependent infancy also provides for longer association with adult members of the group, and this, in turn, enlarges the opportunity for learning from these adults through sharing in their activities. With language the possibility of communication is so enlarged that literally a new dimension is added to experience. Through language the ability to recall that which has been experienced, and to make fine discriminations among objects in the environment is also greatly strengthened. Thus the behavior of the human organism comes increasingly to be controlled by meanings acquired in experience.

"With the animals, an experience perishes as it happens, and each new doing or suffering stands alone. But man lives in a world where each occurrence is charged with echoes and reminiscences of what has gone before, where each event is a reminder of other things. Hence he lives not, like the beasts of the field, in a world of merely physical things but in a world of signs and symbols." [9]

Language also contributes the possibility of abstract reasoning. Without the irrevocable commitments involved in overt action, a preliminary testing in thought can be given to proposed lines of action. With the capacity for abstraction, generalization, and inference which language makes possible, the range of such "internal experimentation" can be indefinitely extended. Ultimately the hypothesis must be tested by overt operations, but many inadequate suggestions can be eliminated in advance of such decisive overt action. We can within limits foretell what outcomes will follow from various lines of procedure without the cost of actually trying them out. When such reliably anticipated consequences become directive stimuli in present behavior, the organism is still further emancipated from sheer trial-and-error response to that which is immediately given. Mind is now present in the interactions of the organism with its environment.

"As life is a character of events in a peculiar condition of organization, and 'feeling' is a quality of life-forms marked by complexly mobile and discriminating responses, so 'mind' is an added property assumed by a feeling creature, when it reaches that organized interaction with other living creatures which is language, communication. Then the qualities of feeling becomes significant of objective differences, in external things and of episodes past and to come. This state of things in which qualitatively different feelings are not just had but are significant of objective differences, is mind. Feelings are no longer just felt. They have and they make *sense;* record and prophesy. That is to say, differences in qualities (feelings) of acts when employed as indications of acts performed and to be performed and as signs of their consequences, *mean* something." [10]

With capacity for learning, and the ability to preserve one's learnings, the manifestation of preferences becomes "a function of the entire life history." As these meanings and preferences accumulate, not infrequently they come into conflict with one another in the face of novel situations. The very excess of preferences growing out of experiences which lie behind prevents us from responding immediately to the present situation. Action is held up because meanings are in conflict. Such a situation is literally a choice-situation. We have to choose, not because we are uninfluenced by previous experience, but precisely because we are so influenced by the various experiences we have already undergone, that whatever lies behind is unable automatically to determine in what direction activity should go. That which is contributed by previous experience is inadequate to guide our operations. Choosing is finding, discovering, and, at its highest, creating a new preference out of the competing preferences called out by the interaction of old habits and ideas with the new situation. In terms of the S—R terminology, it may be spoken of as the remaking of the stimulus. An inadequate stimulus has to be remade into an adequate stimulus. In terms of the conception which views behavior as a function of an organism-environmental unity, such a choice may be considered as an attempt to reconstruct a total experienced situation so as to unify its now disintegrated factors. An ideal choice is one that adequately cares for all the values now in conflict. It is that reconstruction of experience which contributes most to the growth of the individual concerned. As a choice always goes beyond old experience, it is in the nature of an adventure into the unknown future, and consequently involves a certain amount of risk. The risk cannot be eliminated. It can be mitigated, however, if we have acquired the disposition to learn from our experiences of failure as well as from our experiences of success. Even mistaken choices are not an entire loss if learnings have accrued from them.

One of the chief educational aims of the experimentalist is so to control the educative process that this tendency to learn from experience is progressively developed. Freedom is achieved through continuous learning from experience. As the above analysis indicates, it is an affair of constant growth in understanding and in effective means of control. We are free to the degree that we have the capacity to learn, and have acquired the disposition of "learning to learn." Undoubtedly a disciplinary procedure is a preliminary to the development of this disposition. Such a disposition is not something that emerges spontaneously from random hit-or-miss activity, no matter how whole-heartedly that activity may be entered into by the young. On the other hand, the discipline that is required to achieve this sort of growth in understanding is not something that can be imposed on the individual from without. Control of external conditions may facilitate or hinder its development, but the broad habit of "learning to learn" can be acquired only by the active participation of the individual in his own education. The problem of discipline becomes something radically other than that of merely keeping order in a school-room, or of demanding that certain facts be learned, and that a number of specific skills be acquired. It becomes the problem of how to develop respect for consequences; of how to increase ability to observe and to discriminate more adequately, to plan more wisely, to purpose more broadly, to be more resourceful in devising means for achieving one's ends; of how to develop a critical, and yet confident, attitude with respect to one's own efforts. If one be concerned, as the experimentalist is, with the democratic ideal, the problem of discipline also involves the problem of how to help each child learn to coöperate with others, and to evaluate the consequences of his acts and of those of his group in terms of their bearing on the welfare of others as well as his own welfare.

This brings us to the question of responsibility. Responsibility is no more originally given than is individuality. It is something to be developed. He is responsible who can be made to become responsible. The ground of responsibility in conduct is "not in antecedent conditions but in liability for future consequences." That which is done is done. The educator is concerned with that which has been done only in so far as it gives guidance to that which must still be done if an individual is to develop an adequate sense of responsibility for his conduct. Praise and blame, rewards and punishments can be justified only to the extent that they help and do not hinder the attainment of this end. In any given situation due regard must be given to the specific results which the exercise of these forms of control is actually tending to produce. Is it building or destroying the confidence of the individual child in his own possibilities and capacities? Does it tend to make him more careful in his observation, planning, and evaluating in connection with the situations with which he has to do, or does it stimulate him to pay attention to ways of "getting by" through cleverness in appearing to comply with the demands of adults? Above all, does the use of such means of control tend to weaken or to strengthen the habit of assuming responsibility for acts and for active interest in learning from what is done? Capacity for intelligent self-direction, which is capacity for individuality and freedom, is dependent upon acquiring the disposition of continuing to learn from experience.

Some objection may be raised to this whole interpretation of how freedom is to be achieved on the ground that it too greatly stresses intellectual factors, while little attention is given to emotional factors. But is this criticism well taken when one recalls the nature of intelligence as interpreted by the experimentalist? As has been indicated, traditional intellectualism with its split between thought and emotion, or between reason and desire, is far removed from the conception of intelligence held by the experimentalist. His thinking about intelligence and freedom starts with the primary fact of a sentient organism possessed of vital urges and active preferences in interaction with a natural and social environment. The function of thinking for such a creature is not to ignore or suppress its feeling reactions, rather is it to help that organism find the maximum satisfaction for its wants and desires. Now as ethical writers have pointed out, the terms *good* and *bad* cannot be applied to desires taken singly or in isolation. Such single desires are whatever they happen to be. In a human being, however, whose expression of desire becomes a function of its entire history, desires cannot be taken singly, for in life they appear together. Not infrequently they are experienced in actual conflict. The satisfaction of certain desires is incompatible with the satisfaction of certain others. The aim of intelligent inquiry is to help one find in the light of all his desires or preferences that which he really wants, including always the question of the type of person he desires to become and the kind of society he wants to live in. If one is to do this effectively, it is important that he should have knowledge of the consequences of the activities into which his desires would lead him, and, as we are now beginning to realize more fully, it is also important that he should have all the knowledge he can gain of the history of his present desires. The more one can come to know why he feels as he does, the greater the probability that he will be able to modify reactions and preferences which hinder the fullest development of his own possibilities. That every normal individual does desire the most complete development of which he is capable is a working assumption of the experimentalist. That very early experiences have much to do in shaping the general style of the life of the individual cannot be doubted. The more educators can know of how these basic organic attitudes are acquired, the more intelligent will their undertakings become. Without such knowledge education remains something less than an intelligent art in certain of its most fundamental aspects.

4. The Place of Adult Guidance

From all of the foregoing, what are we to conclude about the place the experimentalist gives to adult guidance in the education of children? It is somewhat difficult to answer this question precisely. Part of the difficulty is inherent in the very nature of the philosophy of experimentalism. It determines what should be done in terms of the needs and possibilities in the actual situation. The uniqueness of each situation is as pertinent in relation to this question of adult guidance as it is in relation to other affairs. There is no reason to suppose that wholesale solutions will work better in this connection than elsewhere. On the other hand, it cannot be doubted that experimentalism does have general guiding principles with respect to the function of adults in educational procedures relating to children.

Its understanding of the psychology of the self leads experimentalism to reject any theory of education founded on the principle that education is a process of natural unfolding of inborn capacities. The self develops out of its experiences. It is literally the result of the interaction of the biological organism with its natural and social environment. The traditions incorporated in that social environment inevitably influence the development of the child. It is a form of deception to ignore this fact of the pervasive operative presence of the social environment in the feeling, thinking, and acting of the child. Either the influences of this environment will enter accidentally and furtively into his experiences, or they will enter under conditions provided by intelligent arrangement. In any case, for better or for worse, these social influences are bound to penetrate all processes of self-development.

The experimentalist believes in the possibilities and importance of creative activity on the part of children. But he also realizes that the minds of children cannot create something out of nothing. Children work with, and upon, the materials they have experienced. Any conception of freedom or of creative activity which considers the only appropriate activity of adults in relation to children to be merely that of removing external restraints is altogether too limited and negative to meet the positive demands of the experimentalist's conception of how individuals come to be. Instead of a *laissez-faire* policy, his program presupposes careful, intelligent adult planning in order that the child may have opportunity to experience in the most efficient manner the best the race has discovered.

On the other hand, it is equally apparent that he is hostile to attempts of adults to fix beliefs and habits in the child in such a manner that they shall not be subject to later reconstruction by the individual in case the development of experience is such they should thus be modified. Any religious, economic, social, or political doctrine which is so insinuated into the experience of a child that he is unable to think critically about it in so far forth robs him of his freedom. To illustrate: The experimentalist believes that a person who has been trained in a variety of patriotism through certain types of flag-drill, etc., so that he has not learned to think critically about his nation's policies, but has been conditioned to follow his country's flag wherever it goes and no matter what the nature of its mission, is in this realm of his experience in much the same position as the moth that has only one response to a bright flame. His freedom to act as an intelligent citizen has been confiscated by those who have thus conditioned him to follow unthinkingly the men who, for the time being, control his nation's policies. So also in religion. If a child has been trained to do immediately without reflection that which is the will of God, he is apt to take slavishly many of his purposes from other men, because always some one, somewhere, must do the thinking necessary to discover what is the will of God in each particular conflict-situation. Beliefs and habits can enslave as well as free activity. The experimentalist believes that any response which is so fixed that it cannot be modified in the light of consequences is a dangerous response to acquire. Such fixed ideas, particularly when charged with emotion, are apt to become enslaving prejudices. He believes it an immoral procedure for adults thus to seek to determine the future thought and conduct of the child. As far as possible, he wants his own most fundamental values, such as faith in the experimental method and regard for the principle of social democracy, so to be accepted that the way is kept open for their further critical examination by each individual. Even the process of criticism is not exempt from further criticism.

But the position of the experimentalist with regard to adult guidance is not adequately or fundamentally defined by stating that, on the one hand, he opposes efforts to indoctrinate the child; and that, on the other, he believes the conception of education as a process of natural unfolding to be based on a false psychology. As we have seen, the growing ability to form intelligent purposes, the developing resourcefulness required to carry out those purposes, and the expanding capacity to judge critically the results achieved by such purposeful activities are all fundamentals in the process by which individuality and freedom are attained. His concern is that education be so managed that this entire process can go on in connection with the work of the school. He finds this process to be essentially the experience process, which, in the last analysis, is the only educative process. If the schools were to reorganize their work around the conception that education is learning from experience, the experimentalist believes that the following considerations would receive greater attention:

(1) Experience is an affair of the concrete doings and undergoings of actual individuals. Development is not filling in some standardized ideal pattern; it is an affair of the specific limitations and possibilities of the actual self of each child. Hence the starting point for educational activities is the concrete capacities and interests of individual children. If the activity has no meaning connection with the present experience of the child, it is doubtful if he will learn much of value from it if he undertakes it because of cajolery or coercion. As Dewey emphasized in his clarifying discussion

of *interest* and *effort*, "the genuine principle of interest is the principle of the recognized identity of the fact to be learned or the action proposed with the growing self; that it lies in the direction of the agent's own growth, and is, therefore, imperiously demanded, if the agent is to be himself." At this point the philosophy of experimentalism and the findings of educational psychology seem to be in full accord, as the following quotation from Thorndike and Gates indicates:

"To secure learning we must have activity, and to secure activity some want must be alive. The most effective learning occurs when learning is the means of satisfying some want. A primary consideration, then, in all learning and teaching is the provision of a motive; of an energizing want, desire, or interest which will provide vigorous and whole-hearted activity." [11]

(2) Normally the "energizing interest" should be inherent in the situation with which the child is dealing. On the whole the learnings are better if the child participates in the activity because of an intrinsic interest in what he is doing rather than because he desires to win the approval or avoid the reproof of some adult. Undoubtedly the attitude of older persons toward his activity is always more or less of a factor in what the child does, but more effective educative experiences are achieved when the child is primarily interested in what is happening in the actual situation with which he is dealing. Better emotional and intellectual adjustments are secured when the child is absorbed in the affair at hand than when his attention is divided between the activity and concern for the response of adults whom he is trying to please or deceive. To say that the child should learn from first-hand experience with a wide variety of situations does not imply that he should be given a razor to play with in order that he may

learn that sharp things cut. Neither does it indicate that he
should be given a bottle of acid to drink in order that he
may experience the effect of poison on the human system.
However, to recognize that many such learnings must be
mediated through the experience of others does not destroy
the importance of the principle that the child learns best
when he is participating as a purposeful agent in a situation
of concern to himself and one in which outcomes, to some
extent at least, depend upon what he does.

(3) More effective learning takes place when a child is
permitted to participate in complete units of experience.
The intellectual aspect of an experience is better grasped
when one has shared in the antecedent experience of the
situation which set the problem; when he has participated in
developing a plan for dealing with it and of finding means
for carrying out that plan; and when he has had opportunity
to observe for himself the success or failure of his planned
operations in resolving the situation of difficulty. Without
such complete units of work, learning from experience becomes a mutilated affair. Much of the so-called learning of
the schools fails to provide the latitude for this complete
process of experience which permits the agent to understand
why the acts are undertaken, and to make the back-and-
forth reference between that which is done and that which
happens in consequence of the doing. Until provision is made
for such complete experiences within the schools, much of
the learning which enters most potently into the character
and conduct of the child will take place outside of school
procedures.

(4) If a serious attempt is to be made to meet the above
conditions, the experimentalist believes the activities of the
schools must be more intimately connected with the activities

of the wider community life. As children grow older, artificial school projects are too superficial to call out whole-hearted responses. This is as it should be, for maturing individuals cannot be expected to derive nourishment for significant development apart from contacts with actual life-situations. Dare the schools be adventurous enough to permit children to have meaningful intercourse with the wider community activities? Short of this, some believe they cannot meet the fundamental conditions for educational growth.

In this connection there is danger that we may take the present school system as something inherent in the very nature of things. The vast numbers enrolled as pupils and teachers, and the size of budgets and property interests involved, have conferred upon our schools the prestige that comes from large-scale business enterprises. It is a doubtful asset. We need to remind ourselves that present educational institutions are comparatively a recent development. For the greater part of the history of the race the getting of an education has come mainly through the participation of children in the activities of their social group. It is still an unproved experiment whether by abstracting education as we do to-day from the larger social activities, and by making it something that is pursued on its own account in an institution exclusively set apart for that purpose, we shall better provide for the all-round development of children. It may be a more economical way to make our youth literate, but education in its most crucial sense is something more than an ability to read and write. To be sure, there are impressive reasons which have inspired this movement to provide intentional educational agencies. The experiment has its record of positive achievements. On the other hand, it also becomes increasingly evident that if the experiment is to reach a tolerable success the way must be discovered to make that which goes on under the direction of the school more continuous with that which goes on outside of the school.

Once again let it be said this does not mean that children are to be plunged recklessly into all of the undesirable, dishonest, and painful aspects of present-day adult society. The schools probably do have to decide what phases of our social and political life are too "unsafe" to permit children to have contact with them. On the other hand, a good case could be made for those who would urge that children should be allowed to look into any situation in which they have a serious purpose to find out how and why things go on as they do go on at the present time. Certainly with older age levels all barriers to honest inquiry should be removed. Education which is the continuous reconstruction of experience cannot go on with vitality in the framework of a social order that is insulated from reconstructive experiments. Freedom is achieved within the world of actual events. It cannot be won apart from these wider social movements which condition our whole experience.

(5) Given the above conditions, the experimentalist believes necessary skills and knowledges normally can be acquired in connection with purposeful activities. Much of the time and energy now devoted to forced drill in the so-called "tool-subjects" could be eliminated if the children were engaged in important activities that made the mastery of these tools a vital concern. Here, again, the educational psychologist adds his supporting word:

"Ten minutes of practice with full zeal, when the worker is keen to do his best and when he is thrilled at every advance in his accomplishment may be worth an hour of work done merely to avoid disfavor or reproach, or idly to pass away the time." [12]

(6) In actual experience learnings are never single. For that matter, no more are learnings single even when we try to assign them out one by one with a specific period in the time-table to be devoted to each learning. The implications of this fact of the plurality of learnings for character development are profoundly significant. An educative procedure that is concerned about freedom is of necessity also concerned about education for the nurture of character. As we have seen, freedom is a function of the intellectual and emotional dispositions which an individual builds through his active experiencing. In the opinion of the experimentalist, education for character development will never be effective until our schools recognize that purposes, attitudes, ideals, and habits of all sorts are being built all the time in the give-and-take of ordinary experience. They are functions of the situations with which we interact. The assigned lesson, or the primary activity, is by no means the only thing that is being learned. What Kilpatrick has well called the "concomitant learnings" are often more important than those which have the position of direct concern. Here, also, educational psychology and the principle of experimentalism support the same conclusion:

"In sum, even in relatively simple tasks of learning, the whole person is engaged. One reacts as a whole to the learning situation. All sorts of motor acts, muscular and internal adjustments, emotional attachments, facts, learning techniques, interests, resolves, purposes, aims, ideals, may be acquired in this one act and setting. To say that a person is merely learning to write is to misinterpret almost entirely the process of education and learning. To say that one's entire person or life is being changed in some degree during this experience is more nearly correct." [13]

(7) In a changing world the only person who can become free and who can maintain his freedom is the one who has

"learned to learn." A democratic society can hope to succeed only if it is composed of individuals who have developed the responsibility for intelligent self-direction in coöperation with others. From these two basic considerations the experimentalist draws the conclusion that the most fundamental objective of education is to arrange its procedures so that all of them contribute to the realization of these purposes. He believes that it is a sound psychological principle which states that we learn that which we practice. He urges, therefore, that schools be placed on the experience basis in order that children may practise learning from experience, and in so doing acquire those habits and attitudes, together with the mastery of those techniques, which lead to increasing ability to control their own experience—which is freedom.

Would an educational program based on principles such as these give an important place to adult coöperation and guidance? To review these principles is to find the answer to that question. One could, if it were necessary, list many quotations from the writings of experimentalists to show how explicitly they have emphasized the importance of such adult guidance. The very nature of the program itself, however, gives a more convincing answer. One who does not see the necessity for intelligent adult leadership if the educational program of experimentalism is to be effective has not understood what the experimentalist really means by education for individuality and freedom.

REFERENCES

1. WALTER LIPPMANN, *A Preface to Morals* (The Macmillan Company, 1929), p. 91.
2. JOHN DEWEY, in the *New Republic,* Dec. 13, 1922. (Reprinted in *Characters and Events* [Henry Holt and Company, 1929], II, 489.)

3. JOHN DEWEY, in the *New Republic,* LXII, No. 798, p. 124 (March 19, 1930).
4. RANDOLPH BOURNE, *Untimely Papers* (B. W. Huebsch, Inc., 1919), pp. 20–21.
5. JOHN DEWEY, in the *New Republic,* LXII, No. 798, p. 126 (March 19, 1930).
6. T. V. Smith, *The Philosophic Way of Life* (University of Chicago Press, 1929), pp. 122–123.
7. JOHN DEWEY, in the *New Republic,* LXIII, No. 814, p. 205 (July 9, 1930).
8. JOHN DEWEY, *Human Nature and Conduct* (Henry Holt and Company, 1922), p. 9.
9. JOHN DEWEY, *Reconstruction in Philosophy* (Henry Holt and Company, 1920), p. 1.
10. JOHN DEWEY, *Experience and Nature* (The Open Court Publishing Co., 1929), p. 258.
11. THORNDIKE and GATES, *Elementary Principles of Education* (The Macmillan Company, 1929), p. 85.
12. *Ibid.,* p. 97.
13. *Ibid.,* p. 98.

CHAPTER VII

EXPERIMENTALISM AND THE RANK AND FILE

"The real law in the modern state is the multitude of little decisions made daily by millions of men."

LIPPMANN.

"The importance of the plain man's judgment is, in short, the foundation upon which the expert if he is to be successful must build."

LASKI.

"To draw inferences has been said to be the great business of life. . . . It is the only occupation in which the mind never ceases to be engaged."

J. S. MILL.

1. Experience in Philosophy

IN the field of general philosophy, one of the important features of experimentalism has been its insistence that experience is both subject-matter and method for all valid philosophizing. In supporting this view of experience, experimentalism has found it necessary to be active along two fronts. On the one hand, it has continuously criticized such philosophical formulations as have sought to find in the non-empirical the ultimate sanction and meaning of human affairs. So often have the actual empirical roots of all such "transcendental" systems been exposed that non-empirical method has come to have little standing in general philosophy to-day. On the other hand, experimentalism equally has been concerned to show that ordinary experience, equipped as it now is with experimental procedures, is adequate to develop its own regulative standards. According to the experimentalist, efforts to transcend experience are not only futile, but also unnecessary—futile, because we can only talk and think about events that have entered into our experience in one way or another; unnecessary, because experience can stand on its own feet, and is competent to direct its own activities.

2. Can People Think?

In a genuine sense the counterpart of this conflict in general philosophy is to be found in the field of education to-day. In education the search for some effective means of social control other than that found in the capacity of ordinary experience to guide intelligently its own ongoing affairs has by no means been abandoned. Accordingly the effort of the experimentalists to develop an educational program based on the central premise that intelligent experimental control of experience is the fundamental essential has been subject to much attack.

One group of critics concedes that such an educational program is appropriate for the superior few, but asserts it is absurd to suppose that the rank and file can share creatively in determining the standards by which they shall run their lives. These critics point to the army tests which are reported to have demonstrated that the "average mentality" of our population is slightly over thirteen years. How can a nation of "thirteen-year-olds," they ask, be expected to manage their own affairs? To permit such immature minds to question existing social and moral arrangements is both foolish and dangerous, because they simply do not have the capacity to deal with questions of such far-reaching importance. Consequently it is urged that educationists interested in social stability should endeavor so to train these "average" minds that they will acquire the permanent habit of accepting the established standards of society, and of obeying without criticism the suggestions of expert leaders. If democracy is to be made safe for the world, habits of obedient followership must become fixed in the behavior of the rank and file. Moreover, the knowledge we now have of the process of "conditioning" provides us with a reliable method by which such fixed habits of response can be developed. Among others, Finney in his book *A Sociological Philosophy of Education* has given emphatic expression to this point of view:

"To the educational problem of providing a following for intelligent leaders, the present chapter will accordingly direct the reader's thought.

"For the solution of this problem the usual formula is: Teach the people to think. Every citizen, it is urged, ought to be encouraged to the utmost to think for himself." [1]

"But this solution will hardly bear inspection. In the first place, the barber's IQ is only .78, according to army tests. IQ's below .99+ are not likely to secrete cogitations of any great social fruitfulness. Quite the opposite, indeed. How strange it is that such contradictory ideas should run current at the same time. The mental-measurements movement has given prevalence to a discouragingly low estimate of the average citizen's intelligence, while the Dewey school has exalted the independent thinking of this average citizen as the means of saving democracy." [2]

"The safety of democracy is not to be sought, therefore, in the intellectual independence of the duller masses but in their intellectual dependence. Not in what they think, but in what they think they think. . . .

"The truth seems to be that a mere echo is the best that can ever be expected from the duller half of the population; and the vital question is who secures them as a sounding board." [3]

"To load the dice of popular beliefs with the enlightened beliefs of enlightened leaders is the only preventive. How shall we go about it?

"The psychological secret to the solution of this problem

would seem to be found in the fact that rote behavior in one
person, and reasoned behavior in another, may be so similar as
to be indistinguishable by the observer. One person's reflexes
may be conditioned to a rule, proverb, or slogan the reasons for
which he fully understands; the other's reactions may be conditioned by the same stimulus without his understanding it at all.
But both *behave* alike." [4]

3. Democracy and the "Conditioned Reflex"

An even more drastic criticism of the educational program
of the experimentalist comes from a school of psychology
which believes that thinking has little to do with the behavior of either the "superior" or the "inferior" intellects.
According to this school, habit, and not reflection, plays the
significant rôle in shaping conduct. All activities are viewed
as reactions bound to stimuli through both inherited and
acquired specific neural connections. The reflex is said to be
the proto-type of all behavior. The knee-jerk may be taken as
an example of a reflex. To understand the central principle of
human behavior it is only necessary to cross the legs, and
sharply tap the patellar tendon just below the knee of the
suspended leg. Invariably the leg flies up in a quick, involun-
tary reaction. As often as the stimulus is applied, the same
response occurs. As this simple reflex demonstrates, there is a
one-to-one correspondence between the stimulus and the response. It follows as a consequence that if we can control the
stimulus, we can also control the response, because the stimulus
is the efficient cause of the response. To be sure, the inherited
stock of reflexes is inadequate to provide for all behavior, but
these original reflexes can be elaborated and diversified
through a process of "conditioning." "Conditioning" is accomplished by repeatedly associating some new stimulus with

the original biological stimulus. In time this artificial stimulus becomes adequate to produce the desired response without the aid of the original biological stimulus. Such a response which through repeated trials has become firmly attached to a new stimulus is called a "conditioned reflex." The only important difference between a "conditioned reflex" and an inborn reflex is a difference in origin. The most complex adult behavior is in reality only the sum of these specific inherited and acquired reflexes. Aggregations of such simple mechanisms of response are adequate to explain all varieties of human behavior, and it is both unnecessary and misleading to introduce such explanatory terms as *foresight, purpose, thinking,* and *conscious activity.* The task of education is precisely this task of "conditioning." Let the specialists in the various fields determine what habits of response are most appropriate, and through the process of "conditioning" we have reason to anticipate that individuals can be so modified that they may be fashioned to respond in both emotional and overt behavior as desired. A more fundamental challenge to the educational program of the experimentalist could scarcely be conceived, and its utter simplicity makes its appeal the more subtle.

However, not all of the members of this school of psychology are willing to take such an extreme position. Some believe that at times reflection is a factor in the control of behavior. Most of human behavior, to be sure, is mere mechanical response, but occasionally, with the more intelligent, thinking may enter as a factor in conduct. However, since the ability of even the best minds to control behavior through reflection is relatively very slight, the formation of fixed habits still remains the dominating aim of education. Of course it is recognized that situations do vary. But, for the most part, it is believed that the variations are mainly in the details, and that the essential elements are so alike that fixed responses can successfully be associated with these unchanging dominant elements. This being so, it is unnecessary to rely upon individual deliberation to anything like the degree that the experimentalist suggests. Moreover, the tendency of the experimentalist's educational program to emphasize the importance of learning to control behavior through intelligent understanding and critical examination is, these critics say, based on a false interpretation. Even the genius makes few original responses, and certainly the rank and file have little capacity for such original creative adjustments.

The bearing of this psychological point of view on character education is particularly important. In his book *The Nature of Conduct,* Symonds develops some of these implications for character formation. While he does not deny the value of reflection in conduct, he believes it is easy to exaggerate its significance. As the following quotation indicates, he questions the important place the experimentalist gives to deliberation in conduct:

"The author would not deny the assertion of the previous writers that deliberation is necessary for the highest control of conduct and hence for the highest form of character. To follow the course described by Kilpatrick—(1) to know the elements involved in a situation; (2) to evaluate and weigh these elements correctly in deliberation, considering the expected outcomes of proposed conduct; and (3) to act on the basis of the thought-out solution—would indeed result in a character of high type. Carried to an extreme such a character would mean the cessation of activity because of the difficulty and time necessary to carry out the deliberations. But the question is naturally raised whether the description of character given by Kilpatrick accords with the facts of conduct. Do persons, even of the highest type of character, follow through the steps proposed by Kilpatrick? This is a matter of research and not of definition. Whether character implies conduct which follows deliberation is not known. However, one may venture to express an opinion, using facts of mental life as they are today known. Ideo-motor conduct is a possibility. But evidence points to the fact that taking people as they are found, their ideas control only a very small fraction of their conduct. Even the most intelligent people guide their conduct by ideas only in new and unfamiliar situations which comprise only a small percentage of a day's activities. The average man probably responds a hundred times to sights, sounds, and touches to every one time that he responds to an idea during the course of the day's experiences. Again, many of the ideas to which even the most intelligent man responds are habitual thoughts—the new responses to ideas are rare indeed among all responses to ideas. For the average man perhaps it is safe to say that for every hundred responses to an idea, one is a new response to an idea. In the chapter on reasoning it is pointed out that only rarely do we reason out from knowledge of anatomy and physiology a course of action to follow regarding our health and safety. Such deductions come only at intervals from the greatest minds in the medical profession and they are passed on and used, but not reinvented, as devices by the people. Only an Edison could invent the incandescent light; any child can turn on the switch which sends the current through the lamp. The human race has been centuries evolving a set of *mores* which permit human beings to live together with a sort of security and freedom; and it is only too easy to criticize these *mores,* even though they are the inductions of the best minds of all the ages. It is difficult to believe that we shall be successful in teaching children today to deliberate on their conduct successfully. The writer's opinion is that the character described by Kilpatrick is possible, but extremely improbable. The best that can be done is to teach pupils the habit of responding to their own ideas (probably a habit that can be generalized) and then to put them in the possession of the best solutions to all the problems of conduct that are available. To attempt more than this would probably be unavailing." [5]

4. A Critical Challenge to Experimentalism

It is apparent that the sociological and psychological positions of the above two groups of educators are in serious conflict with those of the experimentalists. The difference in point of view relates to both the type of character which education can and should seek to produce, and also to the educative process by which this character is to be produced. The educational ideals of the experimentalist are indeed visionary if the basic contentions of these critics are well grounded. Now as much as the experimentalist believes in ideals, he believes only in those ideals that point to unrealized possibilities of the actual. His whole philosophy is a protest against the traditional dualism between the ideal and the real—between theory and practice. He has no patience with ideals which are praised in the abstract, and ignored in the concrete. For the experimentalist, ideals are either *working* hypotheses, or they are mere wishful thinking, and of the latter, he believes the world already has had too much. Hence if his educational ideals cannot guide actual practice fruitfully, the logic of his philosophy would demand that they be reconstructed until they can be translated into a practical program.

The balance of this chapter will be devoted to a consideration of the educational aims of the experimentalist in the light of these criticisms. For convenience the issues between the experimentalist and his critics are grouped under three main classifications: metaphysical and social, psychological, and ethical.

(1) *Metaphysical and Social:* How significant are the factors of change and novelty in the natural and social environment with which the average person has to do? Do we live in the kind of world in which the individual can successfully manage his affairs largely on the basis of fixed habit and fixed belief? What is meant by creative activity? Is it to be achieved only rarely by the superior few, or is it a feature of the everyday activity of ordinary people?

(2) *Psychological:* What light do the findings of experimental psychology throw on these differences between the experimentalist and his critics? Is most behavior of the automatic reflex type? As narrowly construed, how adequately does the *S-R* bond formula account for all aspects of behavior? How about the specificity of conduct? Is behavior a mere aggregation of specific positive and negative tendencies, or is there evidence that integration of character is a fact, and that the organized behavior of a normal individual is more than a mere mathematical sum of its parts? Is learning a process of "mere conditioning"? If so, what is meant by "mere conditioning"? What part does the individual, himself, play in the learning process? If he actively participates in the process, what is the nature of his activity and how significant is it? Is it a psychology or a philosophy which demands that we so largely eliminate conceptions of "purposeful activity" and "conscious behavior" from our explanations of human experience? What, if any, rôle does psychology give to thinking in the control of conduct?

(3) *Ethical:* From an ethical point of view, what kind of person are we concerned to develop? Is the experimentalist correct in his contention that to be an individual in any complete sense includes capacity for self-direction? What are the interrelations between social efficiency and individual development? Which is means, and which is end? What about the expert? What is his function in a democratic society? Has civilization become so complex, and is knowledge now so highly specialized, that it is no longer possible for an individual to guide his life on the basis of his own critical evaluation of consequences? Just what have the tests discovered about the nature of intelligence, and about the intellectual possibilities of the rank and file? What are the implications of the find-

ings of these tests for educational procedures in a democracy?

Before beginning the discussion of these various points, it may be well for the writer to indicate his own bias in these matters. His sympathies are frankly with the experimentalists. He believes that we start with a more fruitful premise in education when we assume that very ordinary folks *can,* and *do,* control their conduct through an intelligent understanding of what they are about, than when we start with the contrary premise that for the most part rote behavior is all that can be expected from the rank and file. Manifestly the concrete emphasis and detailed program in educational work will vary profoundly according to which of these two views is made the working hypothesis.

In this connection it is important to remember that in dealing with the plastic material of childhood the very educational procedures adopted are frequently potent factors in determining what the ultimate outcomes shall be. Educators proceeding on one of the above assumptions might in time accumulate a very different set of findings about the intellectual possibilities of the average person than would be achieved by educators working on the opposing assumption. The findings would be different because the human products of the two systems would be different. In other words, our faith, or lack of faith, in the possibilities of the rank and file, once expressed in concrete educational activities for children, may help to create the very facts which, in turn, come to be accepted as ultimately decisive in determining what our subsequent educational procedures should be.

To assume that the average person can become intelligent in the control of his conduct does not mean that the significance of individual differences is ignored. While appropriate educational procedures can do much to develop possibilities which might otherwise go unrealized, they cannot develop possibilities which are not latently present. That the organic equipment of each individual sets certain broad limits to his possibilities of development cannot be doubted. In education we ignore such limitations at our peril. An intelligent understanding of the human material with which we have to do must be the basis for any educational undertaking that is to rely on other than chance factors for its success. Such intelligent understanding will not be gained by those who substitute optimistic views about the unlimited possibilities of each individual for a painstaking consideration of such knowledge about human nature as careful scientific study is slowly accumulating. On the other hand, mere enthusiasm for the "objective" study of human behavior does not lead automatically to an intelligent understanding of human possibilities. This is particularly apt to be true if devotion to "objective" techniques causes us to rest content with a psychology that slights essential factors in human conduct because they do not seem to harmonize easily with certain "ultimate scientific categories" carried over from the physical sciences. In view of the fact that some of these "categories," such as "mechanism," "cause and effect," and "immutable law," are now receiving fundamental reinterpretation in the physical sciences themselves, we should be wary of basing dogmatic conclusions on them in the field of psychology.

5. How Fundamental Is the Factor of Change?

In an earlier chapter, the experimentalist's conception of the dynamic nature of the world was reviewed.* It may be briefly summarized by saying that every existence is seen as

* Chapter III, sections III-VI.

an event. Hence the world of existences is characterized throughout by process and change. One situation develops into another. Each has its own unique character. In such a world of transitive events uncertainty, novelty, and plural possibilities are naturalized. Existence is inherently unstable and precarious. That which is true of the primary order of nature is no less true of the social order. It is particularly true of the social order based on our modern scientific technology. Change, probably increasingly rapid change, is one of the pervasive traits of a civilization that has perfected a process of making discoveries and inventions. This does not imply that all things change equally rapidly, nor that all changes are of equal significance for the educator. It does imply, however, that in such a changing world each individual and each group of individuals will be constantly faced with new and novel situations. It is a basic conviction of the experimentalist that the individual trained to rote behavior is ill equipped to make the adjustments inherently demanded in a rapidly changing society. Efforts to "preadjust" children to a dynamic world are of doubtful value.

So much for the general point of view. Is this conception of the nature of the world we live in, and of the demand it makes for flexible, intelligent behavior, as opposed to fixed habitual response, borne out by the findings of everyday experience? As indicated by one of these critics, "this is a matter of research and not of definition." As an empirical philosophy, experimentalism cannot consistently object to the most severe testing of its theories by the further examination of experience. In this connection, what are the facts of experience, and how are they to be interpreted?

With regard to the larger questions of general public policy, apparently the experimentalists and their critics are in essential agreement. Both seem to admit that such problems as those of war and peace, national and international economic arrangements, immigration policies, control of natural resources, public health, etc., all call for continuous readjustments based on an intelligent apprehension of the changing factors involved. In this wider area there is no dispute about the ongoing nature of experience, nor of the need for fresh creative solutions. Such difference in point of view as exists arises rather because of varying conceptions of the process by which such continuous readjustments are to be achieved, and because of a conflict in views about the relation which the expert should sustain to the rank and file in a democracy. This problem of the expert's function will be considered later. The important point to be noted in this connection is that both the experimentalists and their critics believe that continuous reconstruction of general public policies is required to meet changing conditions.

This would seem to be an important concession on the part of the critics of experimentalism. If in the field of general public policy creative adjustments are continuously called for, why may we not reasonably anticipate that in smaller group and private affairs a similar type of creative activity will be demanded? Once again, however, it is a question of fact and not of definition. In this connection the observation of Walter Lippmann, who is considered by many to be one of the most penetrating minds dealing with social and political problems, is worthy of consideration:

"The essential point is that as the machine technology makes social relations complex, it dissolves the habits of obedience and dependence; it disintegrates the centralization of power and of leadership; it diffuses the experience of responsible decision throughout the population, compelling each man to acquire the habit of making judgments instead of looking for orders, of adjusting his will to the wills of others instead of trusting to custom and organic loyalties. The real law under which modern society is administered is neither the accumulated precedents of tradition nor a set of commands originating on high which are imposed like orders in an army upon the rank and file below. The real law in the modern state is the multitude of little decisions made daily by millions of men. . . .

"The crucial difference between modern politics and that to which mankind has been accustomed is that the power to act and to compel obedience is almost never sufficiently centralized nowadays to be exercised by one will. The power is distributed and qualified so that power is exerted not by command but by interaction." [6]

In his further discussion of the moral situation, Lippmann attributes much of existing moral confusion to the attempt to rehabilitate an authoritarian system of morality. In a society which is changing as rapidly as ours, he believes it is folly to rely on unchanging ethical rules and moral conventions. To rely on fixed codes is held to be folly because so to do is to attempt the impossible. In a progressive dynamic society authority and prestige are soon stripped from unchanging social arrangements because they so obviously fail to meet the requirements of new situations. Consequently the maladjustments which arise from the effort to obey set standards at once bring these social patterns to conscious attention and criticism. This greatly decreases their effectiveness as authoritarian moral controls, because external authoritarian controls by their very nature work smoothly only when they are accepted without question as something inherent in the structure of society. Once social maladjustment causes them to be subjected to scrutiny and criticism, they must henceforth meet the searching demands of reason. This means that such standards are appraised in terms of their present social utility and not primarily in terms of their ancient origin.

What weight shall we accord to this social and political analysis of present-day society? If Lippmann's interpretation is correct, the educational program advocated by the critics of experimentalism would seem to be poorly designed to meet the demands of such a society. Rote behavior for the rank and file seems grossly out of place in a society that compels "each man to acquire the habit of making judgments instead of looking for orders," and one which is governed fundamentally by "the multitude of little decisions made daily by millions of men." From an entirely independent approach, Lippmann reaches a conclusion practically identical with the position of the experimentalist. He also sees human life as continuous interaction with people and things. The nature of this interaction is such that novel individual adjustments are constantly required. Choice, inference, judgment, and decision are necessitated by the new situations which develop in the shifting movement of events. If this be true, thinking for the rank and file would seem to be a necessity, not a luxury, if they are to meet the demands of our present social situation.

According to the experimentalist, the real issue is not whether the circumstances of life are such as to make thinking necessary, but rather, what is to be the quality of the thinking done. The experimentalist believes that the implications of experience are much more truly revealed in the following statement of the logic of John Stuart Mill than they are in the psychology which holds most behavior to be simple mechanical response to fixed external stimuli:

"To draw inferences has been said to be the great business of life. Every one has daily, hourly, and momentary need of ascertaining facts which he has not directly observed; not from any general purpose of adding to his stock of knowledge, but because the facts themselves are of importance to his interests or to his occupations. The business of the magistrate, of the mili-

tary commander, of the navigator, of the physician, of the agri-
culturist, is merely to judge of evidence, and to act accordingly.
. . . As they do this well or ill, so they discharge well or ill the
duties of their several callings. It is the only occupation in
which the mind never ceases to be engaged." [7]

As this quotation from Mill illustrates, the logic of the
experimentalist and the psychology of certain extreme behaviorists are at opposite poles. While this latter group of
psychologists seems to construe human experience so as to
minimize, if not to eliminate altogether, the function of thinking, the experimentalist sees thinking as something which in
one form or another, well or poorly done, is native in all human conduct. Far from conceiving the business of living to be
a mere mechanical routine, he considers it essentially to be a
creative art—creative, because the ongoing nature of experience is such that novel adjustments ever challenge the individual. And such novel adjustments are considered to be
creative for the individual concerned even though they contribute nothing original to society's stock of knowledge.

"When I think of this fresh reaction of little children to the
world, I am led to ask why it so soon gets dimmed; why it gets
so soon covered up and a kind of mental rubber stamp or
phonograph record takes its place. It may be thought absurd to
demand originality of everyone. But I think this idea of absurd-
ity is due to having a wrong measure by which to judge originality. It is not to be measured by its outer product; it is rather
an individual way of approaching a world that is common to us
all. An individual is not original merely when he gives to the
world some discovery that has never been made before. Every
time he really makes a discovery, even if thousands of persons
have made similar ones before, he is original. The value of a
discovery in the mental life of an individual is the contribution
it makes to a creatively active mind; it does not depend upon no
one's ever having thought of the same idea before. If it is sincere
and straightforward, if it is new and fresh to me or to you, it
is original in quality, even if others have already made the same

discovery. The point is that it be first-hand, not taken second-hand from another." [8]

In his home and family life, in his occupation, in the management of his business affairs, in matters of health, and in all of the endless variety of his daily social relationships, each individual is certain to be called upon to face conflicts, to weigh values, to integrate meanings, and to make decisions. Even such a simple activity as crossing the street cannot be safely reduced to a fixed routine. Possibly certain specific items in such an experience can be fixed in habit, but the experience as a whole changes so much from one time to another that ability to size up the entire situation intelligently, and thus to act in accordance with meanings perceived and understood, cannot be replaced by a series of uniform responses to fixed rules and signals. For all who are not institutional cases, the necessity for observation, drawing inferences, and making judgments seems to be immanent in the very nature of experience itelf.

If the necessity for making inferences and choices is rooted in experience, the necessity for thinking is likewise rooted in the process by which life moves along. If this be the character of the experience process, how does it happen that certain psychologists in their analysis of human conduct have tended to make little place for such factors in their explanations of behavior? The hypothesis might be advanced that these psychological explanations have been based less on an actual comprehensive study of ordinary experience itself and are more in the nature of deductions from certain oversimplified premises. We shall now consider certain of these more purely psychological questions. Fortunately the psychologists themselves have already begun a reëxamination of some of these basic propositions. This reëxamination seems to indicate that certain revisions of earlier positions are called for. In any case, in this field, as in all others, macroscopic experience and not the refined products of abstracted analytical processes must be granted the first and the last word.

6. The "S-R Bond" Psychology

From the standpoint of the underlying psychology involved, it is apparent that the present emphasis in education on habit formation as contrasted with intelligent purposeful control of experience is rooted in the conception that the educative process is essentially the process of conditioning responses. As evidence of this we need only to examine the writings already quoted. In the excerpt given earlier in this chapter, Finney explicitly states that in the process of conditioning reflexes we have "the psychological secret" of how "rote behavior in one person, and reasoned behavior in another, may be so similar as to be indistinguishable by the observer." Symonds in the opening chapter of his book, although recognizing that "purpose" and "consciousness" are realities in behavior, tells why they should be avoided as categories of explanation by modern psychology, and also points to the superior value of the "concept of conditioned response."

"Modern psychology is particularly concerned with avoiding the terminology of purpose and consciousness, not because purpose and consciousness are unrealities, but because they imply a point of view which does not yield to the scientific approach or is fruitless for control. There is no need to deny purpose. It exists and is a powerful force. But the psychology which admits purpose as an explanation is a beaten science. It admits failure. It proposes to adopt an unanalyzable concept because it is too lazy to adopt the slow and painstaking experimentation necessary to make the analysis. When psychology falls back on purpose as an explanation of behavior, it stops advance. It says that we have reached the ultimate. Modern psychology holds a different hypothesis. Purpose must fall into line with other behavior phenomena. At present the most hopeful clues are that purpose involves the phenomena of delayed reaction, and that purpose is a conditioned reaction, the stimuli including the great organic processes such as hunger, sex, and other organic, muscular and glandular processes. This is now little more than a hypothesis, but it has the advantage of stimulating experiment and thought, whereas the concept of purpose deadens scientific activity. Purpose as a psychological concept is also useless as a control of conduct. Since purpose resides within the man, we are not told how to form or stimulate it. But a concept of conditioned response, to use one hypothesis of modern psychology, leads immediately to a method of control. Such a concept provides education with a technique." [9]

It is not surprising that the doctrine of the "conditioned response" should have come to enjoy enormous prestige in the field of education. The educator is interested in producing changes in people, and in controlling the direction which those changes are to take. If this can be done effectively through his own activity and immediate control of the situation, manifestly the educator has a more simple and direct route to his goal than though he be obliged to rely on the voluntary cooperation and intelligent understanding of those to be educated. This tendency to slight understanding participation in the process is apt to become particularly pronounced when adults are dealing with children. One scheme after another has been devised whereby the adult educator can directly control processes so as to produce desired outcomes in the behavior and character of the child. Probably the most effective of all of these techniques is that provided in the process of controlling the stimuli which surround the child so that he will be conditioned to behave as designed. To be sure, if this process be broadly enough conceived, all education must rely on it in one form or another. As a matter of fact there is no other way in which human behavior can be modified. For many, however, the special appeal of the "conditioned reflex" procedure is found in the belief that it provides a technique by which the desired habits can be built into the character of the child largely through the *educator's* initiative and exclusive control of the process.

In the second place, the doctrine of the "conditioned reflex" is supported by impressive experimental data. The Russian group under Pavlov have shown how through the manipulation of the environment the response of animals can be conditioned to an apparently endless variety of stimuli. The technique works both ways. By using the same simple procedures habits of response can be either built into, or eliminated from, an animal's behavior. The very simplicity of these experiments, in which the variables are kept under such effective control, has served to deepen the impression that in this process of conditioning the ultimate factors in all learning are revealed. Furthermore, it is a technique that works with children as well as with animals. What is even more significant, it also applies to the hitherto baffling field of emotional behavior. For example, J. B. Watson, using in principle the same techniques, has shown how the response of fear may be attached to the most harmless objects if these objects are shown to a child while a loud, rasping noise is sounded. The native reaction to a loud noise is the fear response of avoidance. If a rabbit be presented to a child at the same time the loud noise is sounded, and this be repeated a number of times, the child will eventually react with fear at the sight of the rabbit alone. Thus, through conditioning, the fear response originally associated with the loud noise has now become attached to the rabbit stimulus. Watson apparently sees no limit to the application of this simple process of forming emotional responses. Many have seen in such techniques powerful resources for the educator faced with the task of shaping the development of both emotional attitudes and motor skills in children. Some enthusiasts have even declared that, if society will only tell them the kind of adults it desires to have produced, and if it will also give them sufficient freedom to control the environment of children, psychologists now possess, in the technique of conditioning, the power to turn out products according to pattern. As we have seen, Finney goes to the extreme of asserting that through this process of conditioning responses a person may be so well trained to rote behavior that he will act in exactly the same manner, judged by all outward results, as does the individual who has an intelligent grasp of what he is about. In other words, the educator through conditioning habits makes intelligence unnecessary for the rank and file. This prospect should be sufficiently alluring to satisfy even the most ambitious educator.

Moreover, these experimental findings have been powerfully reinforced by a widely accepted neurological theory to the effect that all learning is the process of forming and strengthening specific S-R bonds. The S in the formula stands for the stimulus, or the situation; the R for the particular response evoked by the situation, and the "bond" for the connection between the S and the R. This bond or connection is supposed to become stronger and more certain through exercise or practice in making a given response. On the physiological side, a response was once thought to become more firmly attached to a given stimulus through a modification in the synapse, the place where the axone of one neurone discharges its nerve impulse into the dendrite of another. Physiologically learning has been considered to be the process by which these specific modifications in the synapses are accomplished, as the following quotation indicates:

"All learning consists in the modification of synaptic connections by the passage of nerve impulses across them. The exact nature of the nerve impulse, now supposed to be an electrochemical process, is not known, nor is the character of the changes in the synapses brought about by the passage of impulses. A fundamental assumption of physiology, however, is that the transmission of nerve impulses does change the condition of the synapse in a way that makes subsequent passage more easy, certain and prompt. This change brought about by exercise is sometimes spoken of as lowering the resistance, causing greater openness or permeability of the synapse or in other ways, all of which imply the same general hypothesis." [10]

It is not to be inferred from the above discussion that the S-R bond theory of learning is necessarily identical with that of the "conditioned reflex." Much depends on how the theory is interpreted. Undoubtedly the conception of education as the process by which reflexes are conditioned has resulted in a crudely mechanical and atomistic view of the learning process which is foreign to the thought of many who, nevertheless, find it helpful to think of all education as conditioning, and who have found in the S-R bond formula a useful tool with which to work. As far as that is concerned, certain experimentalists have also accepted the stimulus-response description of human behavior and learning, and have found it possible to integrate that approach to education with their central emphasis on the importance of building habits and attitudes of critical, intelligent understanding.

On the other hand, it is also true that many experimentalists have all along had difficulty in giving whole-hearted support to the S-R bond psychology as frequently interpreted.

For them it has seemed only natural that the mechanical, atomistic tendencies in the *S-R* bond theory as narrowly construed should ultimately blossom into the more precise concept of the "conditioned reflex." Moreover, major educational doctrines often associated with the *S-R* bond psychology have also seemed to many to encourage mechanical and atomistic ideas of the nature of the educative process. Among these the following may be mentioned as typical: All learning is habit formation. Learning is the process of forming and strengthening bonds between definite stimuli and responses. Learning is always specific, and such transfer as occurs is to be explained by the presence of identical elements in the several situations. All learning is analytical in character. Trial-and-error learning is typical of all learning. The individual may be essentially explained as an aggregation of specific neural connections native and acquired. In sum, educational conceptions associated with "connectionism" have given intellectual support to an educational practice which has tended to make much of drill and the development of motor skills, but which has not been so well calculated to arouse interest in the creative possibilities of the individual, nor to focus attention upon the importance of the development of procedures which would call out those creative capacities.

Some, at least, believe that if it had not been for the preliminary influence of the narrow interpretation of the *S-R* bond theory in disposing many educators to think of education so largely in the above terms, the extremes of the "conditioned reflex" theory of education might not have made such rapid headway. In any event, criticisms now made of both the conditioned reflex principle and the atomistic interpretation of the *S-R* bond theory of the learning process are sufficiently fundamental in nature to warrant that they be given the most serious consideration. In the next section some of the criticisms which have been directed against these doctrines will be briefly summarized. The aim is not to try to prove that these doctrines fail to give important psychological insight into learning procedures, but rather to show that when these conceptions are modified or reinterpreted as now seems necessary in the light of further studies, they cannot be employed to compel acceptance, on so-called scientific grounds, of the view that mere "conditioning of habits" should replace the "development of intelligent understanding" as the basic objective in education.

7. Psychology Criticizes Itself

(1) One of the conceptions which has given the S-R bond formula such impressive standing has been the view that in learning processes localized modification in synaptic structure takes place. It would now appear that this hypothesis was the product more of inventive speculation than of experimental observation. After years of painstaking and highly skilful experimental research on the neural mechanisms involved in learning, in which the influence of cerebral lesions on the learning process of animals was carefully observed, Lashley comes to the conclusion that the results of his experiments "are incompatible with theories of learning by changes in synaptic structure." [11] This outcome is the more impressive as he states that he began the study with a definite bias in favor of the theory of modification of synaptic structures. His conclusions are so pertinent to our discussion that they are quoted somewhat at length:

"I began the study of cerebral function with a definite bias toward such an interpretation of the learning problem. The original program of research looked toward the tracing of conditioned-reflex arcs through the cortex, as the spinal paths of simple reflexes seemed to have been traced through the cord. The experimental findings have never fitted into such a scheme. Rather, they have emphasized the unitary character of every habit, the impossibility of stating any learning as a concatenation of reflexes, and the participation of a large masses of nervous tissue in the functions rather than the development of restricted conduction-paths.

"Likewise, attempts to analyze the maze and problem-box habits in terms of adequate stimulus and conditioned-reflex response have indicated that the problem is far from solved by the simple mechanical theories of learning. Random activity, association, and retention constitute only a small part of the totality of processes underlying the formation of such habits, and even with the rat in the maze there is more than a little indication that direct adaptive reactions and some process of generalization are of fundamental importance for the learning process. Evidence in support of this statement will be presented later. For the present I wish merely to emphasize that the interpretation of learning in animals as a simple conditioning is by no means established." [12]

While there may well be dissent from Lashley's assertion in the passage that follows to the effect that rejection of doctrines of formal discipline have been based on speculative reasoning more than upon convincing experimental evidence, nevertheless, what he has to say on the problem of transfer is of the utmost significance. His experimental studies seem to challenge the hypothesis of *identical elements,* which hypothesis has been one of the fundamental supports of the view that habit formation is the basic objective in education.

"The doctrine of isolated reflex conduction has been widely influential in shaping current psychological theories. Its assumptions that reactions are determined by local conditions in limited groups of neurons, that learning consists of the modification of resistance in isolated synapses, that retention is the persistence of such modified conditions, all make for a conception of behavior as rigidly departmentalized. Efficiency in any activity must depend upon the specific efficiency of the systems involved; and, since the condition of one synapse cannot influence that of others, there must be as many diverse capacities as there are independent reflex systems.

"The effects of such a theory can be traced in many present-day beliefs. If learning is restricted to particular synapses, there can be no influence of training upon other activities than those actually practiced; any improvement in unpracticed functions must be the result of nervous connections which they have in common with the practiced activities. The rejection of doctrines of formal discipline seems to have been based far more upon such reasoning than upon any convincing experimental evidence.

"The doctrine of identical elements has been applied also to the problem of insight. When similarities between the two situations are recognized, it is because both call out a basic set of reactions involving identical reflex paths. Thus the application of past habits to new situations is limited to those in which an identity of elements can exist; all other behavior must be explained by the selection of random activities.

"There is no evidence to support this belief in identity of nervous elements. On the contrary, it is very doubtful if the same neurons or synapses are involved even in two similar reactions to the same stimulus. Our data seem to prove that the structural elements are relatively unimportant for integration and that the common elements must be some sort of dynamic patterns, determined by the relations or ratios among the parts of the system and not by the specific neuron activated. If this be true, we cannot, on the basis of our present knowledge of the nervous system, set any limits to the kinds or amount of transfer possible or to the sort of relations which may be directly recognized." [12]

The writer does not pretend to be competent to judge of the adequacy of Lashley's data nor of the reliability of the inferences he draws from these data. Until they are challenged, however, by equally thorough experimental work, it would seem reasonable to accept his conclusions in preference to theories which apparently rest so largely on a foundation of speculation. Nor is it to be understood that Lashley's challenge of the synaptic theory is a drive back to mentalism. That there is a physiological correlative of some sort to a change produced by a learning is not in question. The question is rather of the nature of that change and how definitely localized it is. Woodworth, who reviews with interest the finding of Lashley, suggests another hypothesis to replace the one which seems no longer adequate to explain the facts as now known.

"Let no one tell you that we know nothing about the cerebrum, for to assimilate what is known would take years of study; and let no one tell you that the cerebrum simply acts as a whole, for that is either a figure of speech or a gesture of despair. Different areas of the cortex do have different connections, and different functions, though it does not follow, by any means, that every type of behavior or mental activity has its own circumscribed cortical area, nor that every different performance has its own little spot in the cortex that 'presides' over it. The best conception is that the brain acts in patterns, and that each pattern may bring into activity several or many groups of neurons in different parts of the cortex. Corresponding to the many varieties of the individual's knowing and doing, there must be many brain patterns, all different, though not neatly localized in separate bits of the cortex." [14]

(2) In *The Nature of Intelligence,* Thurstone objects to the S-R doctrine because it tends to focus attention on the environment rather than on the individual. He criticizes the stimulus-response conception because in thus tending to locate the source of activity in the environment, it is prone to ignore the individual with his wants, purposes, and aspirations. By conceiving the individual as merely the agent who reacts to these environmental stimuli the way is easily opened to oversimplified mechanical explanations of human behavior because the very point of view adopted makes it almost inevitable

that the individual and his mental experience should be ignored.

"One of the basic differences between the old and the new psychology is in the treatment of the stimulus or environment. Writers of the academic schools of psychology treat the stimulus as the datum for psychological inquiry. They put their subject into the laboratory, and confront him with stimuli of various kinds, colors, noises, pains, words, and with the stimuli as the starting-point they note what happens. The behavior of the person is interpreted largely as a mathematical function of the stimulus or environment. The person's own inclinations are of course recognized as constituting a factor in the situation, but only as a modifying factor. The stimulus is treated as the datum or starting-point, while the resulting behavior or conduct is treated as the end-point for the psychological inquiry. The medical writers on psychology state or imply a very different interpretation of the stimulus. Here, the starting-point of conduct is the individual person himself. He wants certain things, he has cravings, desires, wishes, aspirations, ambitions, impulses. He expresses these impulses in terms of the environment. The stimulus is treated by the new psychology as only a means to an end, a means utilized by the person in getting the satisfactions he intrinsically wants. This is a very basic contrast. In the older schools of psychology we have the characteristic sequence: the stimulus —the person—the behavior. The behavior is thought of mainly as replies to the stimuli. In the newer schools of psychology we have a different characteristic sequence: the person—the stimulus —the behavior. The stimulus is treated merely as environmental facts that we use to express our purposes." [15]

Supporters of the *S-R* bond psychology would reply to Thurstone by saying that it is unnecessary to suppose the stimulus to be something exclusively confined to the external environment. As far as the *S-R* bond theory is concerned, there is no reason why the stimulus may not frequently be some organic change within the individual. But does this reply fully meet the objection? Granting that in strict logic the stimulus may be located in either the organism or the environment, is not the tendency of the conception weighted in favor of making the stimulus an affair of the environment and the response an affair of the individual? If this be not the case, what becomes of the assertion that the S-R bond conception gives the educator a tool superior to that afforded by the notion of behavior as due to some purpose resident within the individual? For, if the stimulus may be defined as some purpose or need of the individual, then it would seem that the "stimulus concept" and the "purpose concept" are subject to the same limitations. Moreover, the typical experiments, particularly those of the "conditioned reflex" variety, do most obviously assume the stimulus to be an external environmental factor that can be freely manipulated by the person controlling the experiment. The superior possibility of control resides precisely in the assumption that if we properly arrange the external situation, we can condition the response that we desire.

The experimentalist believes that we always get into trouble when we assume that the exclusive source of activity resides either in the environment or in the organism. He believes that all activity is a function of both factors, and that behavior always arises from a disturbance in the relationship of the organism and the environmental influences. However, if he were obliged to choose between one or the other of these two factors as a seat of behavior, he would probably agree with Thurstone that the organism is the more fruitful starting place. The theory which has sought to explain and to control behavior by working exclusively with external stimuli has not proved to be as fruitful as some of its advocates have supposed. This is particularly true when one passes beyond the range of the mechanical skills to the deeper and more permanent interests and activities of the individual. As Bode declares:

"The conception of the living organism as spontaneously active is basic for an adequate understanding of behavior, from the standpoint both of psychology and of education." [16]

(3) While apparently Woodworth does not agree with Thurstone in all details, he is in hearty accord with his view that the S-R formula is apt seriously to mislead us. He also objects to the view that it is the S that causes the R. It is the organism that is stimulated, and it is also the organism, not the stimulus, that produces the response. Here, again, we meet with the insistence that the integrated individual with his needs, purposes, and enduring interests be restored to the pre-eminent place in our thinking about behavior. In order to provide for this, Woodworth proposes that the S-R formula be changed to S-O-R, the O in the revised formula standing for the organism. In criticizing the S-R formula he says:

"Sometimes this formula is interpreted to mean that if you know the stimulus, you can predict what the response will be; or that if you wish to secure a given response, all you have to do is to apply the proper stimulus.

"But a little reflection shows that the formula, so interpreted, is incomplete; for the stimulus really acts upon the organism, and the organism makes the response. . . .

"In order to predict the response, we must know not only the stimulus, but also the organism stimulated. . . .

"These three things you must know about the individual stimulated, in order to predict his response; his equipment or repertory of possible responses, his present organic state, and the activity in which he is engaged. The stimulus, then, is not the cause of the response—not the full and sufficient cause." [17]

Not infrequently has it been assumed that the stimulus is to the response on the organic level as the cause is to the effect on the inanimate level. The failure to recognize the qualitative difference between these two levels of reaction has led to unduly mechanical notions of the character of organic behavior. Even in the most simple reflex the one-to-one correspondence between the S and the R does not always hold. To quote Woodworth again:

"But the organism, O, has to be considered even here. Though the reflex is a *fairly* dependable response to the stimulus, it fails in certain conditions of the organism. If O is in a condition of terror, with pupils widely dilated, bright light entering the eye fails to give the pupillary reflex. If O is anxious about his knee jerk, the blow on the tendon fails to elicit the reflex. But if O clenches his fist a second before the patellar tendon is struck, the reflex will be unusually strong. If O is carrying a hot dish which he dares not drop, the heat on his hand does not arouse the usual flexion reflex. So we see that, even in the case of reflexes, we cannot predict the response from knowing simply the stimulus, but must also know the condition of the organism." [18]

Once the whole organism is reinstated in the behavior unit, the hypothesis immediately arises that possibly the organism has a more active rôle to play in the learning process than some of the "conditioned reflex" experiments would seem to indicate. Both in Pavlov's experiments with dogs, and in Watson's emotional conditioning of children, the agent seemed to be largely passive, and his responses were apparently controlled by the stimuli that were placed around him. Closer examination reveals, however, that even in these controlled laboratory situations where every precaution was taken to eliminate distracting influences, the agent was not wholly passive. Discussing Pavlov's most famous experiment, Woodworth declares:

"The contiguity of the bell and the food, in the conditioned reflex experiment, does not attach the flow of saliva to the bell unless the dog is hungry so that the food stimulus actually arouses saliva. The stimuli must not simply be presented together, but they must be responded to together. Connections are established by the activity of the responding individual, and not by the contiguity of the stimuli." [19]

Moreover, in the laboratory the conditions were so controlled that the food always was associated with the ringing of the bell. In other words, the environment was so manipulated that one of these factors became invariably the sign of the other. Suppose the animal were not in the laboratory with the ministering experimenter on hand to present the food each time the bell was rung. Would the saliva response have been attached to the bell stimulus? That it would not is abundantly proved by the fact that the precise method used to uncondition such an acquired response is to fail to produce the food after the bell has been rung. Apparently even in these simple operations the organism is *observing* and *checking up* on what happens. If the *check-up* does not reveal a connection either artificially provided, or inherent in the order of the different events as in actual life-experience, the conditioning does not take place. The bearing of this is supremely important, not only for our interpretation of "conditioned reflex" experiments, but also for our general understanding of what goes on in trial-and-error learning. According to Woodworth the organism does something more than make mere random movements in these trial-and-error situations.

"The characteristics of trial and error behavior are that it is aimed at some goal, that it is relatively blind and unobservant, and that it is varied. The variation of activity results from check-up by the environment. If the first response to the situation reached the goal, there would be no other response on that trial at least. But when the first response results in a check, some other response takes its place. The strange fact is that out of this medley of actions, in the course of repeated trials, the unsuccessful responses gradually disappear, while the successful remain and are organized into a definite action pattern, such as is seen specially well in maze running. Evidently the check-up by the environment does more than arouse the varied activity; it is responsible also, in some obscure way, for the selection of some responses as against others. But whether trial and error behavior is really as blind as it seems, we saw reason to doubt. Almost certainly there is a small amount of observation present, a noticing of places to go to and of places to avoid, if nothing more. The delayed reaction experiment shows that definite adjustment to locations certainly takes place in animal learning." [20]

The significance of admitting that even in trial-and-error learning observation is something of a factor cannot be overemphasized. Just where observation leaves off and inference-making begins is a hard line to draw. Some would say that all observation has something of the quality of prediction in it, that even in the most simple perception the organism responds to relationships, and in so doing adjusts its activity in accordance with these relationships, whether the consequences of so doing are consciously anticipated or not. Thus, to-day, certain psychologists instead of following the extreme behaviorists in their assumption that thinking plays a small part in the behavior of most human beings, are inclined to move in the opposite direction and affirm that experiments in animal learning show that even some of the lower animals exhibit a considerable amount of intelligence in their adjustments to simple but novel situations. The irregularities in the learning curve in the most blind trial-and-error learning situations are also taken to indicate that observation and "insight" have played a part even in these comparativly mechanical adjustments. After reviewing a number of such points that seem to have been overlooked in the earlier interpretations of learning by trial and error or by "conditioning," Wood-

worth is then moved to ask what is meant when it is said that
all learning is simply "conditioning":

"In endeavoring to formulate a theory of the underlying processes of learning, we of course try to get along with as few and
simple processes as possible. We base our theory on simple
types of learning, and then see whether these simple processes
account also for the more complex types. Accordingly we started
from the conditioned reflex and have been trying to account for
the higher types of learning as based upon the same process
that appears in the conditioned reflex. Suppose our attempt has
been successful—or measurably successful—does that prove that
all learning is only a lot of conditioned reflexes? That word 'only'
covers a multitude of real differences which are blithely wished
away when we say that one thing is only something else. What do
these people mean who, having made the acquaintance of the conditioned reflex, proclaim that all learning is only conditioning?
Do they mean to deny the superior efficacy of observant learning,
or of active recitation, or of careful attention to what one wishes to
learn? This is what they sometimes seem to be wishing to say. They
imply that all learning would be just as successful if the learner
were as passive as the dog in the conditioned reflex experiment,
without any trial and error, any observation, or active participation of any sort.

"But the fact is that the simple underlying processes which
we have been speaking of in our theory of learning are simply
the raw material for the efficient learner." [21]

Good logic seems to support Woodworth in his protest
against the tendency of some psychologists to explain things
by explaining them away. Lewis is a recent book *Mind and
the World Order* makes a similar protest against this tendency in psychology from the standpoint of a logician:

"If, for example, the extreme behaviorists in psychology deny
the existence of consciousness on the ground that analysis of
the 'mental' must always be eventually in terms of bodily behavior, then it is the business of philosophy to correct their
error, because it consists simply in a fallacy of logical analysis.

The analysis of any immediately presented X must always interpret this X in terms of its constant relations to other things—to Y and Z. Such end-terms of analysis—the Y and Z—will not in general be temporal or spatial constituents of X, but may be anything which bears a constant correlation with it. It is as if one should deny the existence of colors because, for purposes of exact investigation, the colors must be defined as frequencies of vibratory motion. In general terms if such analysis concludes by stating 'X is a certain kind of Y-Z complex, hence X does not exist as a distinct reality,' the error lies in the overlooking a general characteristic of logical analysis—that it does not discover the 'substance' or cosmic constituents of the phenomenon whose nature is analyzed but only the constant context of experience in which it will be found." [22]

Apparently because he is unwilling to accept such analytical reductions as adequate explanations of all behavior, Woodworth would appear to be in disagreement with the assertion that a "psychology which admits purpose as an explanation is a beaten science." In Woodworth's opinion any effort to account for behavior as a mere concatenation of so many separate, unitary reactions to discrete stimuli fails to give the essential pattern of the daily activities of life. Unless we see behavior in terms of the larger patterns for which the concept of organized purposeful activity provides an intelligent explanation, he believes we are without any adequate means of interpreting what actually goes on in everyday experience.

"The daily activities of life are better represented by the dog coming at the sound of the whistle than by the simple reaction or the reflex. Behavior usually comes in lengths, not in separate reactions. You put on your coat and hat; you go out to the garage; you start the car; you back out; you take on your passengers; you drive them to the station. Thus one might list the acts performed in a certain quarter of an hour. Each of these acts includes a series of smaller acts leading up to some end result. When you start upon each series you are starting towards the end-result of that series. You are set for that end-result. You have embarked upon a certain total activity, which immediately becomes your 'activity in progress.' and motivates all the detailed movements or preparatory reactions composing the total activity. What you are doing in toto determines what you do piecemeal." [23]

Woodworth does not assert that the dog coming at the sound of the whistle necessarily anticipates the end result of his activity. It is possible that such complex animal behavior can be adequately described in terms of an organic set occasioned by a delayed reaction. In the case of human behavior, however, Woodworth is unambiguous in his declaration that this is not the case. Here he believes that we do need the concept of conscious behavior to do justice to the facts in the case, not because consciousness is a noun standing for some discrete mental entity, but because acting consciously is qualitatively a different sort of behavior from acting mechanically or unconsciously. To quote further:

"Whether the dog coming at the sound of the whistle anticipates the end result of his activity, it would be difficult or impossible to prove. What we do know is that the whistle started something going in the dog that did not run down till the end result was reached. So we say that the whistle set him, or adjusted him, for this total activity with its end result. But when the individual is not only set for a certain activity, but also foresees the outcome of the activity, then the activity is purposive. A purpose is a set for a certain activity with foresight of the result of that activity.
"A reflex is not purposive, however useful it may be. The stimulus simply arouses the response, with no preliminary set or motivation. At least this is true of the simpler, prompter reflexes, such as the eyelid or the flexion reflex." [24]

Woodworth describes four special characteristics of human behavior marked by conscious purpose which distinguish it from routine response. Of these four—precision of adjustment, intensity of adjustment, breadth of adjustment, and novelty of adjustment—it is the last which has most bearing on our present discussion. By *novelty of adjustment* he means that a new action pattern is made as the activity proceeds.

"Purposive behavior is new behavior, rather than habitual behavior. It is behavior in the making, rather than behavior already organized." [25]

That Woodworth believes such situations calling for novel adjustments are not infrequently experienced but, on the contrary, are the normal accompaniments of ordinary experience, is indicated by the following statement:

"A total situation, in strictness, should never be recognized, for even if all externals are now the same as on some former occasion, you yourself have changed. You may be sitting in the same room, with the same furniture, same lighting, same temperature, same clothes on, and may even be re-reading the same book. But in the back of your head you are keeping in touch with your life in general, so that, though everything around is familiar, the total situation is new and felt to be new. That is the normal state of affairs." [26]

For Woodworth the concept of purpose is fundamentally important for a psychology of human behavior. In his opinion it "need not be thought of as something lying outside of the general scheme of stimulus and response." [27] It is probably unnecessary to add that he does not believe that a mind-body dualism is required to account for conscious, purposeful activity.

"Conscious purpose is an adjustment still in the making or just being tuned up, and specially an adjustment that is broad and still precise. Purpose is not something foreign to an activity and directing it from outside, or from above. Purpose is the activity itself initiated, but not completed. It is an activity in progress." [28]

On the other hand, the reality of human purpose seems so well established and important to Woodworth as a psychologist that he is willing to "object to any one who would frighten us away from the facts of human purpose, for fear they would disturb some neat philosophical system." [29]

8. Suggestions from the Experimentalists

In addition to the above criticisms from the field of general psychology, the experimentalists themselves have also raised objections to certain current interpretations of the S-R bond psychology and the "conditioned reflex" theory of education. Beginning with a prophetic article published in 1896 in the *Psychological Review* on "The Reflex Arc Concept in Psychology," Dewey has consistently pointed to inherent difficulties in the S-R formula. Although frankly recognizing that the stimulus-response conception marks an important advance over the psychology of sensationism, he nevertheless seems to consider that the S-R conception as currently explained does not adequately provide for certain important aspects of human behavior.

In the first place, he considers the view that the stimulus initiates the activity to be seriously misleading. Here he would seem to have anticipated Thurstone's position that the S-R formula tends to promote the idea that the organism is inherently passive, and is only aroused to activity by the operation of external factors. Since the organism both by nature and the conditions of existence is ceaselessly active, he believes that the notion of "stimulus *to* activity" should be replaced by the better notion of "stimulus *in* activity." When thus conceived stimuli are not thought of as the sufficient cause of the activity, but rather as factors which serve to guide an ongoing activity as it progressively reconstructs itself in the light of developments. Stimuli are cues to response, rather than the primary sources of the response.

Secondly, behavior cannot be adequately understood if viewed as a mere succession of unitary responses to discrete stimuli. Normally in organic behavior the primary fact is an organized activity moving to realize a goal, or an end, even though the organism may not always be conscious of the end. Both stimuli and responses are conditioned by this more inclusive spread of activity. Such an organized activity is marked by continuities; earlier stages are preparatory to later ones. It has a temporal spread. It also is characterized by direction; activity is in favor of certain outcomes and is opposed to others. In such behavior the stimuli are as much determined by the more inclusive project under way as the responses are shaped by the guidance derived from stimuli. If we drop out of our calculations this primary fact of organized activity concerned to achieve certain ends, we are left without the essential clue to what is going on in normal behavior. In *The Psychologies of 1930* Dewey has deemed it important to reëmphasize this serial character of behavior. He says:

"From the standpoint of behavior itself, the traits in question take us beyond the isolated act of the subject into a content that has a temporal spread. The acts in question came out of something and move into something else. Their whole scientific point is lost unless they are placed as one phase in this contextual behavior.

"It is hardly possible, I think, to exaggerate the significance of this fact for the concept of behavior. Behavior is serial, not mere succession. It can be resolved—it must be—into discrete acts, but no act can be understood apart from the series to which it belongs. While the word 'behavior' implies comportment, as well as de-portment, the word 'conduct' brings out the aspect of seriality better than does 'behavior,' for it clearly involves the facts both of direction (or a vector property) and of conveying or conducing. It includes the fact of passing through and passing along.

"I do not mean to suggest that behaviorists of the type that treats behavior as a succession rather than as serial exclude the influence of temporal factors. The contrary is the case. But I am concerned to point out the difference made in the concept of behavior according as one merely appeals to the *effects* of prior acts in order to account for some trait of a present act, or as one realizes that *behavior* itself is serial in nature. The first position is consistent with regarding behavior as consisting of acts which merely succeed one another so that each can be understood in terms of what is actually found in any one act taken by itself, provided one includes the *effects* of prior acts as part of the conditions involved in it. The second position, while, of course, it recognizes this factor, goes further. In introducing into behavior the concept of series, the idea of ordinal position connected with a principle which binds the successive acts together is emphasized." [30]

It is true that in cases of extreme exhaustion, or of nervous disorganization, behavior does tend to become a mere succession of responses to the multitude of stimuli pouring in on the individual. The jerky, destructive character of behavior resulting from such disorganized responses to the wide variety of stimuli bombarding the organism is far removed from the unified, adaptive activity of the normal type. Just so far also is the conception of behavior as a mere succession of responses to bare physical stimuli removed from an adequate interpretation of what normal adaptive behavior really is like. To quote from Dewey's earlier article:

"The discussion up to this point may be summarized by saying that the reflex arc idea, as commonly employed, is defective in that it assumes sensory stimulus and motor responses as distinct psychical existences while in reality they are always inside a coordination and have their significance purely from a part played in maintaining or reconstituting the coördination; and (secondly) in assuming that the quale of experience which precedes the 'motor' phase and that which succeeds it are two different states, instead of the last being always the first reconstituted, the motor phase coming in only for the sake of such mediation. The result is that the reflex arc idea leaves us with a disjointed psychology, whether viewed from the standpoint of development in the individual or in the race, or from that of the analysis of the mature consciousness. As to the former, in its failure to see that the arc of which it talks is virtually a circuit, a continual reconstitution, it breaks continuity and leaves us nothing but a series of jerks, the origin of each jerk to be sought outside the process of experience itself, in either an external pressure of 'environment' or else in an unaccountable spontaneous variation from within the 'soul' or the 'organism'. . . .

"In any case what precedes the 'stimulus' is a whole act, a sensori-motor coördination. What is more to the point, the 'stimulus' emerges out of this coördination; it is born from it as its matrix; it represents as it were an escape from it." [31]

Dewey suggests that the deeper source of the difficulty may be an unexamined assumption to the effect that stimulus and response represent literal distinctions to be found in the existence of the facts themselves. He denies that they are distinctions of this existential sort. Stimulus and response are better thought of as "teleological distinctions, that is, distincions of function, or part played, with reference to reaching or maintaining an end." [32]

Moreover, seeing, hearing, tasting are acts of the organism just as truly as are motor responses. The naïve assumption that certain things are stimuli in and of themselves will not bear critical examination. Nothing stimulates an organism except as it has relation to the total conditions or set of the organism. We avoid the confusion of this naïve dualism of an environment that supplies the stimuli ready-made, and of an organism whose responses are controlled by these stimuli,

if we recall that a complete analysis of any activity reveals
that the activity always implicates both the organism and the
environment. If it be objected that in case of extreme shock
such as that occasioned by a sudden explosion we have an
illustration of a stimulus that is in no way related to the
antecedent activity of the organism, the reply is not difficult
to make. In such an event, according to Dewey, you have
neither stimulus nor response, but merely a bare physical
process:

"In the physical process, as physical, there is nothing which
can be set off as stimulus, nothing which reacts, nothing which is
response. There is just a change in the system of tensions." [33]

The importance of recognizing this fact of organization in
all organic behavior which is characterized by adaptive responses becomes more apparent when we come to interpret
reflective behavior on the human level. If organic activity is
thus typically serial in nature and is literally an ordered
process moving toward a conclusion, and, moreover, a process
which internally reconstructs itself as hindrances and resources are experienced, we are enabled, on the one hand,
to see more clearly why atomistic, mechanical explanations
of behavior involve an over-simplification of the facts; while,
on the other, we are given a positive clue to an interpretation
of reflective behavior which makes a real place for thinking
in conduct without having to resort to the traditional mind-
body dualism. Intelligent behavior is not discontinuous with
the adaptive behavior of the biological organism. It is precisely this adaptive behavior become aware of what it is
about. By thus becoming conscious of its own processes it is
able to take more things into account, to display greater
flexibility in its activity, to define more adequately the ends

for which it is striving, and to utilize and create better means for the realization of those ends.

The inadequacy of the *S-R* bond conception when too narrowly interpreted becomes more pronounced when we seek to do justice to all of the facts of reflective behavior. Reflection starts with a difficulty—with a block in activity. It arises from a situation that is experienced as a problem. In other words, it is not the presence of an adequate stimulus, but the absence of a stimulus adequate to produce an overt response that initiates reflection. Reflection from this point of view may be viewed as the conscious search for means by which the problematic situation may be so apprehended that it does yield a stimulus adequate to release an overt response. Some have sought to remedy this deficiency in the *S-R* formula by extending the meaning of the term *stimulus* so as to make it include the problem itself as stimulus. There is possibly no objection to this procedure if we constantly remember that a problem as stimulus is qualitatively a very different sort of thing from the stimulus which sets off the simple reflex. For example, the one-to-one correspondence between the stimulus and the response breaks down entirely when we stretch the notion of stimulus to include a problematic situation to which the individual must discover or create a solution which constitutes the response finally made. So also when one says that it was the situation in Russia under the Czar which was the stimulus which produced the response of the Communist Revolution, one wonders what that sort of gross stimulus has in common with the simple tap on the patellar tendon that results in the knee-jerk.

Dewey has also suggested that the facts are such that we would do well to recognize the existence of three different levels on which objects interact with one another: the inanimate level, where the terms *cause* and *effect* may be employed appropriately to describe the nature of the interaction; the organic level, where the terms *stimulus* and *response* might better be used; and the level of mind, where the terms *means* and *consequences* seem more adequate to denote the realities involved.

So also have the experimentalists been unwilling to accept the notion of the concept, or the general idea, which has been often associated with the *S-R* psychology. Bode and Dewey have pointed out that the concept, or the universal, is not some existential element present in discrete form in a variety of situations, which we uncover by the process of stripping off the variables until we finally reach the element itself. As Dewey has said, the common element is not in a series of situations or materials, as a piece of salt may be said to be in a piece of meat. You could look at red, green, and blue forever and you would never discover color. Why do we connect red and blue instead of red and odor? Because red and blue may be put in a series, and we find it possible to make a common response to them for certain purposes. The universal is not simply abstracted from the particulars; it is rather a correlative of the particulars. It is a means we have discovered or invented of dealing with the particulars that proves to be fruitful for our purposes of understanding and control. As such, concepts or generalizations are tools with which the individual works to manage the problematic situations with which he has to do.

The difference here is more than formal. It vitally concerns the question of how we shall think of education. If a variety of situations actually contained some common element as their essence, and if through analysis children could be trained so they would always see that common element, we

might find more cogency in the suggestion that they be conditioned to make the right response to that element whenever
it appears as a stimulus in any concrete life-situation. Con-
versely, if the concept or principle is a meaning we have built
up out of previous experience for the purpose of dealing
with certain situations more effectively (because by virtue
of its use we can anticipate better what is to be expected from
the situations), the whole idea of attaching fixed responses
to such universal elements breaks down. Moreover, there is a
vast difference between using a principle as a tool, and guiding behavior on the basis of meanings perceived and understood, where both principles and meanings are continually
reconstructed in the light of further experience; and in accepting general principles as absolute rules which are to control our responses in new and novel situations. The distinction
is equivalent to the difference between being alive and growing
more intelligent by the process of learning from our experiences, and that of behaving as an automaton which interacts
with things on the inanimate level of mechanical push and pull.

9. Indispensability of Intelligent Understanding

What, then, are we to conclude from this review of some
of the criticisms that have been made of the narrow construction of the S-R bond psychology and the "conditioned response" theory? It would be most unfortunate if a study of
these criticisms were to lead any one to conclude that these
conceptions and related experimental studies—particularly
the latter—have not made fundamental contributions to our
understanding of human behavior and the nature of the learning process. That some of the most important discoveries
in the field of educational psychology have been achieved by

the leaders of these movements is so well known as to need no emphasis here. It is also important that investigators should continue to exploit to the limit the hypotheses which these schools of psychology have developed. The more information we can have about these basic processes, the greater will be our possibility for understanding and control.

The point at issue is not the importance of the data achieved by these researches, but is rather what interpretation is to be put upon these findings. That these data are not self-explanatory is evidenced by the various interpretations which are given to them by eminent psychologists. It is possible that a variety of explanations may all be equally true from the strictly descriptive point of view. So much depends in such cases on the purposes we have in mind when we are attempting to make our description. Harm is done, however, when a description or analysis made from one point of view is assumed to be the only possible construction which can be put upon the findings, and hasty educational programs are set up on the basis of these partial interpretations.

Psychologists themselves have often found it necessary to protest against such philosophies of behavior, which frequently are uncritically assumed to be the one inevitable conclusion to be drawn from the findings of their psychological research. As has been shown, many psychologists to-day from various points of approach are moved to protest against what they consider to be just such over-simplified atomistic and mechanical interpretations of human behavior and learning. In the previous section of this chapter the nature of these protests was discussed in some detail, and no attempt will be made to summarize them here. Our present concern is with the original question that prompted this inquiry. Has modern psychology rendered untenable the primary emphasis the experimentalist gives in his educational program to purposeful, intelligent participation of the individual in his own educative experience? The fair conclusion from our survey would seem to be that psychology has not discovered any new processes which enable training in rote behavior and routine habit to substitute successfully for intelligent understanding of what one is about. On the contrary, many psychologists are joining in an insistent demand that the individual, with his interests, purposes, and organized preferences, be restored to the central place in the educative process from which the conception of education conceived primarily as a "mere conditioning of habits" has threatened to remove him. Instead of asking the experimentalist to revise his philosophy of education because it makes so much of purposeful activity and intelligent understanding on the part of each individual, it would probably be more in harmony with the general tendency of thought in the field of psychology to say that any psychological theories which do not recognize the fundamental importance of these factors are themselves in need of drastic reconstruction.

10. Some Ethical Factors

No account of the experimentalist's opposition to the proposal to make habit formation rather than the development of intelligent understanding the central aim in education would be complete which did not deal with the ethical aspect of the problem involved. As was pointed out earlier in this chapter, the experimentalist believes that the changing nature of our world is such that any attempt to proceed on the basis of rote behavior is bound to end in disaster. His notion of experience as a process of continuous interaction between a

changing individual and a world of moving events forever
bars him from placing his trust in an education designed
to achieve "preadjustments" of an automatic sort. Flexibility
and the creative ability to construct new ways of behaving
to meet novel situations are so imperatively demanded by the
dynamic character of existence that the experimentalist considers any educational program which seeks to implant fixed
habits and ideas into the life of the child to be radically
deficient. Particularly does this seem to him to be true of our
modern industrial society, in which wide distribution of
authority and intelligent understanding is necessary if such
an interdependent society is to move forward with reasonable
stability.

However his opposition to this emphasis on rote behavior
is not to be explained wholly by the above considerations. It
also has its ethical foundation. For the experimentalist, the
most fundamental ethical value may be said to be the capacity
and freedom to grow. Growth is defined as that continuous
reconstruction of experience which adds new meanings to
life and yields further power to control subsequent experience. This process of growth is an unending process. It is
believed to be the inclusive end of life, and as such it is the
only end of education. Its essential condition is that the individual attain the power of self-direction. The moral autonomy of each individual becomes then a basic value. Such
moral autonomy implies freedom from the imposed control
of others, and equally freedom from habits that inhibit the
capacity to change and grow. The individual who is controlled
by fixed ideas and habits is no more free to grow than is the
individual whose behavior is dictated by others. However
well intentioned the proposal to control the future of the individual by "conditioning" his responses may be, such an

educational program appears to the experimentalist to confiscate the individuality of those who are thus "conditioned" in so far as it succeeds in realizing its purpose. *Conditioning* is here used in the narrower sense to denote a process of building habits and attitudes that are so fixed they cannot easily be reconstructed when changed conditions may call for their reconstruction. It also implies that primary emphasis is given to an external molding of the responses believed to be the appropriate ones, rather than to aiding the individual achieve an intelligent understanding of the situations with which he is dealing. While the experimentalist believes that in the long run more "social efficiency" of a genuine sort will be achieved on his basis than on the basis of "conditioning," he is not willing to say that "efficiency values" are the most important ones to be weighed in this connection. The capacity of the individual to manage his own experience seems to him to be such a fundamental value that he is willing to conserve this good even at the cost of reduced "social efficiency" of a certain type if this be necessary. For the experimentalist, the significance and goodness of life fundamentally depend upon the individual's having such intelligent control over his own experience.

But the objection will be raised, how about the intelligence of the rank and file? Have we any reason to suppose in the light of the findings of the intelligence tests that the average person has the capacity required to control creatively his own experience? If the individual does not possess this native capacity, can any educational procedures be expected to give it to him? If we put aside inherited, sentimental notions about the "equality of all men," are we not compelled to admit that the results of the testing movement plainly point to the conclusion that the average individual has no such native capacity as is presupposed in the program of experimentalism?

The experimentalists themselves were early in the field with answers to some of these questions. Under critical examination some of the naïve assumptions imbedded in the early tales spread abroad as to what the tests had proved the intelligence of the average person to be began to appear somewhat ridiculous. On formal logical grounds, some of the conclusions were shown to be poorly supported by the data assembled. Certain more responsible leaders of the testing movement all along have been more cautious in the conclusions they drew from the findings of the tests. Through further experimental studies additional facts have been brought to bear on the question which seem to indicate that there is little solid foundation for the earlier pessimistic generalizations. An admirable summary of certain of these points has been given in a recent article by Goodwin Watson. Since the items covered in this summary have important bearing on the basic question of whether the findings of the testing program are such that we can no longer look to the rank and file for intelligent control of their own experiences, it is quoted somewhat at length:

"How seriously should intelligence test scores be taken in guiding the life of a child? Does the I Q give a fair and full index of the worth of an individual to society? Most of the harm that has arisen in connection with the use of intelligence tests seems to have grown out of misunderstandings of the answer to these questions. Even scientifically trained psychologists have not always been careful to emphasize the distinction between a relationship which holds with great masses of data, and that which exists in a particular case.

"Only in extreme cases can individual predictions of a far-reaching nature safely be made. . . .

"When the intelligence test score of an ordinary person is

known, that does not tell very much about him. Even in school work, where intelligence would seem to be more useful than anywhere else, the relationship is far from close. Spelling ability is very slightly related to intelligence. Handwriting shows almost no relationship. Exceptions are numerous even in the more 'intellectual' subjects. If pupils are grouped by intelligence test scores into three sections, one bright, one average, and one dull, and if all three sections are given the same reading test, some of the dull section will prove better readers than some of the bright section. If the test be given in arithmetic, in language or science or history, the same result will be found. . . .

"Once outside the classroom, the significance of an intelligence test score becomes much more doubtful. Tests in other fields have shown that an individual varies in his abilities. Some things he does well. Others he does poorly. The truth of the matter is that individual intelligence test scores do not predict any other known ability of the individual with an accuracy that is 50 percent better than chance. Though we know in general that in the following abilities 1,000 children of high intelligence would excel on the average 1,000 children of low intelligence, we might about as well base our guess as to a particular child's achievement in them on a lottery number, or the length of his big toe, as on his I Q. Personal happiness; popularity with classmates; speed and accuracy of simple learning tasks; mechanical ability; ability to discriminate between good and bad music; ability to sing or play a musical instrument; ability to recognize artistic merit; ability to draw or paint; handwriting speed or quality; coöperativeness, helpfulness; physique, health, athletic ability; persistence; self-control; breadth and variety of play interests; cheerfulness; dependability; speed of decisions; self-confidence; ability to keep out of insane asylum during later years, and ability to keep out of prison during later years.

"This list is not exhaustive. The point, however, may be clear. Whatever may be true about people in large numbers, individual I Q's cannot be taken too seriously." [34]

The experimentalist does not contend that there are no important individual differences. Long before the testing movement began, the experimentalist was urging that education be so conducted as to recognize and respect the individuality of each child. Nor does he proceed on the assumption that there are no organic factors which either favor or limit the possibility of individual success. He does affirm, however, and both ordinary experience and the more careful interpretation of the findings of the intelligence tests seem to support him, that the vast majority of children do have the native capacity to achieve a unique degree of excellence of one sort or another. Particularly is this true if that capacity be encouraged by sympathetic and intelligent educational procedures that deal with the child as one able to grasp and respond to meanings, rather than as one who is to be conditioned so as to behave as an automaton.

Neither does the experimentalist understand that his educational program would render the work of the expert any less socially significant. On the contrary, he sees no possibility of carrying on the undertakings of our interdependent world society without the services of specialists in almost every variety of human activity. He does not see, however, that the expert will be hampered if he is expected to appeal to the intelligent judgment of the population. In a democratic society the true expert will have his chance only where the rank and file can discriminate on the essential points between the charlatan and the genuine leader. The "conditioning program" would seem to work as much to the disadvantage of the honest specialist as it would to the disadvantage of the rank and file. If people were to decide, on the basis of fixed responses to stimuli, the "expert" who would control on that basis would be the one who had the greatest ingenuity in manipulating these stimuli through advertising and propaganda. The true research worker will not be limited in carrying forward his projects because the rank and file have developed the capacity to judge of consequences and to discriminate between the genuine and the spurious. It is to that end that the educational program of the experimentalist is directed. Less than that fails to satisfy him because it seems to do violence to his ultimate philosophy of the nature of the world in which we live and the fundamental values in which the goodness of life consists.

REFERENCES

1. J. Ross FINNEY, *A Sociological Philosophy of Education* (The Macmillan Company, 1928), p. 387.
2. *Ibid.*, p. 388.
3. *Ibid.*, p. 389.
4. *Ibid.*, p. 390.
5. PERCIVAL SYMONDS, *The Nature of Conduct* (The Macmillan Company, 1928), pp. 297–298.
6. WALTER LIPPMANN, *A Preface to Morals* (The Macmillan Company, 1929), pp. 274–275.
7. JOHN STUART MILL, *System of Logic* (Longmans, Green & Co., 1872), Introduction, pp. 8–9.
8. JOHN DEWEY, *Construction and Criticism* (Columbia University Press, 1930), p. 4.
9. PERCIVAL SYMONDS, *The Nature of Conduct* (The Macmillan Company, 1928), pp. 8–9.
10. ARTHUR I. GATES, *Psychology for Students of Education* (The Macmillan Company, 1923), p. 56.
11. K. S. LASHLEY, *Brain Mechanisms and Intelligence* (Chicago University Press, 1929), p. 176.
12. *Ibid.*, pp. 14–15.
13. *Ibid.*, pp. 172–173.
14. R. S. WOODWORTH, *Psychology* (Revised) (Henry Holt and Company, 1929), pp. 531–532.
15. L. L. Thurstone, *The Nature of Intelligence* (Harcourt, Brace and Company, 1924), pp. 5–6.
16. BOYD BODE, *Conflicting Psychologies of Learning* (D. C. Heath & Co., 1929), p. 238.
17. R. S. WOODWORTH, *Psychology* (Revised) (Henry Holt and Company, 1929), pp. 226–227.
18. *Ibid.*, pp. 231–232.
19. *Ibid.*, p. 166.

20. *Ibid.*, p. 167.
21. *Ibid.*, p. 175.
22. C. I. Lewis, *Mind and the World-Order* (Charles Scribner's Sons, 1929), p. 5.
23. R. S. Woodworth, *Psychology* (Revised) (Henry Holt and Company, 1929), p. 238.
24. *Ibid.*, p. 243.
25. *Ibid.*, p. 245.
26. *Ibid.*, p. 107.
27. *Ibid.*, p. 246.
28. *Ibid.*, p. 244.
29. *Ibid.*, p. 244.
30. *The Psychologies of 1930* (Clark University Press, 1930), "Conduct and Experience" by Dewey, p. 412.
31. John Dewey, in the *Psychological Review*, III, 360–361.
32. *Ibid.*, p. 365.
33. *Ibid.*, p. 364.
34. *New York Times,* Sunday, October 12, 1930, Goodwin Watson on the intelligence tests.

CHAPTER VIII

EXPERIMENTALISM AND THE INDIVIDUAL

"The preferences of sentient creatures are what create the importance of topics. They are the absolute and ultimate lawgiver here. And I for my part cannot but consider the talk of the contemporary sociological school about averages and general laws and predetermined tendencies, with its obligatory undervaluing of individual differences, as the most pernicious and immoral of fatalisms."

WILLIAM JAMES.

"A Theory of Experience is a Theory of Art."

EDMAN.

1. Conflicting Criticisms of Experimentalism

FROM the point of view of education, probably no more crucial questions can be asked of any philosophy than what importance it attaches to the individual, and what conception it has of the relation of the individual to the social process. In this concluding chapter, therefore, experimentalism will be examined from the standpoint of its adequacy in providing for these aspects of the life of the individual.

Recently various groups have declared the philosophy of experimentalism to be defective because they believe its net effect is to minimize the significance of the individual. This criticism, originally advanced by writers in the field of general philosophy, is now also shared by certain leaders in the field of education. For many who are sympathetic with the educational aims of experimentalism, the temptation is strong to dismiss this criticism by merely asserting that it is based on such gross misunderstanding as not to merit serious consideration. The fundamental importance of the issue raised, however, and the eminence of some who now voice the criticism would seem to make it unwise to attempt thus summarily to dispose of it.

Before proceeding to a detailed consideration of the grounds on which this criticism is based, it may be well to mention that the philosophy of experimentalism has also been considered by other critics to be open to precisely the opposite objection. All along there have been those who have opposed experimentalism, not because it tends to submerge the individual, but because, as they have thought, it tends to exalt the individual unduly and either to give him an undue priority over institutions or to make excessive demands upon him. We may, then, well begin our discussion of this larger question by first reviewing some of the considerations which seem to support the view that the philosophy of experimentalism does make the individual a central concern.

2. A Philosophy of Concrete Particulars

In the first place, this would seem to be the general influence of the logic of experimentalism. Its logic boldly reverses the traditional arrangement. For the experimentalist, the realm of ends is the realm of particulars, or of individuals. On the other hand, generals, or universals, hitherto intrenched in the realm of ends are declared to belong actually to the realm of means. According to this logic, no individual event can be disposed of adequately by saying that it is a mere specimen of a general class. Each happening is believed to possess a certain unique character of its own and is to be dealt with in terms of its own inherent traits. Moreover, general conceptions and principles are not considered to be ultimate characters; they are viewed as human inventions which were developed because experience proved them to be useful implements in instituting and interpreting experimental inquiries. They have, therefore, the instrumental office of helping us to deal more effectively with the particulars of existence. Their intellectual value, as contrasted with their esthetic value, is to be measured in terms of their fruitfulness in thus aiding us to discover and test the meanings of the concrete situations with which we have to do. This emphasis on the uniqueness and ultimate importance of the individual event and the instrumental character of general conceptions was early stressed by William James in *The Principles of Psychology:*

"From every point of view, the overwhelming and portentous character ascribed to universal conceptions is surprising. Why, from Plato and Aristotle downwards, philosophers should have vied with each other in scorn of the knowledge of the particular, and in adoration of that of the general, is hard to understand, seeing that the more adorable knowledge ought to be that of the more adorable things, and that the *things* of worth are all concretes and singulars. The only value of universal characters is that they help us, by reasoning, to know new truths about individual things. . . . In sum, therefore, the traditional universal-worship can only be called a bit of perverse sentimentalism, a philosophic 'idol of the cave.' " [1]

The general tendency of a logic which thus gives the primary position to the concrete event or particular, and which insists that each event be studied in terms of its own individual traits, would seem to be favorable to a recognition on the human level of the significance of each individual person.

Actually we do seem to find some such connection between the general logic of experimentalism and its ethical point of view. Both friends and foes have frequently criticized experimentalism because it refuses to formulate an inclusive scheme of values. Undoubtedly one of the chief reasons for its opposition to all attempts to set up some such final hierarchy of values is rooted in its respect for the individual and the uniqueness of his experiences and perspectives. This profound respect for human individuality prompts experimentalism to resist the idea that there is some universal pattern of goodness which can be discovered and made into a final authoritative standard. Life is a dynamic affair. Individuals change, and the conditions in which their lives are set also change. Hence goods are many and various. How much any particular good is to be valued is conditioned by the circumstances. It is relative to the actual needs and the possibilities of those concerned. If a general principle be demanded, the experimentalist says that is good which promotes the happiness and growth of individuals and does not interfere with the happiness and growth of other individuals. But here, again, the principle does not fix the end. Such a principle is a "tool of insight." It points to the fundamental importance of the continuous task of finding out in each situation that which is good and that which is bad. It has value only to the degree that it makes us more sensitive to the actual factors that limit and thwart growth as well as to those which lead to expansion and more effective control. If such a general principle directs attention away from the concretes of actual experience, it does more harm than good, as Dewey indicates in the following statement:

"If we still wish to make our peace with the past, and to sum up the plural and changing goods of life in a single word, doubtless the term *happiness* is the one most apt. But we should exchange free morals for sterile metaphysics, if we imagine that 'happiness' is any less unique than the individuals who experience it; any less complex than the constitution of their capacities, or any less variable than the objects upon which their capacities are directed." [2]

The plural nature of the good and the necessity of viewing it as a variable which is a function of the changing experience of particular individuals living in particular situations is the theme of an essay, *On Some of Life's Ideals,* by William James. In this essay James proclaims the opposition of the experimentalist to all attempts to standardize that which makes life good:

"Whenever a process of life communicates an eagerness to him who lives it, there the life becomes genuinely significant. Sometimes the eagerness is more knit up with the motor activities, sometimes with the perceptions, sometimes with the imagination, sometimes with reflective thought. But, wherever it is found, there is the zest, the tingle, the excitement of reality; and there *is* 'importance' in the only real and positive sense in which importance ever anywhere can be." [3]

"The first thing to learn in intercourse with others is non-interference with their own peculiar ways of being happy, provided those ways do not assume to interfere by violence with ours. No one his insight into all the ideals. No one should presume to judge them off-hand. The pretension to dogmatize about them in each other is the root of most human injustices and cruelties, and the trait in human character most likely to make the angels weep." [4]

When we consider the broader social outlook of the philosophy of experimentalism, we find that this tendency to emphasize the significance of each individual becomes even more pronounced. The experimentalist believes the distinguishing characteristic of a democratic society is that it is precisely the kind of society that does cherish individual variations, desires, and aspirations, instead of seeking to crush them out in the interest of some static social arrangement. Consequently a democratic society must ever be a changing society. Its traditions and institutions are to be subjected to continuous reconstruction in order that they may better serve the needs and promote the growth of those individuals whose lives are conditioned by them. The concern of such a democratic society is not to absorb the individual into its already developed social tradition. While such a society seeks to afford fair opportunity for all to nourish their lives on its tradition, it is equally concerned to provide for its own continued growth through the perpetual reconstruction of the social fabric. Concrete individuals with their unfulfilled desires and purposes afford the focal points around which such social reconstruction can take place. The meaning of both individual and collective experience is enriched as this individual-social process proceeds. One of the reasons why experimentalism is an appropriate name for this philosophy is because as a philosophy it desires to promote a society which will be intelligently experimental in carrying forward this reconstructive movement.

"A society based on custom will utilize individual variations only up to a limit of conformity with usage; uniformity is the chief ideal within each class. A progressive society counts individual variations as precious since it finds in them the means of its own growth. Hence a democratic society must, in consistency with its ideal, allow for intellectual freedom and the play of diverse gifts, and interests in its educational measures." [5]

3. Respect for the Actual Self

This brings us to the educational implications of the above considerations. The experimentalist has repeatedly tried to make the educational implications of his social philosophy explicit. A society that is concerned to continue its own growth will find in its children the indispensable resource for achieving this aim. Each new generation of children presents a new opportunity for the infusion of the fresh, impulsive life of primitive nature into our already developed social processes. New vitality and new perspectives for judging our civilization can be gained from this provided we are willing to grant adequate scope to the native tendencies of children, and provided we are also constantly alert to reëvaluate our established ways of doing and thinking in terms of their spontaneous responses to them. In the opinion of Dewey it is this possibility which defines the deeper significance of education:

"With the dawn of the idea of progressive betterment and an interest in new uses of impulses, there has grown up some consciousness of the extent to which a future new society of changed purposes and desires may be created by a deliberate humane treatment of the impulses of youth. This is the meaning of education; for a truly humane education consists in an intelligent direction of native activities in the light of the possibilities and necessities of the social situation. But for the most part, adults have given training rather than education. . . . We have already noted how original plasticity is warped and docility is taken mean advantage of. It has been used to signify not capacity to learn liberally and generously, but willingness to learn the customs of adult associates, ability to learn just those special things which those having power and authority wish to teach. Original modifiability has not been given a fair chance to act as a trustee for a better human life." [6]

Many would say that one of the most important contributions of experimentalism to educational thought and practice arises from its conviction that our understanding of the meaning of respect for individuality should be extended so as to make it include respect for the child as well as for the adult. Children are not to be viewed as mere immature adults. Their childhood activities are not to be conceived as a mere preparation for real life later on. On the contrary, adequate respect for individuality discovers intrinsic value in the present interests and· experiences of children. Moreover, the best preparation for adulthood is declared to be the most zestful experiencing during childhood.

In spite of much criticism and the serious possibility that his views might be so construed as to cause them to appear to give sanction to extreme laissez-faire and anarchistic tendencies in school procedures, the experimentalist has never been willing to sacrifice his view that education should be understood as the process by which the actual self of each child is realized. So also has he consistently opposed the view that education is the process by which the immature self of the child is supposed to grow into an ideal maturity by the passive absorption of a fixed social tradition. Growth is achieved through the interaction of the native impulses and tendencies of the child with the customs and traditions of the group. Where society as well as the child are flexible, both should gain new meanings out of the interaction. Customs and institutions are to be continuously evaluated in terms of their educational effect. We become more conscious of our established ways of doing and thinking as we examine their impact on the lives of children.

The emphasis of the experimentalist on the active nature of the child, and his demand that actual living experiences replace standardized subject-matter assignments as the basic units in school programs, are merely concrete manifestations in education of his general attitude of respect for the individuality of each child. Because the traditional curriculum with its correlative teaching and learning method has seemed to him to ignore too much the concrete interests and purposes of children, he has not hesitated to demand fundamental reconstruction. Instead of viewing the educative process as primarily the process by which adults transmit that which they have already found out to empty, passive minds of children, the experimentalist challenges us to view education as the process of active experiencing on the part of the child. As thus interpreted, school education is not only concerned to conserve whatever of individuality the child has already developed, but it is also so to be managed that its fundamental procedures will contribute to the further growth of this individuality. Meaningful, purposeful activities have been considered to be an indispensable condition if this process is to be carried on within the schools.

It is this same concern for the concrete individuality of each child which explains why the experimentalist in education has never seen the promise in the testing and measurement program that some of his colleagues have seen. In his opinion, much of the significance of the testing program is dependent upon an acceptance of the traditional subject-matter curriculum and lesson assignment procedure. As the following quotation suggests, this whole scheme becomes much less important once one accepts an educational outlook that deals with children as indivduals and not as mere members of classes:

"For example it is natural and proper that the theory of the practices found in traditional schools should set great store by tests and measurements. This theory reflects modes of school administration in which marks, grading, classes, and promotions are important. Measurements of I Q's and achievements are ways of making these operations more efficient. It would not be hard to show that need for classification underlies the importance of testing for I Q's. The aim is to establish a norm. The norm, omitting statistical refinements, is essentially an average found by taking a sufficiently large number of persons. When this average is found, any given child can be rated. He comes up to it, falls below it, or excels it, by an assignable quantity. Thus the application of the results make possible a more precise classification than did older methods which were by comparison hit and miss. But what has all this to do with schools where individuality is a primary object of consideration, and wherein the so-called 'class' becomes a grouping made for social purposes and wherein *diversity of ability and experience rather than uniformity is prized?"* [7]

In sum, it would seem that a very strong case can be made for those who assert that experimentalism holds respect for individuality as one of its most basic values. As we have seen, this seems to be the import of its general philosophical theories, and these same theories when actually tested in the crucial field of education are found to further practical respect for the individual child. Actually its interpretation of what respect for personality means is so far-reaching in its significance that many hesitate to carry out its wider implications. Why, then, do some accuse the experimentalist of having developed a philosophy which in its net effect does less than justice to the individual? To gain an adequate background for the further discussion of this question, it is necessary to turn to the statements of those who thus criticize experimentalism.

4. *Individuality in an Industrial Society*

One of the most vigorous exponents of this view of experimentalism is Lewis Mumford. In his opinion the effects of experimentalism are so blighting to human personality that it would be more appropriate to call experimentalism the "Philosophy of Adjustment," or the "New Mechanism." He finds that the central aim of this philosophy is "to carry

further the processes of life and thought that have given us
the Industrial Revolution, and all its issues and by-products
in politics, social custom, literature and the arts." [8] Again,
for this philosophy "the machine and the world conceived as
a machine are 'real'; the human personality and the products
of personality are, for the mechanist, dead, unreal, empty, impotent—as in fact they are, so long as he holds to his philosophy!" [9] In particular is he critical of the conception of the
nature of the individual, and the rôle of the individual in modern society, which Dr. Dewey has outlined in a recent series
of articles on "Individualism, Old and New." To quote Mumford further:

"To say this, however, is not to acknowledge the primacy of
the 'external environment' or to preach the gospel of adjustment;
that is both bad metaphysics and bad politics. So when Mr. John
Dewey says, as he did in a recent article in *The New Republic*,
that the salvation of the modern individual lies in making his own
chaotic personality conform to the corporate pattern that has been
automatically created by modern technology and finance, one
wonders if he can possibly be conscious of the defeatism involved
in such a position? Has he so much respect for the by-products of
life in the external world, and so little respect for life itself, at
the center? For all his protestations to the contrary, it would seem
that Mr. Dewey in his heart of hearts accepts no values except
those provided by the immediate situation, although intellectually
he is aware of the nature of the social process, and knows that,
as a creature with a social heritage, man belongs to a world that
includes a past and a future as well as a present and can, by his
own selective efforts, create new passages and ends not derived
from his immediate situation. Indeed, the creative act would be
impossible if man lived only in one dimension of time and had
no other resources than those of his local society.

"The mechanist's unbounded faith in the forces and institutions outside of him turns out in practice to be a counsel of
despair: he has no better advice to offer those who wish more
rational ends and more satisfactory modes of life than to get
aboard the industrial bandwagon and permit 'the unavowed forces

that now work upon us unconsciously but unremittingly to have a chance to build minds after their own pattern.' That the minds themselves should achieve a new pattern, and work upon the 'unavowed forces' does not occur to the New Mechanist; or rather, Mr. Dewey faces this point, and says, with a certain show of contemptuous irritation that it cannot be done." [10]

Commenting on this same series of articles, Miss Naumburg, from the viewpoint of education, declares that:

"For Dr. Dewey, individualism can never be that condition of matured and separate growth still discoverable in the old culture of Europe; nor can it apparently be expressed for him in the germinating strength of those who spend their lives in such seclusion as brings forth art and science for the benefit of society as well as of themselves. For to him the individualism of the past is inevitably tied to the *laissez-faire* economics of Big Business; and this he dismisses briefly as unproductive to the group of our future social order. The new individualism as he foresees it is something quite different. 'Assured and integrated individuality,' he says, 'is the product of social relationships and publicly acknowledged functions.'

"Here Dr. Dewey is being the American of Americans. Is this the best that the future holds for a more complete and integrated individualism? A dull and gloomy picture, this technological utopia, to those of us who still hope for a richer and socially balanced individualism—the flowering of a more equitable society." [11]

Inasmuch as these criticisms are typical of others which declare that experimentalism is hostile to the highest interests of the individual, it may be well to give a brief summary of the argument in the articles to which these writers take such vigorous exception. Since these articles also reveal the experimentalist at work on a current social problem, we may gain further understanding of his philosophic method from this concrete illustration of its use.

As has already been stated, the articles deal with a specific

problem, namely, that of the bearing of current social tendencies on individualism. Accepting the experimentalist's view
that ideas and ideals guide us fruitfully only when they are
pertinent to the actual movement of events, Dewey asks what,
if any, new developments indicate that the subject of "individualism" requires fresh consideration to-day. He begins,
therefore, with an analysis of present social tendencies. As a
matter of fact, the primary aim of the entire series of articles
is analytical rather than prescriptive. He finds that our machine technology with its mass production and distribution
has given us a new "collective scheme of interdependence
which has found its way into every cranny of life, personal,
intellectual, emotional, affecting leisure as well as work,
morals as well as economics." In short, we live in a corporate
age.

Now in this new society, corporate in character, and
marked by intricate interdependence, Dewey believes that
the philosophy of individualism developed in our earlier
frontier and agrarian period is not congruent with present
social realities. He sees on every hand evidence of maladjustment due to the fact that in industry, law, and politics we
are trying to maintain conceptions of the individual and
doctrines of individual rights which were appropriate to an
earlier experience, but which do not fit an industrial, urban
civilization. More specifically he declares that the present
situation is chaotic, because our financial and business activities, although literally public in scope and function, are not
planned and conducted primarily with these public interests
in view, but rather with private profit and individual advantage as the controlling purposes. As a result society is divided
against itself. Its activities are public and social in character;
its animating motives are private and competitive. This lack

of unity in our social structure is reflected in countless ways in inner conflicts in the personal lives of individuals. In view of the social nature of the self, it is inevitable that traces of such a conflict in the social order should be found in the personal experience of many individuals. Thus both owners and workers suffer from this fundamental dualism in our economic-social scheme. Nor do the members of the intellectual classes escape its disastrous influence. A society thus divided against itself is too irrational and blindly organized to make a generous use of intelligent guidance and social planning. Intellectual groups will be largely impotent so long as the present state of affairs continues. Dewey asserts that it is time intellectuals stopped compromising with this chaotic social situation and began to direct their attention to what is fundamentally needed if vitality and integrity are to be restored to our social experience. Private roads of escape seem to him unworthy. He demands that we face the larger implications of our actual social situation. He also sketches in broad outlines some of the steps that must be taken if a unified outlook and integrated experience are to be recovered.

In the opinion of Dewey, it is useless to expect that we shall ever return to the simple societal organization of the agrarian period. For better or for worse we must continue to live in the corporate society of the machine economy. Nor does he find this prospect wholly uninviting. On the contrary, he believes that our modern technology has at last made it possible for man to create a society in which an entire population would be sufficiently emancipated from the grinding struggle for the bare physical necessities to permit all to share in the realization of the finer possibilities of existence. But this is possible only on the condition that we are willing to give up traditional notions of individualism and erroneous ideas of personal liberty and property rights which now tragically prevent the management of our new corporate processes for public rather than for private ends. Inherited ideals of individual competition, of private profit, and of the right of each man to do as he pleases with his own, need reconstruction if they are to fit the facts of our interdependent, corporate age. Thus new behavior patterns consonant with the facts of this new social interdependence must be woven into the economic, legal, and political institutions of our country. Such patterns must also be permitted to penetrate into the mental and moral dispositions of individuals. A new social philosophy is demanded.

The stubborn realities of the present social situation cry aloud for such changes. For example, we now find ourselves in panic, depression, and want. Why? Because our crops have failed? Because our factories cannot manufacture enough goods to meet our needs? No! It is because we can manufacture more than we can sell, and we can grow more than we can consume. How can we escape from this irrationality? Through further socialization. The whole tendency of our modern economy points to the need for intelligent, socialized control of our basic processes of production and distribution. Without such socialization of these processes, integration of our collective and individual experience is impossible. Further socialization is now retarded because of traditional notions of the nature of the individual and of the form of his sacred liberties. Dewey demands that these outmoded ideas and practices be modified so as to allow us to claim the new possibilities. He sees a fundamental contradiction in a socialized economy that is so largely irresponsibly controlled for private ends.

Moreover, individuality is not a static term. When conditions change, individuals conditioned by those social changes must also change. We need to-day a new individual, an individual not fashioned after the pattern of the individualism of the agrarian, pioneer life, but an individual integral with the deeper social tendencies of our present industrial corporate civilization. Without some such reconstruction of the individual and of our conceptions of his rights and responsibilities, we shall not find unity, because "assured and integrated individuality is the product of definite relationships and publicly acknowledged functions." Normally individuals find their own highest development only when they are "sustaining and sustained members of a social whole."

Critics have seized upon sentences similar to those quoted above to prove that Dewey desires that the existing machine civilization, with its ugliness, injustice, and brutality, be granted complete freedom to mold the individual according to its present character. Nothing is really farther from his thought. His whole discussion points toward a progressive socialization of these basic activities in order that the very evils now complained of may be eliminated. Undoubtedly Dewey does believe that as long as we hold to a philosophy of individualism which opposes "socialization" and "individuality," we are seriously limited in dealing constructively with these problems. He frankly champions a greater degree of socialization. But socialization in itself is not the end. As he views the present economic and technological situation, an increased socialization is essential if conditions are to be made favorable for the release of a finer individuality. It is scarcely necessary to add that the concern is for that control of conditions which opens the possibility for a richer cultural experience for an entire population and which does not identify culture with the art activities of a leisure class. Because he believes there is this possibility of a finer individuality for our entire people if we will only master the conditions, he is opposed to those who would flee to Europe to live in an alien culture, and he is also opposed to those who would have us return to the past to enjoy vicariously the ornaments of a culture of an earlier day. The real task is to create an indigenous culture out of the materials of the present situation. Nor does this mean a passive acceptance of things as they are. It does involve giving heed to the existing realities, but not in order to conform weakly to them. It is only as we understand these conditioning social factors and see their limitations and possibilities that we are equipped to transform them into something better. In the light of the following statement, also taken from the same series of articles, one wonders how any sincere mind could have supposed that Dewey was asking us to accept passively the existing industrial order:

"The solution of the crisis in culture is identical with the recovery of composed, effective and creative individuality. The harmony of individual mind with the realities of a civilization made outwardly corporate by an industry based on technology does not signify that individual minds will be passively molded by outward social conditions. When the patterns that form individuality of thought and desire are in line with actuating social forces, that individuality will be released for creative effort. Originality and uniqueness are not opposed to social nurture: they are saved by it from eccentricity and escape. The positive and constructive energy of individuals, as manifested in the remaking and redirection of social forces and conditions, is itself a social necessity. A new culture expressing the possibilities immanent in a machine and material civilization will release whatever is distinctive and potentially creative in individuals, and individuals thus freed will be the constant makers of a continuously new society." [12]

What, then, becomes of the "pragmatic acquiescence" which gives so much concern to Mumford and his literary comrades? What is implied by the term *pragmatic acquiescence?* If the epithet is used to signify that the experimentalists accept responsibility for the material phase of existence and what results from this phase, the charge is true. So also is it true to say that they accept an industrial economy made possible by power machinery. The experimentalists do not consider any view of cultural development adequate which refuses to take into account these economic factors. Particularly does this seem to them to be the case when we think of a society organized around conceptions of social democracy. Industry is inside the life of a people and not outside of it. Leaders of a feudal society might be content with a cultural ideal limited to a leisure class and could, therefore, from a narrow cultural point of view ignore the economic foundation of that society. A democratic society by its very nature is forced to accept a more inclusive social ideal, and in so doing foregoes the right to ignore the economic determinants in the collective experience of its people. If accepting responsibility for the entire social problem, including its economic phases, means "acquiescence," the experimentalist then may be truly said to be guilty of "acquiescence." If, on the other hand, it is implied that in accepting our technological culture he tamely accommodates himself to the existing patterns of our machine civilization, nothing could be further from the truth. It is because Dewey does not accept the existing acquisitive and competitive industrialism that he asks us to redefine our conception of the individual and the means by which in our day the individual is to find his highest self-realization. In other words, the experimentalist asks that traditional notions of individualism pass in order that social integrity may be secured. Once such social integration is recovered in our highly interdependent society, the way is at least open for the development of a social medium in which integrated individuals may also be nurtured.

5. Social Change and Individuality

In divergent conceptions of the nature of the individual are to be found the deeper sources of this conflict between the experimentalists and those who believe that the philosophy of experimentalism is subversive of individuality. As has been repeatedly emphasized in this book, the experimentalist does not believe that individuality is something essentially given at birth. The individual self is literally built out of the interactions of the human organism with its natural-social environment. The self is not some psychic core to which experiences are merely added; it is itself a unique pattern of behavior and mind woven out of the raw material of its own transactions with its social environment. Such being the process by which individuality comes to be, it follows that each individual is continuous with these wider social influences which have nurtured his mental and moral disposition. It also follows that if we live in the life of our own day, rather than in the literary records and cultural ornaments of some earlier day, then as social movements change, individuality also will change. That is to say, individuality is not "something static, having a uniform content." "The mental and moral structure of individuals, the pattern of their desires and purposes, change with every great change in social constitution." [13] Moreover, when because of fixation of ideas and emotional outlooks, such inflexibility results that the individual cannot relate his life to the trend of events, serious maladjustment is an inevitable consequence.

In order to avoid further misunderstanding, let it be said that by *adjustment* a two-way process in indicated. *Adjustment* does not mean that the individual is merely fashioned by so-called "external" social influences. On the contrary, being continuous with these social influences, and being in his own person an active center of preferences and a unique manner of interacting with these wider influences, the individual also participates in the shaping of these patterns, both social and personal. Adaptation is thus a continuous process of reciprocal modification. A changed social environment and a changed individual are the normal outcomes of this interactive process which constitutes experience. For the experimentalist, then, individuality is not some soul structure which is simply played upon by "external" environmental forces. Rather, individuality is a unique integration of these larger community influences, and is a particular mode of interacting with them. To the degree that the individual becomes conscious of the forces that have entered into his own mental and emotional make-up, and perceives their deeper tendency and meaning, so also does the possibility of intelligent control over these forces develop. Freedom—effective expression of individuality—is in direct proportion to the degree of intelligent understanding and control which thus has been developed.

Undoubtedly many who have long since rejected metaphysical notions of a soul-substance nevertheless are still controlled by an idea of the individual as something given fully formed, who merely takes on new experiences out of his interaction with an external environment. As a result, the human and the natural, the individual and the social, continue to be thought of as opposed factors. Until such dualistic notions have been eliminated, the experimentalist is bound to be misunderstood when he talks about individuality.

6. The Dynamic View

So also will his position be misunderstood by those who think in static rather than in dynamic terms. Here, again, we find that many who have accepted the principle of evolution, and who have adopted notions of process and change, fail to follow out the full implications of these conceptions for our thought of the relation of the individual to the social process. Every demand for fixed ideals, final descriptions of the goals toward which we are moving, shows that the writer is still controlled by static rather than dynamic notions. The following criticism by Hazlitt of this same series of articles by Dewey on individualism reflects precisely this failure to perceive the larger implications of this dynamic view:

"I have said that I do not know what the 'new individualism' means. Mr. Dewey does not seem to know either. 'I am not anxious,' he writes, 'to depict the form which this emergent individualism will assume. Indeed, I do not see how it can be described until more progress has been made in its production.' Yet it seems to me that only by formulating a clear idea of what we desire can we fix a goal for our efforts; otherwise we must simply drift with events. What would Mr. Dewey think of an architect who told him that he could not say what his building was going to look like until the workmen had made more progress on its construction? In the present situation, thinks Mr. Dewey, 'fixed and comprehensive goals are but irrelevant dreams' and all inclusive ideals are impotent in the face of actual situations; for 'doing always means the doing of something in particular'. Mr. Dewey, I suspect, is guilty of a deep-seated confusion, that between proximate and distant aims. 'Ideals,' he writes, 'express possibilities; but they are genuine ideals only in so far as they are possibilities of what is now moving'. If Mr. Dewey is talking of immediate aims this remark has practical shrewdness; if he is talking of ultimate ideals, it is an abject surrender to whatever forces happen to be dominant at the moment. The sort of imagination that brings success, remarked the late Charles Horton Cooley, 'is one that sees a distant summit, a general route to it, and just where to put your feet for the next ten steps.' In his constant insistence upon the importance of knowing where to put your feet for the next ten steps, Mr. Dewey is fully justified. But his cardinal failure lies in his persistent refusal to tell us where the distant summit is, or what it would look like. For unless we know where we want to go, or whether it is worth while going there, what is the point in moving at all?" [14]

Is a philosophy which fails to give final goals and fixed ideals hostile to the development of individuality? If this be so, then experimentalism may be said to be opposed to the development of individuality. As we have seen, as a philosophy it steadfastly refuses to give any such all-inclusive system of values. It believes that experience is such a living, changing process, capable of taking on so many and varied forms, that it cannot be fastened to any fixed scaffolding of ideals, no matter how attractive these ideals may now appear. Does this refusal to give a completed system thwart the possibilities of individual development? As we have already argued in this chapter, it would seem that by this removing of all fixed conclusions the way is rather left open for indefinite individual variation and growth. Of course, if experimentalism be interpreted to mean that no long-range hypotheses can be evolved, then it would indeed be a philosophy at the mercy of the forces dominant in the immediate situation. As such it would be unfavorable to the growth of finer individuality. But it would seem that an "experience philosophy" is under the inescapable obligation of accepting into its scheme of things anything that experience shows to be

possible and desirable. Now experience does reveal connections and tendencies. Consequently by its own inherent nature
it makes possible the formulation of forward-reaching directive principles. Devotion to the "possibilities of what is now
moving" puts no embargo on hindsights and foresights. On
the contrary, it demands that "the present" be viewed in the
light of its past, and in terms of its probable future direction.
For example, Dewey asks in this series of articles why the
collective ability made possible by this new technology does
not operate to elevate correspondingly the life of individuals.
He also gives his own answer. It would seem that his answer
provides one of those forward-reaching hypotheses that will
be adequate to guide inquiry and effort for a considerable
period of time. He says:

"Our materialism, our devotion to money making and to having a good time, are not things by themselves. They are the product of the fact that we live in a money culture; of the fact that
our technique and technology are controlled by interest in private
profit. There lies the serious and fundamental defect of our civilization, the source of the secondary and induced evils to which so
much attention is given. Critics are dealing with symptoms and effects." [15]

To be sure the belief that "interest in profit" is our root
difficulty is also an hypothesis. Its accuracy in pointing the
way is also to be tested by the results to which it leads.
Doubtless it will take on new meaning as experience proceeds,
but no one can fairly complain that it does not point far
enough ahead to give a generous perspective on the present
situation. For example, can the imagination grasp the profound changes which would be involved if society and the
schools were to experiment with the activities which this
hypothesis would require if it were to be adequately tested?

Surely there is nothing in this directive principle discovered by an analysis of the deeper meaning of present social tendencies which invites us to surrender passively to the forces dominant for the moment in our present social economy.

7. The Instrumental and the Consummatory

Taking a somewhat different approach, another group of critics declares that experimentalism is unfavorable to the all-round development of individuality because of its distorted and partial view of experience. By virtue of its constant emphasis on control and the importance of experimental inquiry, it is said that experimentalism in effect ignores the esthetic and the appreciative phases of experience. Nature is viewed too exclusively as the mere source of supply for raw materials to be exploited, and as the seat of processes that need to be controlled. The natural scene is too little seen by the experimentalist as an object of beauty and wonder holding endless possibilities for human refreshment and delight. By constantly seeking to analyze, to dismember, to formulate, and to control, man tends to lose that innocency of eye and simplicity of response which are essential if he is to grasp the significance of things in their wholeness. Thus the analytical and critical procedures, important as they are in their proper place, give such thin transcripts of the depth of reality as actually experienced that life is bound to be impoverished if such approaches to the world of persons and things are made the exclusive interests of man. As one critic has stated, "the pursuit of truth cannot be made a substitute for living."

Moreover, the mood of the experimentalist is said to be too serious and somber. He tends to reduce the infinite range of significant interests in life to only one—that of "problem solving." The much praised logic of experimentalism seems to construe experience to be simply a continuous passage from one problematic situation to another. Existence is described as a precarious affair. Man, living amid uncertain developments, must be ever wary and alert to guard himself against unfriendly forces which would willingly accomplish his destruction. Even adjustments once satisfactorily achieved cannot be relied upon. Nature is such a shifting, changing scene, and existence is so poignantly unstable, that past solutions cannot be trusted to meet the novel exigencies of the morrow. Because he thus stresses the uncertain and contingent character of all existence, the experimentalist is said to make too much of preparatory and too little of consummatory experience. Thus also criticism comes to be substituted for appreciation, and anticipation for actual realization here and now.

The philosophy of experimentalism is also said to give an undue prominence to the biological factors in human experience. Thinking is construed to be the mere instrument of the physiological organism as it strives to maintain its vital equilibrium. Now experience in its deeper phases is something other than a process by which adjustments are made. Nor is it adequate to say that success and failure are the ultimate categories in human life. Indeed, much of the most meaningful experience for the cultivated individual proceeds in realms to which success and failure as such are utterly irrelevant. For example, what have success and failure to do with the experience of human friendship and communication? What have biological adjustments and organic satisfactions to do with those upper reaches of experience on the imaginative level such as are found in pure science, mathematics, art, poetry, and music? Experience is more than activity. It is not exhausted in the motor and manipulative responses of man. Experience is vision and feeling just as truly as it is "doing and making." The concept of "activity leading to further activity" is quite inadequate to express that which makes life significantly good. Such a conception of the good life could only have gained serious attention in a raw social environment dominated by the busy activities of a people so absorbed in using the machine to exploit nature and make profits for themselves that they have not had the time to reflect deeply about the meaning of experience.

Probably no philosopher has voiced these criticisms of experimentalism with more eloquence than has Santayana:

"What industry or life are good for it would be unsympathetic to inquire: the stream is mighty, and we must swim with the stream. Concern for survival, however, which seems to be the pragmatic principle in morals, does not afford a remedy for moral anarchy. To take firm hold on life, according to Nietzsche we should be imperious, poetical, atheistic; but according to William James we should be democratic, concrete, and credulous. It is hard to say whether pragmatism is come to emancipate the individual spirit and make it lord over things, or on the contrary to declare the spirit a mere instrument for the survival of the flesh. In Italy, the mind seems to be raised deliriously into an absolute creator, evoking at will at each moment, a new past, a new future, a new earth, and a new God. In America, however, the mind is recommended rather as an unpatented device for oiling the engine of the body and making it do double work." [16]

"Finding their intelligence enslaved, our contemporaries suppose that intelligence is essentially servile; instead of freeing it, they try to elude it. Not free enough themselves morally, but bound to the world partly by piety and partly by industrialism, they cannot think of rising to a detached contemplation of earthly things, and of life itself and evolution; they revert rather to sensibility, and seek some by-path of instinct or dramatic sympathy in which to wander. Having no stomach for the ultimate, they burrow downwards towards the primitive. But the longing to be primitive is a disease of culture; it is archaism in morals. To be so preoccupied with vitality is a symptom of anaemia." [17]

Such criticisms as these have long been made in the field of general philosophy. Of late they have been voiced by eminent leaders in the field of education. Our primary concern here is with the educational bearing of this conflict in philosophy. Once again general conceptions in philosophy may well be tested by their actual fruits in the realm of education.

Judging by the consequences already produced in the schools which have utilized the theories of experimentalism, what shall we conclude about the general tendency of this philosophy in the areas of experience above described? When compared with the traditional schools, do the experimental schools disclose a richer and more comprehensive program of activities and interests, or do they offer to children a more restricted range of experience? With regard to the exploration, enjoyment, and study of natural surroundings, which type of school has done the most to provide for such first-hand acquaintance with nature as this requires? Again, has it been the traditional or the experimental schools which have most clearly seen the educational significance of play, of games, of dancing, of music, and of art? When measured by the actual provision made for spontaneous group life, freedom of communication, and joint participation in friendly, purposeful activities, which type of school makes the more creditable showing? Does the actual practice of the experimental schools indicate that appreciative consummatory experiences have been sacrificed to instrumental and preparatory activities? Or, does the record show that the experimental schools have consistently championed the inherent, final worth of child experience as opposed to those who have looked upon childhood as a mere preparation for adulthood? To ask any or all of these questions is to answer them. The whole tendency of the experimental schools has been to stand for the broader interpretation of experience and the richer conception of what may be significantly included within the life of the school. The actual record of the educational reforms made possible by the experimental schools is entirely convincing on this point.

Of course it would be unfair to claim that the philosophy of experimentalism has been the only factor at work which has made for these educational changes. There is no one-to-one correspondence between progressive thought in education and belief in the principles of experimentalism. On the other hand, it is conservative to say that the ideas and practices of educators inspired by the philosophy of experimentalism have been one of the most powerful influences making for these very improvements.

When we pause to think about it, is this not exactly the sort of result in education which one would have anticipated the philosophy of experimentalism might produce? Experimentalism is preëminently a philosophy of experience. As such, if it is to be consistent with its own central principle, it is impelled to expand its educational program so as to make it as broad and as deep as human experience in its manifold forms shows itself to be. To be sure, each individual experimentalist will have his particular interests and emphasis, but the philosophy as a whole can never be true to its own experiential character if it is to be identified with some one phase of experience at the expense of others equally validated in the history of the race. It may happen that James and Dewey as individuals emphasize certain particular interests, but that is no reason why educators who accept their broad philosophic formulations should confine themselves to the particular activities of these two leaders. The inherent logic of a philosophy of experience forbids that its range of interest be thus circumscribed. As long as experimentalism continues to be a living movement in, and of, experience, it can never limit its subject-matter to anything less than the full scope of experience itself. It is interesting in this connection to observe that as an actual movement at work in the schools, experimentalism has exhibited precisely this catholicity of outlook. Its total effects as shown in the schools do not support the conclusion that its tendency is to exalt certain aspects of experience at the expense of others.

When we come to examine more closely the charge that experimentalism interprets experience so as to emphasize the preparatory and the instrumental, and to minimize the final and the consummatory, we find that this criticism apparently rests upon a logical misunderstanding. Two things are confused which experimentalists have taken great pains to distinguish. It would seem that the critics who make this charge assume that the cognitive phase of experience is all there is to experience. Now, as was indicated earlier, this is exactly contrary to what the experimentalist believes. Primary experience is not a form of knowing at all. It is an affair of "doing and undergoing," of "suffering and enjoying," of "being and having." Each such primary experience is whatever it is qualitatively experienced to be. It is because experience in its most primary modes is qualitative through and through— marked by genuine initiations and finalities—that we find it both possible and necessary to distinguish between those experiences which are judged good and those which are judged not good. This leads to reflection, which is a second-

ary and derived form of experience. There is a difference between having things and knowing about them. However important the activity of thinking may be, its broad function is
nevertheless instrumental in character. Its aim is to help us
know more about these primary experiences of "doing and
undergoing" in order that those occurrences which are valued
may be rendered more stable and significant and those which
are not desired may be more surely eliminated or avoided.
Thus to regard thinking as instrumental in function is not to
say that intellectual activity itself is devoid of its own intrinsic value and esthetic quality. Manifestly the reverse is
the fact.

However, if the purpose of thinking is to help us to know
more surely about the happenings of primary experience,
it must be something more than a mere rapturous beholding
of the movement of events. To find out anything, we have to
do something. It is also necessary to observe what consequences follow from our doing. As the connections between
developing events and between acts and consequences flow-
ing from those acts are understood, meanings are achieved.
The more and better organized our meanings, the more intelligent our behavior becomes. In other words experimental,
knowledge-getting experiences are instrumental. To be instrumental they must be instrumental to something. That
something is primary experience characterized throughout by
qualitative differences of every variety of suffering and enjoyment. Now it by no means follows that, because the experimentalist says that cognitive experience is instrumental to
primary experience, he believes that all experience is instrumental in character. The whole significance of his interpretation of experience when properly understood points in exactly
the opposite direction. Primary experience is an affair of be-

ginnings and endings. Endings are final. But not all endings are equally good. Some happenings end in suffering and evil; others in satisfaction and enjoyment. Consummations are endings desired and achieved by the means of intelligent selection and control. Thinking, knowing, are indispensable activities, if primary experience is to be ordered so as to produce satisfying consummatory experiences. It is because consummatory experiences are valued as ends that the experimentalist is unwilling to be careless about the means by which they alone can be secured. It is unfair, however, to charge him with having made no place in his logic of experience for the final and consummatory. In fact, his interest in instrumental activities is without intelligent meaning unless there be other final consummatory experiences for the sake of which these instrumental activities are undertaken.

Nor does the experimentalist by his own arbitrary choice define the nature of the world in which we live. If the empirical evidence points to the conclusion that we do live in an unstable, precarious universe, he thinks that we shall do well to recognize that trait of existence and plan our affairs accordingly. He is unwilling to blink unhappy facts and believes we shall make a better world in which to live if we recognize its genuine uncertain character. And instead of seeking to idealize it in purely fanciful operations, he believes rather that we should seek to understand it and to control it practically for our purposes, wherever such control is possible.

That he is not unmindful that the effort to control may at times conflict with the quiet enjoyment of the appreciative approach to nature is abundantly evidenced by the following quotation:

"Surely there is no more significant question before the world than this question of the possibility and method of reconciliation of the attitudes of practical science and contemplative esthetic appreciation. Without the former, man will be the sport and victim of natural forces which he cannot use or control. Without the latter, mankind might become a race of economic monsters, restlessly driving hard bargains with nature and with one another, bored with leisure or capable of putting it to use only in ostentatious display and extravagant dissipation." [18]

This problem is still ours. We shall only be better able to find its solution as we become adequately aware of its seriousness. On the other hand, we shall not find even an approach to a solution if we assume that one of these attitudes and methods must conquer the other. The experimental method has contributed too much to the welfare of the race to suppose for one moment it can be relegated to a minor position. The problem is to find out how the same individual may be both active and contemplative, inquiring and appreciative. Possibly the truly imaginative and creative workers in the field of science and the field of art do not find as much difficulty in reconciling the two attitudes as do the technicians who have become so burdened with their tools and techniques that they are no longer free to approach nature and life in the spirit of the artist-inquirer.

8. Experimentalism and the Future

As we come to the conclusion of this discussion of experimentalism, the conviction deepens that there is no conclusion in any important sense. The inherent nature of experimentalism is such that it precludes all final formulation. A philosophy which is rooted in experience, and is not a mere theory about experience, must change and grow as experience develops. If experimentalism ever should be reduced to a smug, completed system, it will by that very fact reveal that it is no longer an experimental philosophy. Just as experimentalism believes there is no final, all-inclusive knowledge—only a continuing development of more adequate perspectives with their correlative hypotheses more or less well verified—so also must it be admitted that no insight or statement of any of the prophetic leaders of experimentalism can ever be taken as final. All of these—even the best—must forever remain as hypotheses, subject to revision in the light of further experience.

As was earlier pointed out, this does not mean that experimentalism is merely a method. It is a method. But it is also a philosophy which has developed certain extremely important points of view that give needed guidance as we seek to orient ourselves and others to the task of learning to know and to live more adequately in our common world. So basic are some of these principles of orientation that it seems to the writer only fair to admit that they have an important metaphysical bearing.

But it is also important for those who work in education to bear in mind that experimentalism is by its very nature something other than a completed system. As teachers and administrators we cannot find ready-made answers to our problems in the statements of leading experimentalists. Much less should we seek to find in experimentalism final standards by which all further school experience is to be measured. Our answers to our problems must be framed in terms of the problems themselves as they appear in actual experience. The standards for our work must also be evolved from within the process of education itself. Both standards and solutions are to be tested by the consequences they produce. Both are to be reconstructed when an adequate examination of all the consequences indicates that they no longer satisfy the requirements of our ongoing educational experience.

This does not mean that the conceptions of the experimentalists are not important. They are supremely important. But as is true of all principles, they are instruments for further discovery, not a system of rules to be followed slavishly. The writer believes the basic conceptions of the experimentalist form an indispensable resource for the educator who would be an intelligent student of his task. But these existing conceptions do not constitute an orthodoxy to be defended; they are tools to be used. They will be judged, as is the case with all tools, by how well they are fitted to accomplish their purposes. They should and will be superseded when better tools are found.

REFERENCES

1. WILLIAM JAMES, *Principles of Psychology* (Henry Holt and Company, 1890), I, 479–480.
2. JOHN DEWEY, *Influence of Darwin on Philosophy* (Henry Holt and Company, 1920), pp. 69–70.
3. WILLIAM JAMES, *On Some of Life's Ideals* (Henry Holt and Company, 1900), pp. 9–10.
4. *Ibid.*, pp. 49–50.
5. JOHN DEWEY, *Democracy and Education* (The Macmillan Company, 1922), p. 357.
6. JOHN DEWEY, *Human Nature and Conduct* (Henry Holt and Company, 1922), pp. 96–97.
7. JOHN DEWEY, *Progressive Education and the Science of Education* (Progressive Educational Association, 1928), p. 5.
8. LEWIS MUMFORD, "A Modern Synthesis," *Saturday Review of Literature,* April 12, 1930, p. 920.
9. *Ibid.,* p. 921.
10. *Ibid.,* p. 921.

11. MARGARET NAUMBURG, "The Crux of Progressive Education," *New Republic,* June 25, 1930, p. 146.
12. JOHN DEWEY, "The Crisis in Culture," *New Republic,* March 19, 1930, p. 126.
13. JOHN DEWEY, "Toward a New Individualism," *New Republic,* Feb. 19, 1930, p. 14.
14. HENRY HAZLITT, "Individualism, Old and New," *Nation,* Oct. 22, 1930, p. 447.
15. JOHN DEWEY, "America by Formula," *New Republic,* September 18, 1929, p. 119.
16. GEORGE SANTAYANA, *Winds of Doctrine* (Charles Scribner's Sons, 1914), p. 17.
17. *Ibid.,* pp. 18–19.
18. JOHN DEWEY, *Reconstruction in Philosophy* (Henry Holt and Company, 1920), p. 127.

INDEX OF SUBJECTS

INDEX OF SOURCES

263

AMERICAN EDUCATION:
ITS MEN, IDEAS, AND INSTITUTIONS
An Arno Press/New York Times Collection

Series I

Adams, Francis. **The Free School System of the United States.**
1875.

Alcott, William A. **Confessions of a School Master.** 1839.

American Unitarian Association. **From Servitude to Service.**
1905.

Bagley, William C. **Determinism in Education.** 1925.

Barnard, Henry, editor. **Memoirs of Teachers, Educators, and
Promoters and Benefactors of Education, Literature, and
Science.** 1861.

Bell, Sadie. **The Church, the State, and Education in Virginia.**
1930.

Belting, Paul Everett. **The Development of the Free Public High
School in Illinois to 1860.** 1919.

Berkson, Isaac B. **Theories of Americanization: A Critical Study.**
1920.

Blauch, Lloyd E. **Federal Cooperation in Agricultural Extension
Work, Vocational Education, and Vocational Rehabilitation.**
1935.

Bloomfield, Meyer. **Vocational Guidance of Youth.** 1911.

Brewer, Clifton Hartwell. **A History of Religious Education in the
Episcopal Church to 1835.** 1924.

Brown, Elmer Ellsworth. **The Making of Our Middle Schools.**
1902.

Brumbaugh, M. G. **Life and Works of Christopher Dock.** 1908.

Burns, Reverend J. A. **The Catholic School System in the United
States.** 1908.

Burns, Reverend J. A. **The Growth and Development of the
Catholic School System in the United States.** 1912.

Burton, Warren. **The District School as It Was.** 1850.

Butler, Nicholas Murray, editor. **Education in the United States.**
1900.

Butler, Vera M. **Education as Revealed By New England News-
papers prior to 1850.** 1935.

Campbell, Thomas Monroe. **The Movable School Goes to the
Negro Farmer.** 1936.

Carter, James G. **Essays upon Popular Education.** 1826.

Carter, James G. **Letters to the Hon. William Prescott, LL.D., on
the Free Schools of New England.** 1924.

Channing, William Ellery. **Self-Culture.** 1842.

Coe, George A. **A Social Theory of Religious Education.** 1917.

Committee on Secondary School Studies. **Report of the Committee on Secondary School Studies, Appointed at the Meeting of
the National Education Association.** 1893.

Counts, George S. **Dare the School Build a New Social Order?**
1932.

Counts, George S. **The Selective Character of American Secondary Education.** 1922.

Counts, George S. **The Social Composition of Boards of Education.** 1927.

Culver, Raymond B. **Horace Mann and Religion in the Massachusetts Public Schools.** 1929.

Curoe, Philip R. V. **Educational Attitudes and Policies of Organized Labor in the United States.** 1926.

Dabney, Charles William. **Universal Education in the South.** 1936.

Dearborn, Ned Harland. **The Oswego Movement in American Education.** 1925.

De Lima, Agnes. **Our Enemy the Child.** 1926.

Dewey, John. **The Educational Situation.** 1902.

Dexter, Franklin B., editor. **Documentary History of Yale University.** 1916.

Eliot, Charles William. **Educational Reform: Essays and Addresses.** 1898.

Ensign, Forest Chester. **Compulsory School Attendance and Child Labor.** 1921.

Fitzpatrick, Edward Augustus. **The Educational Views and Influence of De Witt Clinton.** 1911.

Fleming, Sanford. **Children & Puritanism.** 1933.

Flexner, Abraham. **The American College: A Criticism.** 1908.

Foerster, Norman. **The Future of the Liberal College.** 1938.

Gilman, Daniel Coit. **University Problems in the United States.** 1898.

Hall, Samuel R. **Lectures on School-Keeping.** 1829.

Hall, Stanley G. **Adolescence: Its Psychology and Its Relations to Physiology, Anthropology, Sociology, Sex, Crime, Religion, and Education.** 1905. 2 vols.

Hansen, Allen Oscar. **Early Educational Leadership in the Ohio Valley.** 1923.

Harris, William T. **Psychologic Foundations of Education.** 1899.

Harris, William T. **Report of the Committee of Fifteen on the Elementary School.** 1895.

Harveson, Mae Elizabeth. **Catharine Esther Beecher: Pioneer Educator.** 1932.

Jackson, George Leroy. **The Development of School Support in Colonial Massachusetts.** 1909.

Kandel, I. L., editor. **Twenty-five Years of American Education.** 1924.

Kemp, William Webb. **The Support of Schools in Colonial New York by the Society for the Propagation of the Gospel in Foreign Parts.** 1913.

Kilpatrick, William Heard. **The Dutch Schools of New Netherland and Colonial New York.** 1912.

Kilpatrick, William Heard. **The Educational Frontier.** 1933.

Knight, Edgar Wallace. **The Influence of Reconstruction on Education in the South.** 1913.

Le Duc, Thomas. **Piety and Intellect at Amherst College, 1865-1912.** 1946.

Maclean, John. **History of the College of New Jersey from Its Origin in 1746 to the Commencement of 1854.** 1877.

Maddox, William Arthur. **The Free School Idea in Virginia before the Civil War.** 1918.

Mann, Horace. **Lectures on Education.** 1855.

McCadden, Joseph J. **Education in Pennsylvania, 1801-1835, and Its Debt to Roberts Vaux.** 1855.

McCallum, James Dow. **Eleazar Wheelock.** 1939.

McCuskey, Dorothy. **Bronson Alcott, Teacher.** 1940.

Meiklejohn, Alexander. **The Liberal College.** 1920.

Miller, Edward Alanson. **The History of Educational Legislation in Ohio from 1803 to 1850.** 1918.

Miller, George Frederick. **The Academy System of the State of New York.** 1922.

Monroe, Will S. **History of the Pestalozzian Movement in the United States.** 1907.

Mosely Education Commission. **Reports of the Mosely Education Commission to the United States of America October-December, 1903.** 1904.

Mowry, William A. **Recollections of a New England Educator.** 1908.

Mulhern, James. **A History of Secondary Education in Pennsylvania.** 1933.

National Herbart Society. **National Herbart Society Yearbooks 1-5, 1895-1899.** 1895-1899.

Nearing, Scott. **The New Education: A Review of Progressive Educational Movements of the Day.** 1915.

Neef, Joseph. **Sketches of a Plan and Method of Education.** 1808.

Nock, Albert Jay. **The Theory of Education in the United States.** 1932.

Norton, A. O., editor. **The First State Normal School in America: The Journals of Cyrus Pierce and Mary Swift.** 1926.

Oviatt, Edwin. **The Beginnings of Yale, 1701-1726.** 1916.

Packard, Frederic Adolphus. **The Daily Public School in the United States.** 1866.

Page, David P. **Theory and Practice of Teaching.** 1848.

Parker, Francis W. **Talks on Pedagogics: An Outline of the Theory of Concentration.** 1894.

Peabody, Elizabeth Palmer. **Record of a School.** 1835.

Porter, Noah. **The American Colleges and the American Public.** 1870.

Reigart, John Franklin. **The Lancasterian System of Instruction in the Schools of New York City.** 1916.

Reilly, Daniel F. **The School Controversy (1891-1893).** 1943.

Rice, Dr. J. M. **The Public-School System of the United States.** 1893.

Rice, Dr. J. M. **Scientific Management in Education.** 1912.

Ross, Early D. **Democracy's College: The Land-Grant Movement in the Formative Stage.** 1942.

Rugg, Harold, et al. **Curriculum-Making: Past and Present.** 1926.

Rugg, Harold, et al. **The Foundations of Curriculum-Making.** 1926.

Rugg, Harold and Shumaker, Ann. **The Child-Centered School.** 1928.

Seybolt, Robert Francis. **Apprenticeship and Apprenticeship Education in Colonial New England and New York.** 1917.

Seybolt, Robert Francis. **The Private Schools of Colonial Boston.** 1935.

Seybolt, Robert Francis. **The Public Schools of Colonial Boston.** 1935.

Sheldon, Henry D. **Student Life and Customs.** 1901.

Sherrill, Lewis Joseph. **Presbyterian Parochial Schools, 1846-1870.** 1932 .

Siljestrom, P. A. **Educational Institutions of the United States.** 1853.

Small, Walter Herbert. **Early New England Schools.** 1914.

Soltes, Mordecai. **The Yiddish Press: An Americanizing Agency.** 1925.

Stewart, George, Jr. **A History of Religious Education in Connecticut to the Middle of the Nineteenth Century.** 1924.

Storr, Richard J. **The Beginnings of Graduate Education in America.** 1953.

Stout, John Elbert. **The Development of High-School Curricula in the North Central States from 1860 to 1918.** 1921.

Suzzallo, Henry. **The Rise of Local School Supervision in Massachusetts.** 1906.

Swett, John. **Public Education in California.** 1911.

Tappan, Henry P. **University Education.** 1851.

Taylor, Howard Cromwell. **The Educational Significance of the Early Federal Land Ordinances.** 1921.

Taylor, J. Orville. **The District School.** 1834.

Tewksbury, Donald G. **The Founding of American Colleges and Universities before the Civil War.** 1932.

Thorndike, Edward L. **Educational Psychology.** 1913-1914.

True, Alfred Charles. **A History of Agricultural Education in the United States, 1785-1925.** 1929.

True, Alfred Charles. **A History of Agricultural Extension Work in the United States, 1785-1923.** 1928.

Updegraff, Harlan. **The Origin of the Moving School in Massachusetts.** 1908.

Wayland, Francis. **Thoughts on the Present Collegiate System in the United States.** 1842.

Weber, Samuel Edwin. **The Charity School Movement in Colonial Pennsylvania.** 1905.

Wells, Guy Fred. **Parish Education in Colonial Virginia.** 1923.

Wickersham, J. P. **The History of Education in Pennsylvania.** 1885.

Woodward, Calvin M. **The Manual Training School.** 1887.

Woody, Thomas. **Early Quaker Education in Pennsylvania.** 1920.

Woody, Thomas. **Quaker Education in the Colony and State of New Jersey.** 1923.

Wroth, Lawrence C. **An American Bookshelf, 1755.** 1934.

Series II

Adams, Evelyn C. **American Indian Education.** 1946.

Bailey, Joseph Cannon. **Seaman A. Knapp: Schoolmaster of American Agriculture.** 1945.

Beecher, Catharine and Harriet Beecher Stowe. **The American Woman's Home.** 1869.

Benezet, Louis T. **General Education in the Progressive College.** 1943.

Boas, Louise Schutz. **Woman's Education Begins.** 1935.

Bobbitt, Franklin. **The Curriculum.** 1918.

Bode, Boyd H. **Progressive Education at the Crossroads.** 1938.

Bourne, William Oland. **History of the Public School Society of the City of New York.** 1870.

Bronson, Walter C. **The History of Brown University, 1764-1914.** 1914.

Burstall, Sara A. **The Education of Girls in the United States.** 1894.

Butts, R. Freeman. **The College Charts Its Course.** 1939.

Caldwell, Otis W. and Stuart A. Courtis. **Then & Now in Education, 1845-1923.** 1923.

Calverton, V. F. & Samuel D. Schmalhausen, editors. **The New Generation: The Intimate Problems of Modern Parents and Children.** 1930.

Charters, W. W. **Curriculum Construction.** 1923.

Childs, John L. **Education and Morals.** 1950.

Childs, John L. **Education and the Philosophy of Experimentalism.** 1931.

Clapp, Elsie Ripley. **Community Schools in Action.** 1939.

Counts, George S. **The American Road to Culture: A Social Interpretation of Education in the United States.** 1930.

Counts, George S. **School and Society in Chicago.** 1928.

Finegan, Thomas E. **Free Schools.** 1921.

Fletcher, Robert Samuel. **A History of Oberlin College.** 1943.

Grattan, C. Hartley. **In Quest of Knowledge: A Historical Perspective on Adult Education.** 1955.

Hartman, Gertrude & Ann Shumaker, editors. **Creative Expression.** 1932.

Kandel, I. L. **The Cult of Uncertainty.** 1943.

Kandel, I. L. **Examinations and Their Substitutes in the United States.** 1936.

Kilpatrick, William Heard. **Education for a Changing Civilization.** 1926.

Kilpatrick, William Heard. **Foundations of Method.** 1925.

Kilpatrick, William Heard. **The Montessori System Examined.** 1914.

Lang, Ossian H., editor. **Educational Creeds of the Nineteenth Century.** 1898.

Learned, William S. **The Quality of the Educational Process in the United States and in Europe.** 1927.

Meiklejohn, Alexander. **The Experimental College.** 1932.

Middlekauff, Robert. **Ancients and Axioms: Secondary Education in Eighteenth-Century New England.** 1963.

Norwood, William Frederick. **Medical Education in the United States Before the Civil War.** 1944.

Parsons, Elsie W. Clews. **Educational Legislation and Administration of the Colonial Governments.** 1899.

Perry, Charles M. **Henry Philip Tappan: Philosopher and University President.** 1933.

Pierce, Bessie Louise. **Civic Attitudes in American School Textbooks.** 1930.

Rice, Edwin Wilbur. **The Sunday-School Movement (1780-1917) and the American Sunday-School Union (1817-1917).** 1917.

Robinson, James Harvey. **The Humanizing of Knowledge.** 1924.

Ryan, W. Carson. **Studies in Early Graduate Education.** 1939.

Seybolt, Robert Francis. **The Evening School in Colonial America.** 1925.

Seybolt, Robert Francis. **Source Studies in American Colonial Education.** 1925.

Todd, Lewis Paul. **Wartime Relations of the Federal Government and the Public Schools, 1917-1918.** 1945.

Vandewalker, Nina C. **The Kindergarten in American Education.** 1908.

Ward, Florence Elizabeth. **The Montessori Method and the American School.** 1913.

West, Andrew Fleming. **Short Papers on American Liberal Education.** 1907.

Wright, Marion M. Thompson. **The Education of Negroes in New Jersey.** 1941.

Supplement

The Social Frontier (Frontiers of Democracy). Vols. 1-10, 1934-1943.